DRIVER SEAT

DRIVER SEAT

NAVIGATING TRANSITIONS, TRAUMA & TRIUMPH

JONATHAN EVERETT

Dedication

THIS BOOK IS DEDICATED TO THE PEOPLE WHO SHAPED ME, WALKED WITH ME, AND, IN SOME CASES, COULD NOT STAY THE ENTIRE JOURNEY. FAMILY IS THE FIRST PLACE WE LEARN DIRECTION, RESISTANCE, LOVE, AND RESPONSIBILITY, AND WHETHER NEAR OR FAR, PRESENT OR REMEMBERED, FAMILY LEAVES AN IMPRINT ON HOW WE MOVE THROUGH THE WORLD. TO MY MOTHER, **WANDA EVERETT**, WHOSE STRENGTH AND FAITH FORMED MY EARLIEST UNDERSTANDING OF RESPONSIBILITY; TO MY SON, **JONATHAN EVERETT JR.**, WHOSE LIFE REMINDS ME THAT EVERY DECISION AT THE WHEEL ECHOES BEYOND ME; TO MY BROTHERS AND SISTERS, WHOSE SHARED HISTORY, SHARED WOUNDS, AND SHARED RESILIENCE REMIND ME THAT NO ROAD IS TRAVELED WITHOUT FAMILY SOMEWHERE IN THE REARVIEW, SHAPING HOW WE SEE WHAT'S AHEAD. AND MOST TENDERLY, THIS BOOK IS DEDICATED TO THE SACRED MEMORY OF MY SISTER, **TRIANNA EVERETT**. BEING IN THE DRIVER SEAT TEACHES YOU A HARD TRUTH: OBEDIENCE COSTS, PURPOSE SEPARATES, AND ALONG THE WAY YOU WILL LOSE PEOPLE WHO PLAYED MAJOR ROLES IN YOUR BECOMING, SOMETIMES TO DISTANCE, SOMETIMES TO SEASONS, AND SOMETIMES TO DEATH. TRIANNA'S ABSENCE IS NOT A FOOTNOTE IN MY STORY; IT IS A WEIGHT I CARRY WITH REVERENCE. I THINK OF HER EVERY SINGLE DAY, AND ON SOME DAYS I STILL WISH SHE WERE IN THE PASSENGER SEAT, REMINDING ME OF THE SMALL THINGS, LIKE HOW TO TAKE MEDICINE THE RIGHT WAY, EVEN WHEN IT COMES IN THE FORM OF PILLS. BECAUSE LOVE DOESN'T DISAPPEAR WITH LOSS; IT JUST FINDS QUIETER WAYS TO STAY PRESENT. THIS BOOK IS WRITTEN WITH GRATITUDE FOR THOSE WHO STAYED, HUMILITY FOR THOSE I LOST, AND RESOLVE TO KEEP DRIVING WITH INTEGRITY, MEMORY, AND PURPOSE.

TABLE OF CONTENTS

Why I Wrote Driver Seat:

The Book I Needed Before I Became a Leader

There comes a moment in every leader's life when you realize something unsettling: You have a dream, but you don't yet have direction. You have potential, but no process. You have calling, but no clarity. Everyone talks about purpose. Few talk about preparation. Everyone celebrates elevation. Few sit with the shadows of development. Everyone preaches destiny. Few teach the discipline that destiny demands. This book was born from the tension between being called and being ready. Joseph's story is one of the most misinterpreted leadership narratives in Scripture. We shout about the palace, but whisper about the prison. We celebrate the dream, but skip past the discipline. We admire the elevation, but avoid the excavation that made him whole. Joseph did not go from prophecy to promotion. He went from pit to house to prison to palace to purpose. Every environment shaped him. Every environment exposed him. Every environment trained him. Every environment demanded a different version of himself. As I walked through my own life through betrayals, transitions, leadership failures, misread seasons, false accusations, internal trauma, delayed promises, and unexpected opportunities, I began to see something sacred: God does not waste environments.

He uses every one to build the leader your destiny requires. Joseph's story is not just ancient history. It's the blueprint for modern leadership.

It is the psychology of calling, the system of stewardship, the anatomy of influence, and the emotional journey of becoming. This book is not written for perfect people. It is written for those who have survived pits, escaped unsafe places, navigated systems they didn't choose, carried

dreams they couldn't explain, and endured seasons where nothing seemed to move. This is the book I wish I had when I didn't understand why God delayed me, why people betrayed me, why promotion scared me, why my emotions shocked me, and why the path to purpose felt nothing like the promise. If you have ever felt gifted but untrained, called but underprepared, chosen but overlooked, elevated but unstable, responsible but emotionally exhausted, powerful but deeply human, then Driver Seat is for you. My prayer is that Joseph's journey becomes your permission slip to lead without apology, to heal without shame, to build systems without fear, to navigate culture without losing identity, and to stay in the Driver Seat even when the road bends unpredictably. Welcome to your formation. You're not here because you're ready. You're here because God refuses to let you waste your calling.

Let's drive.

—Jonathan Everett

Everybody Is Leading Somebody

Everyone is a leader.

I know this is a general concept of leadership. I know the argument is whether people were born a leader or if you can produce or develop a leader. But I've discovered this, and this is from God's perspective, that before the earth met you and I, God developed us and made us leaders. Scripture affirms that our leadership begins in God's intentional design, not in human appointment. The Bible shows us that leadership didn't start with people choosing us or selecting us to lead. It started with God forming us. You are a leader not because you carry a title, but because you carry God's image.

Leadership is, in essence, not necessarily a position. It is your presence. It is your influence. It is the way you shift a room without announcing your presence. It is the way your story strengthens someone else who thought they were too broken to continue. Leaders influence somebody. Your influence as a leader, to some degree, is saving somebody right now. Your leadership ability is encouraging somebody else to endure. Some lead with their voices. Some lead with their scars. But no one in the room is exempt from influence or responsibility. You're leading someone, whether you realize it or not.

God never wastes a breath creating passive beginnings. He breathes purpose, authority, and stewardship into us all. From the very beginning, God entrusted humanity with responsibility and dominion, not passivity. He didn't create us to sit back and spectate. He created us to steward, to cultivate, and to carry weight. To lead. You are leading even when you don't realize anyone is watching. Matter of fact, I think one of the craziest things about leadership is that some can lead from the front, some can lead from the middle, and some can lead from the back. Everybody looks like a leader when life is light, but leadership is really proven in the dark, in the moments of uncertainty, in the middle of transitions, and in the seasons when God hands you the wheel and you have to keep driving without seeing the full road ahead.

And that's the power behind *Driver Seat*.

This book walks through the life of Joseph, not just as a biblical story, but as a mirror of the realities leaders face today. Joseph's journey, betrayal, transition, misunderstanding, silence, confinement, elevation, and responsibility, is the same terrain most leaders will face at some point in their lives. His life becomes a blueprint for how to move, how to navigate seasons you didn't choose, how to stay steady on roads you didn't ask to travel, and how to let God mature you while you're still in motion.

One of the things I'm discovering more and more about leadership, and what you are going to take away from this book, is that there are different forms of leadership, different styles of leadership, and different seasons of leading. How God uses you to lead is totally at His discretion. Your resilience is teaching someone. Your faithfulness is guiding someone. Your quiet strength is stabilizing someone. Leadership isn't loud. Sometimes it whispers, "If I made it through this, then you can too."

I'm not sure what age or stage you are in your life, whether you're leading an organization, leading your family, or leading your friend group or people in your church, but you are a leader. You were born. You have value. Your presence has purpose. Because God said so.

Now, as we start talking about everyone being a leader or leading in something, we also have to confront one of the dangers of leadership, and that is an identity crisis. One of the dangers in becoming or evolving into what the Lord has designed us to be is becoming something we were not created to be in an attempt to be better than what we were. It is a temptation that has driven people to embrace falsehoods, false narratives, and even, to some degree, become successful at the wrong thing or complete a task wrongly.

You know, living what you don't learn from instruction, God often teaches us through experience. And whenever we start talking about leadership from a lived-in perspective, the Bible reminds us in Proverbs that there is a way that seems right to a man, but it ends in destruction (Proverbs 14:12; Proverbs 16:25). In other words, sincerity without alignment can still lead to damage.

God has a strategic way to ensure that the lessons necessary for the next season of our lives are imprinted within the blueprint and the fabric of our attitudes, our disposition, our integrity, and our loyalty to His Word. Leadership is not only about living and learning. It is also about leveraging. There are two types of people that exist in any form of leadership or existence, and that is movers and managers.

One of the leveraging realities of leadership is discovering who is motivating the mover and who is developing the manager. Both have distinct operational functions. Many people have the misconception that you have to be either-or, when in reality you can be complex enough to be both. But if you don't allow someone to motivate you to move beyond yourself, God will often send a problem to move you out of a place you stayed in far too long. Sometimes pressure is not punishment; it is propulsion.

The other aspect of leverage is that many of us feel we don't need someone to develop the manager because we have mastered managing things that are sometimes broken, but we have not yet understood wholeness. Management has layers. It is complex. It is always scaling. And without development, it will eventually collapse.

Another essential part of leadership, as we drive into this book and talk about the driver seat, is the lust of leadership. It is the temptation to think everybody is qualified to lead, and the lust of what leadership brings, whether it is material, the spotlight, or the platform. Those things are seductive. I'm not saying that everyone who desires leadership is lusting after it, but I do want to caution you to discern whether this is a lust or a call from God.

In today's society, I don't believe people always know the difference between a call from God and a career in church, or between what God is calling us to and what we simply want. Scripture says that when we are driven by the success of our neighbors or the jealousy of our neighbors, it is like chasing the wind (Ecclesiastes 4:4). Comparison produces motion without meaning.

This book is not just about leadership. It is about living, leverage, and legacy. And one of the most important things I pray this book gives you is the ability to think about legacy. Think about legs. L.E.G. Who are you leaving legs behind for so they can walk faster, go higher, jump higher, and soar higher than you did. That is legacy. Legacy, in its essence, is making sure the next generation can see Him faster, walk faster, and reach His desired place.

And as we continue throughout this book, we are going to tap into Joseph's life and watch how God used him quietly to foreshadow the coming of the Lord Jesus Christ. We will see how he led through some of the most challenging terrains, ambiguity, and attacks. Joseph's life shows us that leadership is shaped in pits, prisons, households, and palaces, in transition, not comfort. He did not have a title. He did not have a position. He did not have a role. The only thing Joseph did was remain obedient to God, allowing God to develop him into a God-sized version of who he was created to be.

And that is the heartbeat of this book. Learning how to sit in the driver seat of your calling, even when the road is unfamiliar, and trusting God to guide you through every transition and every terrain.

Come on. Let's continue to read.

SECTION ONE

THE MAKING OF A DRIVER

CHAPTER ONE

GIFTED BUT NOT DEVELOPED: BECOMING WHAT YOU NEVER SEEN

Why This Story Must Be Told

There are certain stories in Scripture that are too important to leave inside church walls. They are not merely spiritual narratives; they are human case studies. They are mirrors for leadership, psychology, power, family, trauma, systems, and survival. Joseph's story is one of those stories. It is not simply the story of a young dreamer who eventually became powerful. It is the story of what happens when calling collides with immaturity, when destiny meets dysfunction, and when divine revelation lands inside a human life that is still under construction.

For centuries Joseph has been preached as a success story. The pit, the prison, the palace, a clean arc that comforts believers and inspires perseverance. But the reality is far more complex than the simplified sermons many of us grew up hearing. Joseph's life is not just a testimony of promotion; it is a study in formation. It is about what happens to a person who receives vision before they receive maturity. It is about how systems treat gifted people who do not yet understand their own power. It is about family dynamics, jealousy, betrayal, incarceration, economic systems, political leadership, and emotional survival. It is about the brutal space between revelation and readiness.

And that space is where most people live.

Joseph's life matters on a large scale because it speaks to more than church culture. It speaks to entrepreneurs trying to steward vision before they have the infrastructure to sustain it. It speaks to leaders who see further than the rooms they occupy. It speaks to young professionals whose gifts outpace their experience. It speaks to families fractured by envy and misunderstanding. It speaks to systems that exploit potential before they recognize humanity. It speaks to people who have been trafficked by circumstances, imprisoned by accusations, and misunderstood by those closest to them.

Joseph's story is not simply ancient history. It is modern reality wearing biblical language.

This is why the story must be revisited honestly. Because too many people have been taught to admire Joseph without being prepared for Joseph's process. We celebrate the palace while ignoring the psychological and relational immaturity that preceded the pit. We quote the dreams without studying the emotional intelligence Joseph lacked when he first spoke them. We applaud the outcome without examining the inner development required to survive the journey.

And that is where this chapter begins.

Because the first thing we must confront is uncomfortable: the dream was real, but Joseph was not ready.

Not yet.

Opening Reality: Gift ≠ Maturity

Joseph is seventeen when we meet him, not seasoned, not processed, not prepared. The dreams are accurate; the destiny is real, but vision does not equal readiness. Gift does not equal maturity. Calling does not equal competence. Revelation does not equal readiness. Joseph can see the future, but he cannot yet steward the present. He has insight without integration, awareness without wisdom, revelation without restraint. He carries a true God-given glimpse of what will be, but he lacks the social, emotional, and relational intelligence to handle what is.

Early vision without relational intelligence creates isolation, not because the vision is wrong, but because the delivery is premature. Joseph does not yet understand that timing is part of calling, audience is part of prophecy, and discretion is part of destiny. His dream is accurate, but his handling is immature. He speaks truth in the wrong tone, to the wrong people, at the wrong time. And when vision outruns wisdom, people withdraw, not from the calling, but from the carrier. Joseph isn't rejected because he dreamed; he is rejected because he announced what he didn't yet know how to manage.

Before You Touch the Wheel

When we look at Joseph's life, we see brilliance wrapped in immaturity. We see a gift that was so loud that it spoke before Joseph learned how to steward his own voice. We see in the household of Joseph that because he was favored by his father, the misconception was that he was the favorite. We see that in organizations. We see that at church. We see that in families. We see that in friend groups. We see that in all different types of structures where there are multiple people and people think your favor automatically creates this notion that you are the favorite. Favor does not always mean people love you. Sometimes favor just means God marked you, and the people around you misread it.

We also see that even in the midst of that, Joseph did not know how to steward his voice, to speak to the right safe spaces that could value the weight of his words. Like many gifted people that we run into today, Joseph had a dream before he had discipline, a vision before he had the vocabulary to articulate what it actually was, and the calling before he had the character to carry it. And if we are honest, most of us have lived in that same tension, gifted enough to see something but not developed enough to walk in it yet.

Speaking Too Soon

This is no different than some of us today. Without having the proper understanding of how valuable we really are, understanding that our existence is not something merely thrown together but shaped with purpose, we mishandle ourselves. I want to challenge each and every person reading this book right now to be careful with your words and to realize your words have weight and your voice has value. Sometimes we speak too soon, not because we are arrogant, but because we have not yet learned the power of silence, timing, and discernment.

Joseph, in his entire story, and as we read through it and understand the parallels between Joseph's story and our story, teaches us that the undeveloped part of a gifted person is not the absence of potential. It is the absence of processing. What this means for the reader is important: when a person is gifted, we often assume the gift should automatically translate into readiness, maturity, or leadership capacity. But Joseph shows us that gifting alone is never the full picture. A person can have divine insight, supernatural potential, and a clear sense of calling, and still be unprepared for the weight, responsibility, and relationships connected to that calling. The gap isn't a lack of greatness; it's simply a lack of growth. The raw, unrefined parts of a gifted person are not proof that the gift is missing. They are proof that the gift has not yet been developed, stretched, disciplined, or matured through real-life experiences.

Joseph's entire life reminds us that potential must be processed. Dreams must be developed. Calling must be cultivated. What looks like weakness or immaturity in an early season is not evidence that God chose the wrong person, it is evidence that God is still forming the right person. Joseph had the gift at 17, but the gift had to go through pits, houses, prisons, and systems before it could be trusted in a palace. His immaturity was not failure; it was phase one. His ignorance was not incompetence; it was a signal that development was necessary. His early missteps were not disqualification; they were invitations to processing.

So when we look at our own undeveloped places, the areas where we feel behind, unprepared, or emotionally underbuilt, we must remember Joseph's example. We are not seeing an absence of potential. We are seeing areas where God is still shaping, still strengthening, still maturing, still processing us into the leaders our destiny requires.

God takes us through processes to develop us into a God-sized version of ourselves so we can carry a God-sized anointing, a God-sized gift, and a God-sized type of glory. Before God enlarges your territory, He enlarges your capacity. Before God hands you the wheel, He strengthens your hands.

The Coat: Identity Before Development

Genesis 37:3–4 — Jacob gives Joseph a coat of many colors. The coat signals favor, identity, distinction, visibility. But Joseph's identity is still externally reinforced (father's favor, visible garment, affirming dreams). Visibility arrives before humility; attention arrives before emotional intelligence. Being favored by God does not mean you are ready for influence.

Here's what this means on a deeper level: When Joseph receives the coat, it becomes the first thing people notice about him. It is loud. It is colorful. It is public. It is symbolic. It marks him as "chosen" long before he understands what being chosen requires. In other words, Joseph's identity at this stage is not rooted in internal maturity. It is rooted in external reinforcement, in what is put on him, not what has been formed in him.

Joseph is favored, but not formed. Visible, but not grounded. Distinguished, but not developed. The coat gives him a sense of significance he has not yet grown into. His father's affection becomes his confidence. His dreams become his validation. His garment becomes his introduction. This is dangerous, because external identity is fragile identity. When your sense of self is built on what someone else gives you, someone else can also take it away.

That is exactly what happens. Joseph's brothers strip the coat from him to attack the identity he has not yet internalized. They know something Joseph does not: if your identity is built on something you wear, then stripping the garment strips the confidence. If your value is tied to attention, then losing attention collapses the ego. If your stability is based on favor, then losing favor destabilizes the soul.

This is why the text emphasizes that visibility arrives before humility and attention arrives before emotional intelligence. Joseph is seen before he is strong. He is elevated before he is educated. He is visible before he is stable. He is admired before he is wise. That sequence is common among gifted people, especially those called early. But it is also spiritually dangerous, because being favored by God does not mean you are ready for influence.

Favor is not competency. Visibility is not maturity. Calling is not character. Dreams are not development. Identity placed on you is not identity formed in you.

God often introduces destiny before He introduces discipline. He lets you see the future long before He builds the emotional strength needed to survive it. The coat is proof of future purpose, but it is not proof of present readiness. So Joseph wears honor he hasn't yet grown the shoulders to carry. He carries favor with an undeveloped identity. He has recognition without regulation. He has affirmation without awareness.

That is why the coat becomes the first thing taken from him. Because God will never let you build your identity on what someone else put on you. He will strip away everything you depend on externally so He can build something internally that cannot be stolen. In Joseph's story, the coat is not the beginning of leadership. The coat is the beginning of processing.

Blind Spots Behind the Vision

Joseph could see the palace, but he could not see how to handle the politics of it. There is always a blindside to gifted people. There is a grace that God gives us. Joseph could interpret dreams, and we are going to see that in the storyline, but he could not interpret people. How often do we see that? Oftentimes we are very accurate in understanding the imagery of God, but we misunderstand people and the ramifications of their mental instability. He could foresee greatness, but he could not foresee how his own unhealed places would provoke jealousy, tension, and misunderstanding. It was not that Joseph was wrong. He was just unaware, and unawareness will cost you just as much as disobedience.

One of the craziest things about being underdeveloped is that you have to manage the unhealed areas of your life before they contaminate everything that God has prepared for you. I am discovering that gifted people often do not realize that their unhealed wounds shout louder than their gifts. Sometimes your pain walks in the room before your purpose does.

Dreaming Out Loud in Unsafe Spaces

Joseph told his dream to his brothers, to his own family, to the people he naturally assumed were the safest place to share what God showed him. And that's where many of us relate to Joseph, not in the dreaming, but in the disappointment that follows. Most of us do not intentionally announce our dreams to hostile or insecure people; we announce them to people we trust. We share them with the ones we assume will celebrate, protect, and understand us. But Joseph's story gently exposes a truth most of us learn only after the fact: not everyone you think is a safe space actually is. And sometimes the insecurity of others is invisible until your dream brings it to the surface.

This is why discernment matters. When God gives you a dream or a vision, you must be careful and prayerful about who you invite into that conversation. Joseph was not wrong for dreaming. We clearly understand that. He was simply young enough to believe that sharing what God showed him with his family wouldn't cost him anything. His gift was divine, but his emotional intelligence was still under construction. He assumed that family equaled safety, that closeness equaled covering, that familiarity equaled celebration.

But influence requires wisdom that youth has not yet developed. And this is the tension we navigate as believers, CEOs, entrepreneurs, creatives, and leaders: you may not always recognize insecurity when you're looking at it. It doesn't always announce itself. It doesn't always look like jealousy. Sometimes it looks like quiet discomfort, passive resistance, or a subtle shift in tone when your vision grows louder than their comfort zone. Sometimes it looks like a family member who smiles but never supports. Sometimes it looks like a friend who says, "I'm just trying to protect you," when really they're trying to protect themselves from their own disappointment.

Insecurity shows up in conversations where someone dismisses your dream with, "Everybody is doing that," or, "Are you sure that's realistic?" It shows up when you share an idea and someone rushes to tell you why it won't work before you even finish the sentence. It shows up when you tell a sibling you're launching a business, and suddenly they're doing the same thing, not from inspiration, but from competition. It shows up when you tell a coworker your promotion goals, and they conveniently "share" your idea with your boss before you have a chance. It shows up when you're excited about a new opportunity, and someone close to you responds with caution laced in fear: "Don't get your hopes up." "Be careful." "Don't set yourself up for disappointment."

For entrepreneurs, insecurity can look like someone telling you your dream is "too much," "too big," or "too risky"—not because it is, but because it exposes the dream they never chased. For CEOs, it can look like team members who pretend to support you publicly but undermine you privately because your growth threatens their comfort. For creatives, it looks like inspiration being stolen, ideas being "borrowed," or someone dismissing your unique voice because they never developed their own. For pastors or believers, it looks like people spiritualizing their insecurity: "Is that really God?" "Are you sure that's wise?" "Maybe you should slow down."

Insecurity does not always scream. Sometimes it whispers. Sometimes it avoids eye contact. Sometimes it minimizes accomplishment. Sometimes it imitates. Sometimes it withdraws support. Sometimes it uses "advice" as a disguise for discouragement. And the hardest part? You often don't realize it until after you've shared something tender with someone who wasn't emotionally equipped to hold it.

Joseph didn't share his dream with enemies. He shared it with brothers. He shared it with family. He shared it with people who should have been safe. But here's the truth most of us learn only by experience: insecurity is not always visible until your dream exposes it.

Joseph teaches us that some people don't struggle with your dream, they struggle with what your dream awakens in them. Some people do not hate your vision; they hate that your vision exposes the places they stopped dreaming. His anointing was undeniable, but his awareness was underdeveloped. And the unhealed parts of a gifted person are dangerous because they can lead us into mistakes rooted not in arrogance but in innocence, mistakes connected to attention, affirmation, and premature exposure. We can confuse applause for identity, elevate dreams above development, and rush into spaces our character has not caught up to yet.

Joseph's story invites us to grow in discernment, not fear. To share wisely, not loudly. To dream boldly, but protect carefully.

The Danger of Untrained Giftedness

Joseph shares dreams that imply family hierarchy reversal, he is accurate, but unaware. He is seeing something God will eventually perform, but he is announcing it in a room emotionally unprepared to hold it. The leadership skills not yet formed: timing, discretion, relational stewardship, emotional regulation, strategic silence. The modern parallel is clear: you can be spiritually gifted, entrepreneurially talented, visionary in calling, and still be socially unaware. Dreams reveal destiny; they do not replace development.

What Joseph Didn't Know Yet and Every Rising Leader Must Learn

Joseph wasn't merely sharing dreams; he was announcing a shift in power to the very people who benefitted from the current structure. His brothers didn't just hear his testimony; they heard a threat to their place. That's not pride—it's unawareness of hierarchy dynamics.

> **Driver Seat Quote:** "Announcing elevation before relationships can emotionally handle it creates unnecessary conflict."

What they heard: "Your position is shrinking." What he meant: "God showed me something I don't understand yet." What happened: Insecurity was activated. Conflict accelerated. Isolation followed.

Joseph is accurate in revelation and underdeveloped in delivery. He knows what; he does not yet know how or when.

Why Vision Without Relational Wisdom Meets Resistance

Influence disrupts established structures. People rarely resist your gift; they resist what your gift changes. People fear what they cannot control. People protect the roles that define them. People interpret your future through their present. People often prefer a predictable order over a providential shift.

This is why relational sensitivity is part of leadership. If your announcement destabilizes identity, people will defend themselves against your destiny.

Driver Seat Quote: "Meaning is irrelevant when emotional intelligence is missing."

Maturity Markers Before You Share

Before you speak publicly about a dream that could reshape roles, ask: Timing: Is now wise, or is now just exciting? Discretion: Have I shared this with the smallest faithful circle first? Should I share it at all? Relational stewardship: How will this land on the people most affected by it? Emotional regulation: Can I remain grounded if my sharing is met with silence or pushback? Strategic silence: What needs incubation before exposure?

Driver Seat Quote: "Revelation without restraint creates resistance. Revelation with restraint creates partnership."

Modern Parallels

Family: You share a scholarship, a move, or a ministry call at dinner. A relative "smiles" but minimizes, redirects, or quietly imitates. And because family feels safe, you don't expect sabotage, but sometimes the people at your table become the first to question your credibility, discourage your momentum, or actively block the very opportunities God opened for you. Like Joseph's brothers, their proximity gives them power to wound you in ways strangers cannot.

CEOs / Leaders: You preview a restructuring to a senior team that will lose status. They nod in the room and resist outside the room. And before you realize it, they are subtly undermining you in meetings, misrepresenting decisions to staff, or aligning with board members to slow your progress, not because your vision is wrong, but because its success would mean they no longer hold the same authority.

Entrepreneurs: You float a product idea to a "supportive" cousin; the next week they've registered the domain. And suddenly you're in a legal or competitive fight you never wanted, sabotaging timelines, destroying trust, and forcing you to defend a dream that wasn't even ready to launch. Like Joseph's robe, the idea you shared can be seized and weaponized.

Creatives: You unveil a concept to peers; they "borrow" your frame and question your originality. And in a single conversation, they can drain your confidence, beat you to the market, or make you second-guess your value, not because you lacked creativity, but because you shared tender work with someone who saw it as competition instead of collaboration.

Believers: You testify about a calling; someone wraps fear in spiritual language: "Are you sure that's God?" "This might not be your season." And sometimes that kind of spiritualized insecurity can paralyze your movement, bury your conviction, or delay obedience, not because God hesitated, but because you trusted a voice that masked fear as wisdom.

Why This Matters

Every one of these scenarios mirrors Joseph's story: He shared something sacred with people he trusted… and they weaponized what he revealed. Not out of hatred for the dream itself, but because of what the dream awakened in them. Joseph's life teaches us that: Not all harm is obvious. Not all sabotage is bold. Not all danger looks like danger. Not all "safe spaces" are spiritually, emotionally, or relationally safe.

Insecurity doesn't always scream. Sometimes it whispers, cautions, imitates, withholds celebration, or changes the subject when your vision grows louder than their comfort zone. And often, you don't recognize it until after you've entrusted something sacred.

The Leadership Lesson Buried in Joseph's Moment

Joseph's story reveals a leadership truth many learn only through painful experience: vision requires relational sensitivity. You cannot announce role shifts to people whose identity is invested in keeping the current order intact. When God begins to elevate you, the people around you will not all have the capacity to celebrate it. Some have been strengthened by your stability, not your rise. Others have defined themselves through your predictability, not your potential. Vision, therefore, demands discernment, not because the dream is wrong, but because not every relational environment is strong enough to carry the weight of your revelation.

Hierarchy shifts require maturity, and Joseph learned that the hard way. A divine prophecy spoken out loud in the wrong timing, in the wrong room, and in the wrong tone can create fallout that was fully preventable. The dream was right, but the announcement was unwise. Many leaders sabotage favor not because they misheard God, but because they misread the moment. Revelation is perfect; delivery requires growth. God often gives us dreams in raw form, but He expects us to cultivate the relational wisdom to know *when* to speak, *how* to speak, and *to whom* it should first be spoken.

This becomes even more complex when you recognize that your growth may be felt as someone else's loss. Your horizon can feel like another person's sunset. Your rising can feel like their diminishing. This is not always jealousy, sometimes it is insecurity, identity confusion, or fear. But whatever its source, spiritual maturity teaches a leader to read the room before they reveal the dream.

And that leads to the Driver Seat Leadership truth at the heart of this moment: Some relationships only thrive as long as you play a minimized version of yourself. When you stand upright, doors shift. Roles shift. Dynamics shift. Not everyone wants that shift, which is exactly why vision must be stewarded with both boldness and emotional intelligence.

Driver Seat Quote: "Your growth threatens those who benefit from your smallness."

A Mini Driver Seat Coaching Moment

Before you speak, lead, or unveil what God is growing inside you, slow down long enough to reflect. Ask yourself: Who actually feels safer when I share, and who feels smaller? Some people add strength to your revelation. Others drain the oxygen from it. Discernment in this area is not suspicion, it is stewardship.

Next, discern what part of the dream still needs incubation: prayer, planning, counsel, and timing. Not every dream is ready for daylight. Some grow best in the unseen until your character and capacity can sustain the weight of its visibility.

Then decide: Who are the first one to three people I can trust with an unformed vision? Choose those who are wise enough to guide you, honest enough to correct you, and secure enough not to compete with you.

When you begin sharing, share in layers, not blasts. Offer implications, not proclamations. Float the direction, not the destination. This gives your relationships and your leadership room to adjust without unnecessary shockwaves.

And finally, set guardrails around your calling: No public announcements without a private strategy and a prepared core. Vision should never be exposed before you've built the strength to hold it.

Knowing When to Accelerate and When to Pull Over

I want to challenge you throughout this book, as you read the transitions, triumphs, and traumas of Joseph, to realize that the unhealed parts of you will demand a healed version of you in order to process what God has in store. Every level will require a different you, not a different gift.

Joseph had to learn the hard way that your gift can announce you before life has prepared you. He was trying to outrun the growth process. We see this often in society. I have seen it. I have experienced it. That temptation to get to a place first instead of getting to that place prepared. That internal urgency that pushes us to accelerate when we haven't even stabilized. That subtle pressure to prove we're ready, even when our emotional maturity has notified us that we are not.

This is one of the substratums of Christian development, the process we try to skip because we are not prepared or patient enough for God to process us for promotion, prosperity, or leadership. We tell ourselves every season is our season, every moment is our moment, and every yes is our yes. But it takes a healed and mature person to say, "This is not my season. This is not my season to prosper. This is my season to be disciplined. This is not my season to go after everything I see. This is my season to subtract, because I am creating boundaries that protect my emotional stability."

A healed person does not rush into visibility. A mature person knows that acceleration without alignment is danger. And a wise person understands that the road to destiny includes moments where God keeps the car in park so He can work under the hood.

Maturity is knowing when to accelerate and when to pull over, when to respond, and when to rest, when to pursue, and when to pause, when to knock on the next opportunity, and when to let the next opportunity knock on you. In leadership, this discernment is everything. You can outrun timing. You can outrun boundaries. You can even outrun people. But you cannot outrun the need for processing. You cannot bypass the inner work and hope the outer world doesn't collapse.

This is why God disciplines our pace before He increases our platform. He teaches us to listen to internal warning lights. He teaches us to recognize emotional fatigue before it becomes moral failure. He trains us to slow down before speeding becomes self-destruction.

The Driver Seat principle is simple: God gives direction... but He will also whisper "slow down" or "pull over" when your soul is overheating. Acceleration without spiritual awareness is wreckage waiting to happen. The truth is: Your destiny is not just about where you're going. It's about who you are becoming on the way. And timing, God's timing, is the tool that makes sure both stay aligned.

Necessary Roads

God was not punishing Joseph. He was developing Joseph. When we think about development and processing, we often think about how God does it. That is not our responsibility. Our responsibility is obedience, to say yes to God's will. When people think about Joseph's story, they ask why the pit. Was the pit rejection? No. The pit was preparation. Was prison necessary? Was Egypt necessary? While you are reading this book, I want to declare that the pit, the prison, and Egypt were not negative. They were necessary. Necessary seasons do not always feel good, but they always do good.

Egypt was the place where an unhealed, underdeveloped boy became a wise, whole, disciplined leader. God develops us in certain environments to bring out raw gifting and to clarify what He is doing in our lives. In order for God to transform Joseph's life, He had to transform his sight. Joseph is a perfect picture of that.

Staying Humble in the Driver Seat

Every brilliant person attracts jealousy. Brilliance that shows up early feels threatening to those who are older but not wise, present but not progressing. Joseph did not realize it yet, but giftedness reveals two things at the same time: your destiny and other people's insecurities. They were not reacting to Joseph. They were reacting to the reminder that they were stuck. Your movement exposes their stagnation. Friend groups break up. Organizations fracture. Systems destabilize, not because the dream is offensive, but because elevation confronts places where others have grown comfortable.

This is the rarely discussed danger of early giftedness: your rising can feel like someone else's falling. Joseph shared dreams that announced future influence, but he lacked the humility and perspective to recognize that his brothers could not hear those dreams without hearing their own displacement. Jealousy distorts relationships. It turns celebration into comparison, proximity into suspicion, and family into quiet rivalry. The ones you assume are safe can become the ones most unsettled by your growth, not because they dislike you, but because they do not know what to do with what God is doing in you.

Joseph's immaturity came from growing up in a space that felt safe but was not actually safe. He believed his brothers were the safest space. That misconception still misleads leaders today. Closeness does not equal covering. Proximity does not equal protection. Shared blood does not always mean shared vision. Some people are close enough to observe your gift but not healed enough to celebrate its future.

So in His mercy, God introduced Joseph to responsibility earlier than he realized. Not to punish him, but to protect him. God was teaching him how to drive in terrains that others would retreat from. God trains His leaders in environments that intimidate the unprepared. He uses pressure to produce humility, resistance to reveal character, and unexpected responsibility to teach emotional regulation.

Joseph had to realize that with every mile he drove, God wasn't just moving him toward purpose, He was shaping the posture of the man behind the wheel. God wanted him wise and humble in the Driver Seat of his own destiny. Not reactive. Not arrogant. Not insecure. Not validation-driven. But mature enough to carry influence without collapsing under it, and grounded enough to rise without resenting who didn't rise with him.

This is the humility of a Driver Seat leader: being elevated without becoming entitled, being gifted without becoming inflated, and being trusted without becoming careless.

Why Raw Calling Needs Refinement

Raw calling without refinement isolates leaders before it elevates them. Joseph's life is proof that being favored by God does not mean you are ready for influence. Favor reveals potential, but only formation reveals capacity. Early affirmation without adversity produces fragility; acceleration without formation creates collapse. A calling announced too soon becomes a burden you cannot carry, and a platform gained too early becomes a pressure you cannot survive.

This is why Joseph's first leadership lesson is simple but foundational:

before God lets you drive destiny, He teaches you to govern yourself. Before God trusts you with people, He must trust you. Before He promotes you in public, He trains you in private. Before He hands you visibility, He hands you responsibility. Before He promotes your voice, He strengthens your character. Before He enlarges your influence, He excavates your identity.

Joseph's journey shows us that God will not place you in a position where your gifting is louder than your integrity. He will not open a door your emotional maturity cannot walk through. He will not accelerate a life that would fall apart under the weight of its own future. God doesn't just prepare the destination, He prepares the driver. And in Joseph's early years, that preparation required stripping him of external identity, separating him from unsafe familiarity, and walking him through terrain that demanded humility, emotional sobriety, and internal discipline. God was not withholding the palace; He was safeguarding Joseph's soul so the palace wouldn't destroy him once he arrived.

Because destiny is not just about where you're going. It's about who you are when you get there. And God refuses to elevate what you won't let Him refine.

Driver Seat Insights

Gift ≠ Maturity. Vision is not the same as readiness; calling is not the same as competence. The Coat Is a Test. Visibility without inner stability breeds fragility. Timing Is Leadership. Information without discretion destabilizes relationships. Unhealed ≠ Unused, but Unhealed = Unsafe. Pain can walk into the room before purpose does, tend it. Formation Is Mercy. Pits and prisons aren't punishment; they are preparation for weight. Drive Yourself First. The Driver Seat begins with self-governance, not public authority. Favor Isn't Immunity. You can be anointed and still be opposed, learn relational wisdom early.

Prayer

Father, thank You for gifts I don't yet fully understand. Anchor me while You form me. Teach me silence when I want to speak, humility when I'm seen, and discernment when I'm excited. Heal what would sabotage my future and train my reflexes for responsibility. Before You expand my reach, deepen my roots. In Jesus' name, Amen.

Driver Seat Key Takeaways

- **Gift does not equal readiness.** Joseph proves that you can carry a true God-given dream and still lack the maturity, emotional intelligence, and relational awareness needed to steward it. Early vision is accurate, but unprocessed.

- **Vision without timing becomes sabotage.** Joseph isn't rejected for dreaming, he's rejected for announcing. Vision spoken in the wrong room, at the wrong time, to the wrong people creates unnecessary conflict that wisdom could have prevented.

- **Favor is not the same as formation.** The coat made Joseph visible, but not stable. Visibility came before humility, and attention came before emotional grounding. Favor can put you on display before your character is ready to carry it.

- **External identity is fragile identity.** Anything built on what someone else gives you—attention, titles, affirmation, garments—can be taken from you. God strips what is external to strengthen what is internal.

- **Dreams reveal potential; processing reveals capacity.** The pit, the prison, and Egypt are not punishment. They are God's leadership academy. Dreams show where you are going; processing shapes who you must become to get there.

- **Unhealed areas speak louder than giftedness.** Joseph teaches us that your wounds can enter a room before your purpose does. Unhealed places distort perception, provoke insecurity, and can sabotage your own elevation if left unmanaged.

- **Not every "safe space" is spiritually safe.** Joseph shared his dreams with people he trusted, not realizing their insecurity until after the fact.

The lesson: discernment is not suspicion; it is stewardship.

- **Influence exposes insecurities—including in others.** People rarely resist your gift; they resist what your gift changes in their world. Your rising can feel like they're diminishing, and without relational wisdom, vision triggers unnecessary resistance.

- **Elevation requires emotional intelligence, not just revelation.** Joseph knew *what* God said, but not *how* or *when* to say it. Leadership requires timing, discretion, relational stewardship, emotional regulation, and strategic silence.

- **Before God expands your reach, He strengthens your roots.** Joseph's early years reveal the core Driver Seat truth: God prepares the driver before He reveals the destination. He refuses to elevate what we will not let Him refine.

***

Before Joseph can manage Egypt, he must face envy at home. The same dreams that revealed destiny exposed insecurity in familiar places. Chapter 2 opens the first hard truth of leadership: vision does not protect you from betrayal, but betrayal can protect you from immaturity. The brothers are coming, and the road from favor to formation runs straight through their hands. Let's keep reading.

CHAPTER TWO

THE BROTHERS: WHEN THE PEOPLE CLOSEST TO YOU PUSH YOU THE FURTHEST

When Your First Attack Comes From Familiarity

Joseph's first opposition did not arrive from a far-off nation; it rose from within his own household. The contours of the wound are familiar to many: the faces that should have been a refuge became the faces that formed a plan. Before elevation, formation. Before the palace, pressure. Before influence, identity. Joseph's story insists that what shapes us most deeply is not the applause of crowds but the pressure applied by the closest circle. He is not sent into danger by a divine whisper he fully understands; he is sent on an errand by his father, Joseph sent by Jacob to check on his brothers, and he approaches them with the innocence of loyalty, not the armor of suspicion. He is met not by welcome but by calculation: "They conspired against him to slay him." The conspiracy is intentional, relational, and intimate; the injury is not abstract but personal. And then, the unspeakable: "They stript Joseph out of his coat... and cast him into a pit." We will pause the story there, on the brink, with torn fabric and family voices in the air, because this chapter is about the brothers, about what happens to a soul when the first attack comes from familiarity.

When Home Becomes the Detour

One of the things about Joseph's story is that when people look at his story and look at the context by which his narrative really develops, they do not realize that Joseph, at the time of his betrayal from his brothers, is only 17. He is a teenager while experiencing one of the darkest realities a human heart can endure. Most adults cannot survive what Joseph went through at 17, yet he was still expected to function, still expected to trust God, and still expected to move forward with a fractured heart.

Before Egypt ever claimed him, his own household trafficked him. The ones he ate with, laughed with, grew up beside, organized all kinds of things with, and played in the field with did not just betray him. They sold him. They converted their jealousy into currency. And isn't it something how jealousy will always find a buyer and insecurity will always find a transaction.

Joseph's first major transition into destiny came wrapped in the hands of those who shared his blood. This is not a small moment. This is what psychologists now call betrayal trauma and family-of-origin trauma. It is the kind of wound that forms when the people assigned to protect you become the source of your pain.

This is really an ongoing trauma that exists within our inner cities. Young people are often wounded not by strangers, but by systems, homes, families, and environments that were supposed to be safe. The same betrayal Joseph faced is the same betrayal many face today, abandonment, favoritism, survival environments, and unsafe homes.

When Betrayal Wears a Familiar Face

There is a reason this kind of hurt cleaves so close to the bone. Betrayal mines the deepest seams of our belonging. Psychologists call a wound like this **betrayal trauma**, injury inflicted by someone we depend on, which can scramble memory, trust, and even a person's sense of reality, precisely because the betrayer is a needed other. The theory explains why victims sometimes minimize, numb, or "not know" what is happening: the mind bends to survive a relationship it was never meant to fear.

Joseph's brothers do not simply oppose him; they strip him, of his coat, of his place, of the story that garment symbolized. Modern life has its own ways of stripping: the sibling who mocks your calling in the family group chat, the friend who turns your private confession into a public cautionary tale, the ministry partner who uses Scripture as a stick rather than a staff. Such injuries echo the ancient scene because they target identity and trust, not just circumstance.

Leadership Reality

The first threat to your calling may come from people who know your history. The first attack does not come from strangers. It comes from familiarity (Gen. 37:18).

It's a hard truth in leadership, your anointing will often be challenged first by those who helped raise you, those who watched you grow, those who feel they've "seen too much" of you to believe what God placed on you. Familiarity breeds a blindness that makes people misread your calling as competition, your growth as arrogance, and your dreams as delusion.

Joseph wasn't attacked because outsiders misunderstood him; he was attacked because insiders underestimated him. The people who knew his past could not tolerate the possibility of his future. And that is often where the deepest wounds form, not from the blow itself, but from who dealt it.

And this is where the story touches our humanity: When your first wound comes from familiarity, the trauma stays familiar too. It doesn't stay in childhood. It travels. It matures with you. It shows up in moments you thought you had healed from.

How This Shows Up Now—Home, Friendships, Work, and Ministry

In families: Sometimes you're assigned a role you never auditioned for, the "problem," the "too much," the one who must shrink for everyone else to be comfortable. When care becomes conditional, a child learns to perform instead of rest. That's classic betrayal territory: the very place designed for safety becomes the site of wound, and the psyche adapts to preserve the bond at any cost. **Among friends and inner circles:** The pain isn't always loud. It can be the quiet erasure of ostracism, texts stop, invitations dry up, you are present but not included. Research shows that being ignored/excluded threatens core needs of belonging, self-esteem, control, and meaningful existence; even short episodes sting, and chronic exposure depletes coping resources. This is why "the silent treatment" feels like a small death. **In workplaces**: A colleague you trained sidelines you in a meeting; a manager chips away at your dignity with eye rolls and barbed "jokes." That's not trivial. Studies on workplace incivility show it lowers creativity, effort, and retention, and even harms customer trust. In short: disrespect is expensive, for people and for organizations. And the antidote is not just niceness; it's psychological safety, a culture where it is safe to speak up, admit mistakes, and take interpersonal risks. Teams with psychological safety learn and perform better; leaders who coach, listen, and honor candor create the soil where people can heal and do their best work. **In ministry settings**: Church families are not immune. When power is used to control, shame, or silence, especially in the name of God, we call it spiritual abuse. Survivors describe manipulation, enforced secrecy, and the demand to ignore their own God-given conscience to preserve an image. It is still abuse, and it confuses a person's sense of God along with their sense of self. Naming it gives people language to seek help and leaders a mandate to repent and repair.

Betrayal Hits Harder When It's Familiar

You learn something in this moment with Joseph. Betrayal always feels heavier when it comes from familiarity. The people who are close enough to bless you are also close enough to break you. Closeness does not equal character, and proximity does not guarantee purity or safety.

If you do not realize that, you will always fail to detect it. Some of your greatest blessings will come from a person or people closest to you, and some of your greatest pain will come from them as well.

Here is the tension most leaders do not talk about. The same people who helped shape you can also be the ones who shake you. The same hands that held you can be the same hands that hurt you. And when the hurt comes from home, it hits differently. It destabilizes you, it confuses you, and it forces you into decisions you never planned to make.

It is often this kind of familiar pain that God uses as a breaking point, a turning point, and a launching point. And this is the very betrayal that pushed Joseph out of his comfort zone. To be honest with you, sometimes God uses these different types of pains to push us. Sometimes the only thing strong enough to get you moving is the thing that wounded you.

Attachment science helps explain why "brothers'" betrayal feels different. When a trusted other fails you at a moment of need, it creates what therapists call an attachment injury, a rupture so pivotal that the event becomes the new "measure" of whether the relationship is safe. This is why one moment, one meeting, one conversation, one Sunday, is enough to flip the story you thought you were living. The body remembers. The heart re-narrates everything around that breach.

Ostracism and exclusion, even when subtle, strike those same needs, belonging, self-esteem, control, meaningful existence, and, over time, can spiral into depression and helplessness if left unaddressed. This is not "thin-skinned"; this is human. God created us for covenant and community; the science simply traces the contours of what Scripture has declared about our design.

Trauma That Travels With You

This is a trauma that transfers into our careers because unaddressed childhood betrayal creates adults who struggle with trust, collaboration, and leadership confidence. This is a trauma that transfers into our pain and into our pursuit of various career choices. Many of us pick careers, ministries, friendships, and even partners trying to outrun or overcorrect the wounds our childhood gave us. Joseph's trauma followed him into Egypt just like ours follows us into adulthood.

This trauma, if it is not managed properly in private, will sometimes burst out in public. Trauma does not disappear. It disguises itself. It speaks in our tone, in our fears, in our defensiveness, and in our inability to rest or to trust. It shows up in how we lead and how we love.

People do not always see the childhood wound behind the adult reaction, but it is there. It leaks into leadership, into love, into relationships, and into decisions. It explains why strong leaders sometimes panic, why gifted people sometimes withdraw, and why talented individuals sabotage opportunities because the pit of their past is still speaking in the palace of their present.

And this is why leaders must learn to do the work within. You cannot lead others while outrunning what is pursuing you. You cannot build strong teams on a shaky inner foundation. You cannot steward a calling while ignoring the wounds that keep calling your name.

How Leaders Must Address "Brothers' Betrayal"

This chapter is not only for those who have been hurt; it is also for shepherds, supervisors, and team leads who want to **stop** this pattern where they serve. Joseph's brothers formed a conspiracy; leaders must cultivate the opposite, cultures that confront envy, refuse secrecy, and protect the vulnerable. Practically:

- **Build psychological safety on purpose.**
  Normalize candor ("We tell the truth here"), model fallibility ("Here's what I missed"), and protect dissent ("You won't be punished for raising a concern"). Psychological safety is a leading predictor of team learning and performance, and it starts with how leaders respond when people risk honesty.

- **Call incivility what it is and correct it quickly.**
  Eye-rolling, sarcasm, and subtle sabotage corrode dignity and output. Research shows incivility hurts creativity, effort, retention, and reputation. Address behaviors, clarify standards, and reinforce honor as a non-negotiable.

- **Refuse spiritualized harm.**

If someone is shamed, silenced, or controlled "for their own good," you're not building disciples, you're breeding deception. Set transparent processes for reporting harm, involve independent oversight when needed, and center the care of the wounded over the protection of the platform. The literature on spiritual abuse urges precisely this clarity and protection.

- **Shepherd reconciliation without coercion.**
  Forgiveness is biblical and deeply healing, but it cannot be rushed or weaponized. Evidence-based forgiveness interventions (such as Enright's model or Worthington's REACH) show real benefits for depression, anxiety, and hope, yet they respect pacing, agency, and safety. Leaders should offer pathways and resources, not pressure or performative reconciliations.

- **Repair attachment injuries with presence and protection.**
  When trust is shattered, the repair is not a memo; it is reliable responsiveness over time. In close relationships (and church families), we heal when those who failed become emotionally accessible and accountable, and when structures prevent repeat harm. That is the way bonds are re-knit.

The First Step: Naming the Trauma

Healing begins with honesty. What you refuse to name, you cannot address. Trauma grows in silence, but it loses power when brought into the light. Biblically, God has always invited His people to name the truth: Adam was asked to name what was in front of him. Jacob had to name himself before God renamed him. David named his fear, his grief, and his wounds in the Psalms. Jesus asked sick people, "What do you want Me to do for you?"—an invitation to acknowledge the real issue.

Psychologically, naming the trauma is called integration, bringing the fragmented parts of our story into awareness so they stop controlling us from the shadows. You cannot heal what you pretend does not hurt.

The Work of Healing

Healing is both spiritual and practical. God can deliver you in a moment, but as we discussed earlier, He often develops you through a process, one that is intentional, layered, and deeply formational. Biblically, healing begins with confession, not as a performance but as an act of truth-telling, admitting the wound rather than hiding it in the shadows where shame likes to grow (1 John 1:9; Proverbs 28:13; Psalm 32:3–5). It continues in the renewing of the mind, confronting the false narratives trauma has planted, stories that whisper you are unworthy, unsafe, unseen, and replacing them with the truth God has spoken over you (Romans 12:2; 2 Corinthians 10:5; Philippians 4:8). Healing deepens through prayer and lament, where you give your pain to God without editing it, filtering it, or dressing it in religious language. Real lament is holy ground; it is the soul telling the truth in God's direction (Psalm 34:17–18; Psalm 13; Lamentations 3:19–24; Hebrews 4:16). Then comes forgiveness, not the excusing of harm but the releasing of its hold, loosening the grip that bitterness tries to keep on your identity (Ephesians 4:31–32; Matthew 6:14–15; Colossians 3:13). And intertwined through it all is community, the presence of safe relationships that model healthier patterns, hold space for your growth, and remind you what love is supposed to feel like (Hebrews 10:24–25; Galatians 6:2; Proverbs 27:17; Ecclesiastes 4:9–10).

Psychologically, healing also requires courage. It involves identifying triggers and understanding how past wounds disguise themselves in present reactions. It asks you to process your story with language rather than suppression, because what you cannot articulate will continue to animate you from the shadows. Healing requires rebuilding trust slowly and deliberately, allowing your nervous system to relearn what safety feels like. It requires establishing boundaries, not walls of isolation but gates of wisdom that protect new growth. And for deeper wounds, it often involves engaging therapy or counseling, where trauma can be integrated rather than ignored, named rather than numbed, understood rather than avoided. Research on forgiveness-based interventions shows that when this work is done gently and with proper pacing, people experience measurable decreases in depression and anxiety along with increases in hope and emotional stability. Pace and safety always matter.

When leaders engage in this inner work, their leadership gains clarity. Their influence becomes safer. Their decisions become grounded. Their hearts rest easier. Their relationships become healthier. Because healed leaders lead differently, they don't bleed on people they were called to bless, and they don't confuse authority with control. Healing does not erase the past, but it removes the past's permission to lead the present. It loosens the grip of old memories and allows new patterns to take root. It transforms survival into stability, reaction into discernment, and instability into wisdom. It restores the leader before it ever touches the leadership.

A leader who embraces this process begins to change in ways both subtle and profound. They no longer rush to defend themselves, because their worth is no longer on trial. Their correction becomes steady rather than sharp because they are no longer reacting from old wounds. Their presence becomes a shelter, firm without being harsh, honest without being harmful. They make space at the table for others, because someone else's rise no longer feels like their fall. They listen with intention, speak with restraint, and choose accountability over ego.

Healed leaders carry authority without intimidation, vision without paranoia, and strength without dominance. They can remain calm in conflict because peace has finally taken root internally. They make decisions from clarity, not fear; from conviction, not insecurity. They are able to apologize without crumbling, delegate without micromanaging, and correct without crushing. And their teams, families, and ministries feel the difference, because where a wounded leader exhausts a room, a whole leader steadies it.

Healing reshapes leadership from the inside out. It replaces urgency with patience, defensiveness with wisdom, reactivity with discernment, and emotional volatility with spiritual maturity. The result is a life, and a leadership, marked by depth, steadiness, and integrity. A healed leader doesn't just lead better; they *love* better, they *see* better, they *discern* better. They become the kind of leader God can trust with people, because they no longer need people to heal the parts of them they have already surrendered to Him.

Thrown Out of Comfort and Into Calling

Joseph did not leave home. Home left him. There is a difference between walking out and being pushed out, between choosing a path and having the ground taken from beneath your feet. Some people's journeys begin with opportunity; others begin with a tear in the fabric of belonging. When home leaves you, it is not just a change of address, it is a rupture in the soul. The place that should have wrapped its arms around you instead became the backdrop of your heartbreak. You didn't pack a bag and say goodbye; you woke up one day and realized the place you called safe had quietly decided you were no longer welcome.

What pushed him out of his comfort was not a calling he understood. It was the cruelty of the brothers he trusted. Sometimes our lives are redirected not by visions and voices but by the sharp edges of betrayal. Destiny can begin with disorientation. You thought you were stepping into the next chapter with family beside you, but the pages curled in the heat of envy and misunderstanding. Their cruelty didn't just bruise your body or your reputation, it bruised your sense of worth. The ones who should have shielded you became the ones you had to shield yourself from. And it wasn't a clean break. Cruelty from those we love lingers, echoing in the hallways of memory, replaying conversations, re-lighting old scenes at 2 a.m. when sleep refuses to come.

He was thrown into a pit by those whose faces he recognized. That's the worst of it, isn't it? It wasn't a stranger. You knew their laughter. You could recognize their footsteps on gravel. You could identify their silhouette against the dusk. The mind falters when suffering wears a familiar face. That kind of wound becomes more than a moment; it becomes a question: How could you? And eventually, a second question: Who am I, if even you could do this to me? The pit is not just a location, it is a season where trust, identity, and innocence fall into the dark together. You don't just climb out of that; you have to be lifted, slowly, by grace and truth.

There is somewhere in Scripture where the text essentially says, "An enemy I can handle, a hater I can handle, but you were my family." David puts words to this kind of pain in Psalm 55:12–14 in the NLT. "It is not an enemy I could bear that, but it is you, my close friend, the one I walked to the house of God with." That is the kind of wound Joseph endured. And it is the kind of wound that still bleeds in our world: the mother who favored one child and made you the family scapegoat, the spouse who promised forever but left you standing in the shards of trust, the friend who knew your secrets and turned them into a weapon, the church that preached grace but practiced gossip, the manager you trained who quietly undercut your name. These are pits with familiar faces looking down, faces that don't reach in.

If this is you, hear this with tenderness: you are not weak for still hurting. You are not faithless for feeling shattered. Deep wounds take time because they touch deep places, places where you learned what love is, what safety is, what "home" is. When those foundations crack, you grieve not only what happened but what should have happened. You grieve the version of your story where they stayed, protected, believed, and held. You grieve the birthdays that became battlegrounds, the holidays that felt like hostage situations, the pew that became a courtroom. Your tears are not a lack of faith; they are evidence that your heart was made for covenant, for constancy, for the unbroken.

And yet, here is holy ground: God does not waste pits. The same God who met Joseph in the dark meets you in yours, not asking you to pretend it didn't happen, but offering to touch the wound without flinching. He does not say, "Get over it." He says, "Give it to Me." He does not trivialize the betrayal. He transforms it. In time, the pit becomes a place where lies are unlearned: the lie that you were forgettable, the lie that you were too much or not enough, the lie that love must be earned by shrinking yourself. In time, the pit becomes the workshop where God reforges your identity: chosen, seen, held, and sent, not by cruelty, but by calling.

In the modern world, "home leaving you" might look like being written out of the family group text after you set a boundary; being the child who protected everyone but no one protected; watching your father walk out and carrying the ache of his absence into every room; facing a spouse's secret life and wondering if anything you shared was real; asking a pastor for help and discovering your pain became a sermon illustration you didn't consent to; rebuilding from financial sand because a sibling you trusted scattered the inheritance. These are not stories you simply "move on" from. They are stories you must move through, with God.

How do you combat a wound like this without becoming hard yourself? You begin where David began: with truth. Name it. This hurt me because it came from someone close. Refuse to spiritualize the harm into silence. Lament is not complaining; it is worship that tells the truth. Then, guard your heart with wisdom. Forgiveness is not access. Love is not the absence of boundaries. You can bless from a distance. You can honor God without allowing repeated injury. Let trusted people hold space for your healing: a counselor who can help you untangle the knot of shame and blame; a small circle of friends who know when to speak and when to sit in the ashes with you; a mentor who can remind you who you are when your own voice sounds like an echo.

Next, refuse to internalize their actions as your identity. What they did reveals them, not you. You are not disposable, not extra, not "too much." When the old narratives rise—See? You're unlovable; you're always left; you're the problem, answer them with a better Word: I am loved with an everlasting love. I am not forsaken. I am being led, even here. Let God reframe the story, not by denying the evil, but by overruling it with purpose. The same way Joseph eventually discovered that what others meant for harm, God could weave into good, you too will discover that rejection can become redirection, that loss can become holy space for new life to grow, that the pit can become the place you learned to hear God without the crowd.

And finally, practice release, not as a one-time moment, but as a rhythm. Release the need to be understood by people committed to misunderstanding you. Release the audition for rooms that shrink you. Release the story where they become the person they promised to be if it means losing the person God is forming in you now. Release the bitterness that hardens your edges and silences your song. This is not denial; it is deliverance, handing the gavel back to God and stepping out of the courtroom you've been carrying in your chest.

If this is your story...

If you are reading this and recognizing your own brothers, at home, at work, or in church, take heart. You are not weak for still hurting. You are human. Name the wound (lament is worship). Set wise boundaries (forgiveness is not access). Seek safe people, counselors and friends who can hold space rather than rush you past your pain. Evidence suggests that, when you are ready, practicing forgiveness with good guidance can improve mental and even physical health; but no one should demand it on their timeline or use it to bypass accountability.

And for the one tempted to "join the brothers"—to conspire in whispers or strip someone's dignity because their favor agitates your insecurity, hear the warning and the invitation. Envy feels powerful for a moment, but it always robs the family and wounds the Father's heart. If you have participated in harm, confess it fully, make restitution, and choose a better way. Leadership begins with self-leadership.

Prayer

Father, You see wounds with familiar faces. Where betrayal has stripped identity and trust, wrap Your child in a better garment, belonging that no envy can tear. Give leaders the courage to confront harm, and give the wounded wisdom for boundaries, companions for the journey, and, in time, the grace to forgive without returning to danger. Guard our circles from conspiracy. Teach us covenant. In Jesus' name, amen.

Driver Seat Key Takeaways

- **The first wounds often come from the closest circle.** Joseph's story shows that the earliest threats to calling do not emerge from enemies but from familiarity. Home can become the first battlefield, and the people who should have protected you can become the ones who oppose you.

- **Familiar betrayal cuts deeper because it targets identity, not just circumstance.** His brothers did not simply harm him; they stripped him of his coat, his place, and the story it symbolized. Modern betrayals work the same way, striking at worth, belonging, and trust.

- **Familiarity creates blindness that distorts how others see your calling.** People who watched you grow may misread your gift as arrogance, your growth as threat, and your destiny as delusion. Proximity does not guarantee understanding, safety, or character.

- **Betrayal trauma reshapes a person's inner world until it is healed.** Psychology calls this betrayal trauma because the wound comes from a needed other. It can scramble memory, trust, and even your sense of reality. Unhealed, it travels with you into work, ministry, relationships, and leadership.

- **Jealousy always finds a transaction and insecurity always finds a buyer.** Joseph's brothers converted jealousy into currency. The same pattern plays out today in homes, friendships, churches, and workplaces where insecurity fuels sabotage.

- **The deepest attacks are intimate, not distant.** Insiders underestimated Joseph and rejected the possibility of his future. The blow hurts more because of who delivered it. Leaders must face the reality that betrayal from home hits harder and lingers longer.

- **Trauma that is not addressed in private will eventually leak in public.** Pain disguises itself. It shows up in defensiveness, withdrawal, irritability, distrust, perfectionism, or fear. Leadership is shaped by what lies beneath the surface.

- **Healing requires naming the trauma with honesty before God and trusted people.** What you refuse to name you cannot heal. Scripture and psychology agree: truth telling, confession, lament, and integration are the doorway to restoration.

- **Boundaries are holy stewardship, not a lack of forgiveness.** Forgiveness is biblical, but access is wisdom. You can bless from a distance. You can forgive without returning to harmful patterns or unsafe relationships.

- **God does not waste pits; He transforms them into places of reformation.** What Joseph endured was not the end of his story but the beginning of his formation. God uses the pain caused by familiar hands to redirect, reshape, and refine leaders into who they must become for destiny.

***

Holding the line at the pit

This chapter closes where Genesis 37:23–24 closes at the edge of the pit, with fabric in their hands and dust in the air. They stripped him and cast him into a pit. And here, we pause. We do not follow Joseph down just yet, because Chapter 3 will descend into the darkness that swallowed him. Let's keep reading.

CHAPTER THREE

The Pit: When Alignment Feels Like Abandonment

PART 1: WHEN YOU'RE DOWN BUT NOT DONE

There are seasons in life when the fall happens so suddenly that your mind cannot immediately interpret what your heart is feeling. One moment you are walking in confidence, certain of where you are headed, and the next moment you find yourself somewhere you never expected, somewhere dark, somewhere lonely, somewhere empty. The Bible describes Joseph's pit in simple terms, but the impact of that moment was far from simple. Joseph was not merely dropped into a hole; he was thrust into an experience that would strip him of everything familiar, everything comfortable, and everything he once associated with identity. Yet paradoxically, this moment of being thrown down became the foundation of who he was destined to become.

This experience is not isolated to Joseph. Anyone who has walked through a sudden collapse, emotionally, financially, relationally, spiritually, knows that the human heart cannot immediately interpret shock. Psychology calls this "emotional whiplash," a rapid and unexpected disruption that overwhelms the mind's ability to categorize what is happening. You know something shattered, but you cannot yet articulate which part of you absorbed the impact. This is why pit seasons feel suffocating, your heart knows you fell, but your mind is still searching for the moment gravity changed.

Joseph's journey to the pit began before the fall itself. It began with a plan, a plan originally intended to kill him. His brothers had moved from jealousy to malice, from irritation to intention. What started as dislike had matured into a strategy for destruction. And right as that strategy was about to be carried out, Reuben intervened. Reuben didn't rescue him entirely, but he disrupted the plan enough to prevent Joseph's death. This moment is critical, not only in Joseph's story but in the story of anyone walking through purpose: God will often send a partial intervention to keep you alive until His full plan unfolds. Sometimes the hand of God shows up not in a total rescue but in a subtle interruption, enough to protect you, even if it doesn't feel like deliverance. Reuben's idea was simple: don't kill him. Throw him into a pit instead. His intention was to return later and pull Joseph out.

But even good intentions cannot override divine process.

Every person called by God will eventually experience a moment when human intention, both good and bad, bows to divine orchestration. Reuben's intervention was necessary, but it was not sovereign. God did not allow the rescue because He had already ordained the route. You may have people who want to help you, soften the blow for you, or rescue you, and yet God will still lead you through a season they cannot intervene in. Sometimes the protection you want is denied so the development you need can occur. The pit was not a punishment; it was part of Joseph's curriculum.

PART 2: THE STRIPPING AND THE FALL

Genesis 37:21–24

The brothers stripped Joseph of the robe before they threw him into the pit. This detail is not incidental; it is deeply symbolic. Joseph's robe represented more than clothing, it represented identity, favor, approval, and distinction. That robe reminded the brothers daily that Joseph was chosen in a way they were not. To them, tearing off that robe wasn't just about removing a garment; it was about attempting to remove Joseph's significance. People will often attack the symbol of your calling when they cannot attack your calling itself. They will go after what they can reach, not realizing they cannot touch what God has ordained.

Joseph stood there, likely stunned as hands ripped away what had once set him apart. A robe he didn't ask for. Favor he didn't choose. A calling he didn't fully understand. The stripping was violent and humiliating, but it carried a deeper message: anything external can be taken away, but what God places within you cannot be touched. That robe distinguished Joseph, but it didn't define him. Losing it didn't diminish his assignment, it simply exposed what was truly inside him.

Driver Seat Quote: "If losing something changes who you are, that thing was defining you more than God was."

This moment is far more than a garment being torn. Psychologically, relationally, and spiritually, this is the moment Joseph's identity detaches from externals and anchors in God. And the exact same moment plays out today in entrepreneurs, pastors, leaders, families, and anyone navigating identity transition.

Let's break this open.

Identity Detachment: A Psychological Break That Leads To Wholeness

From a psychological perspective, the robe represented external validation, parental approval, special status, social identity, and belonging and significance. When something symbolizes identity, losing it creates what psychology calls an identity rupture, a forced separation between who you think you are and who you actually are without the role, recognition, or symbol. Joseph's brothers didn't tear fabric. They tore the thin layer between external identity and internal identity. That's why God allowed it. If you need the robe to feel chosen, you aren't ready for the palace. If you need the coat to feel called, you can't yet be trusted with nations. If approval or status defines you, leadership will destroy you. The robe distinguished Joseph. God intended the pit to define him. Because the pit stripped him of everything external so that everything internal could be built.

Symbolic Stripping: Who You Are Without The "Robes" Of Life

I believe every person has a "robe"—a role, a relationship, an achievement, or a status that becomes a substitute for identity. For entrepreneurs, the robe might be a title, revenue number, or market validation. For pastors, it might be platform, applause, or the size of the congregation. For leaders, it might be influence, respect, or position. For individuals, it might be a relationship, a job, a talent, or an appearance. Joseph losing the robe parallels the emotional collapse people feel when they lose a job, a title, a relationship, a place in a family, a ministry role, financial stability, a reputation, or a dream they put their worth into. Psychologically, this triggers what's called an ego collapse. Spiritually, it triggers a divine rebuild. God will strip the robe to save the soul.

The Driver Seat Quote That is a Revelation of True Selfhood

"If losing something changes who you are, that thing was defining you more than God was." This is a clinically accurate and biblically sound truth. In psychology, anything you cannot lose without losing yourself is a false self-structure. In theology, anything you cannot surrender without breaking is an idol. Joseph didn't lose himself when the robe came off, which proves the robe wasn't identity, only presentation. What was inside him (gift, integrity, favor, calling) was untouched by external loss. Today's leaders face the same test. If the robe was your title, if the robe was your beauty, if the robe was your talent, if the robe was your marriage, if the robe was your money, if the robe was your platform, then losing that thing exposes what you built identity on. This quote isn't condemnation, it's correction. God reveals what you're resting on so He can shift you to what can't be taken away.

Biblical Lens: God Always Strips Before He Builds

Every great biblical leader underwent a stripping. Moses lost royalty before leading Israel. David lost position before becoming king. Paul lost reputation before preaching Christ. Jesus was stripped before resurrection. Stripping is not shame, it is sanctification. God never elevates what He hasn't first separated. Joseph's robe was taken, but his anointing remained. Joseph's dignity was assaulted, but his destiny was untouched. Joseph's external significance was removed, but his internal significance was intact. That's why after he loses the robe, Scripture shifts focus to his character, his integrity, his discipline, his favor, his leadership, his interpretation gift, his stewardship, and his resilience. In other words, everything God needed was inside him. Everything his brothers hated was inside him. Everything the robe represented was a reflection of what was already in him. The stripping exposed the truth: Joseph wasn't chosen because of the coat. He had the coat because he was chosen.

Let's Dive A Little Deeper Into How Leaders Today Experience "The Stripping"

For entrepreneurs, the robe is the brand, valuation, praise, funding, or success narrative. When the "robe" gets stripped, the failed launch, public criticism, financial downturn, the founder either collapses or transforms. Joseph teaches: You are not the company you built. You are the character you bring. And that cannot be stripped. **For church leaders**, the robe is the applause, platform, title, or people's approval. God strips these gently or forcefully to anchor identity in calling rather than crowd. Pastors preach differently when they no longer preach for validation. The pit makes ministry authentic. In family dynamics, some people have been the "responsible one," "the gifted one," "the strong one," "the achiever," or "the parentified child." When life strips that identity, you learn whether those roles were labels or truth. The pit invites you to lead from who you are, not from the role the family assigned. **For self-leadership,**

losing a job, relationship, community, or role often strips the identity we tied to that thing. The pit teaches you to build selfhood on God's voice, not on circumstances.

For founders and builders, the robe may be valuation, title, a blue-chip client logo, or the public narrative of momentum. The throw can be a term sheet pulled hours before closing, a cofounder's sudden exit, a platform policy change that crushes your CAC, or an unexpected cash-flow winter. The shock isn't only the loss, it's how quickly the ground disappeared. Joseph's cistern teaches you to separate identity from optics. In the pit, faithful leaders narrow to the mission that will matter ten years from now, not just the metric that flatters this quarter. Prayerful pruning clarifies product, strengthens unit economics, and matures governance. Wisdom means slowing the announcement cadence to match reality, tightening burn, and surrounding yourself with counselors who tell the truth (Proverbs 11:14; James 1:5). Your true unfair advantage is not hype; it is holiness, integrity that compounds over long obedience.

For Church Leaders — When Ministry Strips Your Robe

For pastors and ministry builders, the robe can be platform, invitations, or congregational applause. The throw might be a staff betrayal, a public misunderstanding, a scandal not of your making, or a season where fruit seems to vanish. Joseph's experience reminds you that Jesus Himself was stripped (Matthew 27:28); yet the stripping did not diminish the Kingdom, it revealed it. Pit seasons recalibrate the soul away from crowd-sized identity (Galatians 1:10) to Shepherd-sized obedience (John 10:27). This is when you reclaim sabbath as resistance to performance, reconnect your preaching to tears and truth (2 Corinthians 4:1–2), and lead with a limp that refuses to romanticize ministry. God is forming in you a tenderness and durability that programs cannot manufacture. In time, your people will eat from fruit grown in this soil.

For Family Dynamics — When Your Own Strip The Robe

In families, the robe might be the role you always played, golden child, rescuer, peacemaker, achiever. When God begins re-authoring your identity, systems attached to the old dynamics can react. Like Joseph's brothers, some may "strip" symbols that remind them you are changing. Healthy discipleship embraces both honor and boundaries. You can love your people without letting them define you. Romans 12:18 offers nuance: live peaceably "as far as it depends on you," which acknowledges that it doesn't always depend on you. Joseph's story frees you from performing roles to keep peace that isn't real and invites you to become a non-anxious presence whose identity rests in God's voice.

For Self-leadership — When Your Own Life Throws You

If you are leading only yourself right now, the robe could be the routines that once made you feel competent: the job you held, the apartment you curated, the study track you were proud of, the friend circle that framed your weekends. The throw might be a layoff, a break-up, a denial letter, or a diagnosis. Self-leadership in this cistern looks like building a small, brave rule of life: Scripture before screens, prayer before planning, movement before meetings, and one honest conversation each week with a safe, wise person. Psalm 27:13–14 becomes breath-prayer: "I will see the goodness of the Lord... wait for the Lord; be strong; let your heart take courage." You are not what you lost. You are who God is forming beneath the losses.

For Organizational Leaders — When You're Thrown By Your Own System

Executives and team leaders can be "thrown" by board decisions, market shocks, or internal politics that escalate overnight. The robe might be authority you assumed was secure. Joseph's pit offers three anchors. First, emotional regulation is leadership oxygen; respond after prayer, not just after pressure

(Nehemiah 2:4–5). Second, strategic silence is not passivity; it is timing, release information in layers that match your people's capacity (Proverbs 15:23). Third, rebuild trust with transparent processes and principled decisions, even when outcomes are costly (Daniel 6:4). The pit tests your governance so that future elevation does not outpace the soul of your system.

The Stripping Is Not Loss — It's Revelation

Joseph's robe came off so he could see himself without props, so his identity could detach from approval, so his calling could detach from favoritism, so his anointing could detach from symbols, so his leadership could form in truth, and so his development could begin in private. The robe revealed what others saw. The pit revealed who God saw. And that is why stripping seasons, while painful, are holy.

After the robe came the fall. The text says they "threw him" into the pit, not lowered, not guided, but thrown. The violence of that action matters. Trauma often comes not from what is lost but from how it is lost. Joseph didn't get time to prepare. He didn't get time to process. He didn't get time to pray, strategize, or understand. He was there one moment and gone the next, dropped into a darkness that swallowed all sense of stability.

Many people underestimate how disorienting this moment must have been. Joseph was seventeen, still forming his identity, still navigating the complexities of family dynamics, still learning himself. And suddenly, he found himself in a pit with no water, no ladder, no escape, and no explanation. That is the very nature of a pit season: it comes without warning, removes your control, and forces you into a space where nothing looks like the dreams God showed you. Joseph had seen images of rulership, leadership, and elevation. None of those pictures included being thrown into a hole by the same people he loved.

The pit is where dreams collide with reality. It is where God allows the stripping away of everything that could interfere with authentic growth. It is where the noise of approval, expectation, and identity external to God is silenced. Joseph's pit was empty because God needed him empty, empty of validation, empty of assumptions, empty of illusions. The pit removes everything external so you can discover everything internal. That is the heart of the Driver Seat thesis: God will isolate you from what you thought you needed so He can introduce you to what you truly carry.

What Stripping And Falls Do To The Soul

Psychologically, stripping moments attack the scaffolding around the self. When the symbol that once introduced you to rooms is removed, the brain scrambles to rebuild a narrative of who you are. Sudden betrayal by insiders compounds the trauma because it ruptures attachment, which the nervous system reads as danger. The "throw" captures the shock component of acute stress, there was no ramp, only impact. In this space, disorientation is not failure; it is a normal human response. Healthy processing includes naming the event before it names you, allowing lament to ventilate the soul (Psalm 13; Psalm 42), grounding the body through breath and stillness (Psalm 46:10), and letting Scripture stabilize your inner world when externals are volatile (Psalm 119:50). Theologically, God is not threatened by your questions; He invites them onto the anvil where faith is hammered into resilience.

> **Driver Seat Quote:** "If losing something changes who you are,
> that thing was defining you more than God was" is not a shaming
> sentence; it is an invitation."

The pit is the place where God asks, "Who told you that you were only yourself when you wore that robe?" In His kindness, He removes what can be removed so He can reveal what cannot be. The unstrippable core is Christ in you (Colossians 1:27). Everything else is accessory.

The Pit As Holy Emptiness

Joseph's pit was empty because God needed him empty, empty of borrowed voices, of second-hand confidence, of outcomes masquerading as identity. Biblically, God often meets people in emptiness: an empty wilderness that becomes a tabernacle of presence (Exodus 16–33), an empty jar that becomes oil (2 Kings 4), an empty tomb that becomes the world's most disruptive news (John 20). Emptiness in God is not absence; it is space. The pit is room made for the right filling.

What Scripture reveals, and what psychology confirms, is that emptiness is never neutral. When God allows everything familiar to drain out of your hands, it is not because He is abandoning you; it is because He is making space for something truer, stronger, and more eternal than what you were holding before. Emptiness is the place where all the noisy identities fall silent so the real identity can rise. When Joseph hit the bottom of that empty cistern, he had nothing left to lean on: not his robe, not his father's approval, not his brothers' acceptance, not the dream's applause. He had no props left. No external reinforcement. No performance to hide behind. Psychologically, this is the moment where the false self collapses and the true self begins to form. Spiritually, it is the moment when God says, "Now that everything else is gone, I can build you from the inside out."

And this is where your story comes in. Your own emptiness, those hollow places where it feels like everything has been removed, may actually be the clearest evidence that God is preparing you, not punishing you. The relationship that ended, the plan that failed, the door that closed, the season that dried up, the job that slipped through your fingers, the people who walked away, the opportunities that seemed to evaporate, these are not indicators of divine neglect. They are signs that God is clearing the room of your heart so He can fill it with Himself. Emptiness is painful because it breaks attachments. But emptiness is holy because it births identity.

When life empties you, you are forced to confront what was holding you together. For some, it was approval. For others, control. For many, it was productivity, applause, the job title, relationships, or validation. But when those things fade, and the soul feels stripped and silent, this is where God steps closest. Emptiness becomes the meeting place where God says, "I never needed you to carry that. I only needed you to carry Me." It is in emptiness that your faith becomes intimate. It is in emptiness that your confidence becomes internal. It is in emptiness that your calling becomes purified. God often waits until our hands are empty so He can place something in them that won't compete with Him.

So if you feel empty, take courage, because emptiness is not the end. It is an invitation. It is evidence that God is preparing to fill you with something that cannot be stripped, shaken, or stolen. Emptiness is the space where God pours oil, multiplies resources, resurrects what was dead, and reveals who you truly are apart from everything you used to depend on. It is the place where purpose is conceived, resilience is born, and destiny begins to take shape. There is hope in your emptiness. There is purpose in the hollow space. What feels barren is actually fertile. What feels vacant is actually sacred ground. God does His best work in empty places, not because you have nothing left, but because now He can give you everything He intended.

PART 3 — THE EMOTIONAL FRACTURE & THE PSYCHOLOGY OF THE PIT

Emotionally, Joseph's pit represented the first major fracture in his worldview. Psychology calls this "acute trauma response"—the immediate shock that occurs when safety collapses without warning. There is the shock of betrayal. The shock of rejection. The shock of realizing people you trusted saw you as disposable. The shock of seeing how quickly life can change. Every part of Joseph's sense of belonging was interrupted in that moment. And yet, even in the shock, even in the darkness, something essential was happening: Joseph's identity was detaching itself from his circumstances.

Purpose often requires a season where everything familiar is stripped away not as punishment but as preparation. God uses pits to break the dependency on external affirmation. The pit is designed to teach you that identity cannot come from a robe, a role, a relationship, or a reward. It must come from God alone. Most people never step into purpose because they never survive the pit with their character intact. You cannot lead nations if you collapse when people withdraw their approval.

Driver Seat Quote: "Being thrown down is not the same as being disqualified."

From a leadership development perspective, the pit is essential training ground. Leaders must learn to endure sudden loss without losing clarity. They must learn to regulate emotions in moments of shock. They must learn to stand firmly in identity even when stripped of symbols. They must learn to trust God when explanations are absent. Great leadership requires a soul that has been fortified through seasons where nothing made sense yet God remained God.

The Psychology Of Disorientation

Joseph's first emotional fracture mirrors what psychologists call *disintegration of narrative identity,* the moment your inner story suddenly contradicts your outer experience. Before the pit, Joseph's world was coherent: a loving father, a prophetic future, and dreams that made sense. After the pit, his internal map broke. This is what happens when your expectations of life collide with the reality of life.

Modern trauma research shows that sudden betrayal from trusted people produces more psychological shock than harm from enemies. This is because betrayal disrupts the brain's sense of safety at the deepest attachment level. Joseph wasn't just hurt; he was *disoriented*. The ground beneath his worldview dropped out. And that's exactly what pit seasons feel like: life no longer adds up.

Yet spiritually, God sometimes allows this disorientation because the identity you built before the pit cannot carry you into the destiny after the pit.

Joseph, David, Jeremiah, And Jesus

Joseph's fracture echoes David crying, "My closest friend has lifted up his heel against me" (Psalm 41:9). There is somewhere in Scripture where the text essentially says, "An enemy I can handle, a hater I can handle, but you were my family." David puts words to this kind of pain in Psalm 55:12–14 in the NLT. "It is not an enemy I could bear that, but it is you, my close friend, the one I walked to the house of God with." That is the kind of wound Joseph endured. And it is the kind of wound that still bleeds in our world. It echoes Jeremiah, thrown into a cistern by people he preached to (Jeremiah 38). It echoes Jesus, betrayed by one disciple and deserted by the others. Biblically, betrayal is not proof that God abandoned you, it is proof that God is *transitioning you*. God did not save Joseph *from* the pit; God saved Joseph *through* the pit. He did the same with David, Jeremiah, and Jesus.

Every major biblical leader faced a moment where identity had to detach from approval and attach to God alone.

The psychology of disorientation appears differently in entrepreneurs, pastors, families, leaders, and individuals, yet its root is the same: a sudden fracture between what you expected and what reality delivered. For entrepreneurs, the emotional fracture looks like a cofounder you trusted exiting with information they shouldn't have taken, a business partner backing out the night before launch, a board vote that happens without you present, or a client that carried 40% of your revenue suddenly leaving. The shock is not just financial, it's identity-level. You ask, "How could they?" "Why now?" "Does this mean I'm unfit?" "Was the dream even real?" Just like Joseph, the pit becomes the place where your motivations get purified. You stop building for applause and start building from assignment. The pit separates ego from calling. It separates ambition from obedience. It separates who you are from what you built. For pastors and ministry leaders, the fracture might be a volunteer you trusted spreading quiet discontent, a staff member leaving and pulling others with them, a sermon clip taken out of context, or a ministry win immediately followed by a painful internal shakeup. Like Joseph, the shock is compounded because the betrayal was "in-house." Pit moments for spiritual leaders strip away people-pleasing, self-reliance, and platform-dependence. You learn to minister from God's affirmation, not from your congregation's applause, and this is where God grows your interior fortitude so your calling no longer collapses under criticism. For those navigating complex families, emotional fractures include siblings who downplay your achievements, parents who cannot see your calling, a family member who weaponizes your vulnerability, or being the one they "depend on" but never the one they "celebrate." The pain hits harder because you didn't expect the wound to come from within your house. Yet Joseph's story shows us that God will allow familial rejection if familial acceptance would have hindered destiny. Sometimes God removes you from a family dynamic to save you for an assignment the family could never steward. For people leading only themselves, the fracture feels like a closed door you were sure God had opened, an unexpected life transition, divorce, relocation, financial collapse, losing a dream job without warning, or realizing the life you planned no longer fits the person you're becoming. Joseph's pit teaches you that identity cannot depend on circumstances that shift; your identity must anchor in the One who does not. And for leaders of any kind, the pit removes the false structures you built identity on, affirmation, outcome, talent, visibility, predictability, and relational validation. God uses the pit as a sacred deconstruction. Not to destroy you, but to stabilize you. Leaders who avoid pits remain shallow; leaders who survive pits become unshakeable. The pit develops emotional regulation under pressure, clarity without consensus, identity without applause, vision without external validation, integrity when no one is watching, and resilience when everything is unstable. This is why every great biblical leader had a pit season. Joseph had a pit. David had caves. Moses had Midian. Daniel had lions. Jesus had Gethsemane. The pit is not the enemy. The pit is the womb of purpose. Down run from the pit, embrace it.

PART 4 — THE PIVOT OF THE PIT

Joseph's pit season was not long, but it was pivotal. It was the incubator of emotional resilience. It was the birthplace of internal strength. It was the extraction point for every form of dependency that could destroy destiny later. Some seasons feel like chastening, but in hindsight they become the most vital chapters of preparation.

The truth is, your pit season is not about what you have lost; it is about who you are becoming. When God intends to elevate you, He first ensures that no external symbol holds your identity hostage. The pit is isolation, but it is also formation. It is silence, but it is also strengthening. It is empty, but it is not purposeless.

Driver Seat Quote: "Your pit is not the end—it is the excavation before the elevation."

And while Joseph sat in that darkness, unaware of what would come next, heaven was still writing the next chapter. The pit was never meant to be permanent. It was a passage, painful, yes, but purposeful. It was a breaking point, but it was not a burial. It was a low place, but it was not a lost place. God allowed Joseph to hit the bottom so he could discover what foundations could truly hold him.

What Joseph didn't know in that moment mirrors what many of us don't know when we're sitting in our own pits. You may not be in a literal hole in the ground, but you may be in a place where you cannot see what comes next, where your strength feels emptied out, where the people you depended on have stepped away, or where life has dropped you so suddenly that your heart is still catching up to the shock. Yet just like Joseph, heaven is still writing while you sit in the dark. Your pit is not permanent. Your pit is not punishment. Your pit is not proof that God has forgotten you. It is simply the stage you cannot see being built for the chapter you are not yet ready to walk into.

The pit you are facing right now might feel like a breaking point, the moment where something in you cracks under pressure, but God calls it preparation. It feels like burial because it is beneath what you expected, beneath where you thought you'd be, beneath the dreams you saw. But burials and plantings look the same from the outside. What feels like being buried may actually be the planting of something God intends to raise.

Your pit may be a low place, but it is not a lost place. You are not lost to God just because you feel lost to yourself. You are not forgotten just because nothing is moving. You are not abandoned just because the people who hurt you walked away without remorse. God allowed you to hit this bottom not to break you, but to teach you what can actually hold you. Because when everything else falls away, titles, roles, relationships, expectations, certainty, strength, you finally discover which foundations remain unmoveable.

For Joseph, the pit exposed what was fragile and revealed what was eternal.

For you, this pit might be doing the same. It is loosening your grip on what cannot sustain you. It is teaching you what your identity cannot rest on. It is stripping away the lesser foundations so that God can establish the true ones. This dark place you're in might be the very place where God rebuilds you in ways the spotlight never could.

And if Joseph's story teaches us anything, it's this: if you're in the pit, you're not done, you're being drafted. Heaven is writing while you're waiting. God is preparing while you are processing. And the chapter in front of you requires the depth being formed in you right now.

He Cruelty Of Jealousy & The Silence Of God

Joseph's brothers didn't walk away after throwing him in. They sat down to eat as if nothing had happened. That detail alone shows the cruelty of jealousy, the ability to destroy someone else's life and feel no emotional weight. But Joseph's story was not in their hands. Destiny is never at the mercy of those who try to bury you. God controls the storyline, even when humans attempt to edit the script.

When the brothers sat down to eat, it was more than a meal, it was a moment that revealed the chilling disconnect between Joseph's agony and their appetite. Scripture doesn't say they hesitated, prayed, or felt conflicted; instead, they moved from violence to lunch without emotional interruption. That is the psychology of jealousy: it numbs empathy, distorts perception, and creates a world where someone else's suffering feels justified, deserved, or invisible. The same brothers who shared Joseph's childhood, laughter, memories, and table were now able to eat in peace while he cried out from a pit within earshot. This is one of the most painful human experiences, when people who know your heart can harm you and carry on with their day as if nothing happened. When those who promised protection choose betrayal. When people who shared your life refuse to share your pain.

For many of us, this scene mirrors moments in their own lives where the ones who wounded them walked away emotionally unaffected. It's the parent who goes on with their routine after speaking words that shattered identity. The spouse who sleeps soundly after inflicting deep emotional wounds. The friend who betrays trust and then smiles in public. The coworker who undermines you and then laughs in the break room. The family member who tears you down and then serves dinner like nothing happened. Emotional cruelty often shows itself not just in the act of harm, but in the quiet, casual normalcy that follows it.

And yet, this is where Joseph's story becomes profoundly comforting: even when people treat you as disposable, God treats you as destiny-filled. Even when humans disconnect from your pain, heaven is deeply invested in your future. The brothers were eating, but God was orchestrating. The brothers felt nothing, but God felt everything. They sat down to lunch, but God was preparing a caravan of ishmaelites. Their indifference did not interrupt God's involvement. Their cruelty did not threaten God's covenant. Their appetite did not alter God's assignment for Joseph.

And this is the healing truth for you: people may walk away with full hands and full plates, but God never walks away from you. People may forget the damage they caused, but God does not forget the promise He made. People may sit down to eat while you are still bleeding, but God is already writing the next scene of your story. Your life is not controlled by the ones who hurt you but by the One who called you. Destiny is never at the mercy of jealousy. Assignment is never suspended by betrayal. Your future is not fragile because people are fickle, your future is secure because God is faithful.

In fact, the brothers' ability to eat while Joseph was in agony only reinforces the sovereignty of God. If they had felt remorse, if they had looked back, if they had changed their minds, Joseph might have been pulled out prematurely, and premature deliverance can be more dangerous than the pit. Their coldness kept Joseph in position for God's intervention. Their appetite kept Joseph available for God's assignment. Their indifference opened the path to Joseph's destiny.

What people did casually, God used intentionally. What they did in cruelty, God used for calling. What they meant for harm, God was already bending toward healing. And the same is true for you, because this is the anchored truth woven throughout Scripture. Romans 8:28 declares that *all things work together for good to those who love God, to those who are called according to His purpose,"* meaning that every act intended to break you becomes raw material in God's hands to build you. Nothing done against you can override what God has spoken over you. While people respond out of jealousy, insecurity, or indifference, heaven responds with orchestration, alignment, and purpose. The cruelty of others can never cancel the calling of God. Even when humans operate casually, even when they move with coldness or malice, even when their decisions disrupt your life without remorse, God is already weaving those same threads into a storyline that honors His will for your life. Their actions may have surprised you, but they did not surprise God. Their betrayal may have wounded you, but it cannot wound God's plan. What others mishandled, God will redeem. What others broke, God will rebuild. What others used to strip you, God will use to strengthen you. Because all things, even the painful ones, the unfair ones, the sudden ones, the confusing ones, work together according to His will, not according to their intentions.

Why Short Seasons Can Have Long Impact

Here's a different perspective, Joseph's pit season was brief in duration but monumental in impact. Scripture consistently shows that God does not measure transformation by time, but by depth. Elijah's fire fell in seconds, but the drought lasted years. Paul was blinded for three days, but the encounter changed centuries. Jesus spent only forty days in the wilderness, yet those days set the trajectory of His entire earthly ministry.

The Pit As Trauma And Transformation

Psychologically, what happens in brief traumatic seasons often shapes identity, confidence, attachment patterns, and core beliefs. Yet trauma researchers also note a parallel phenomenon: "post-traumatic growth." This is not minimizing pain; it is acknowledging what can form *through* pain.

Joseph's pit experience rewired several psychological pillars: self-concept, as he discovered he was more than a robe; resilience, as he learned stability without external support; agency, as he learned to trust God's sovereignty when he lost all control; attachment, as he shifted from family-affirmation dependence to God-dependence; and meaning-making, as he reframed suffering as formation. This is why God allows certain "falling" seasons. They root identity in something fortified

Let's look at how THE PIT turns TRAUMA into TRANSFORMATION and shows up in our lives. Entrepreneurs often mistake short downturns for death sentences. But the healthiest founders learn that bankruptcy can birth reinvention, a failed product can birth a clearer model, a lost investor can birth healthier ownership, and a derailed plan can expose the plan that truly aligns with calling. Joseph's pit season teaches entrepreneurs that the pit becomes your incubator for refined strategy, identity-anchored leadership, smarter risk analysis, better team discernment, and more Spirit-led decision-making. Many great companies were born after their founders hit bottom, not because the fall was pleasant, but because it was purifying.

For church leaders, THE PIT becomes SPIRITUAL REFORMATION. For pastors and ministry leaders, the pit season is where God deepens you. Many ministers experience volunteer betrayal, moral fallout in the team, unexpected decline in attendance, harsh criticism, relational loss, and burnout or exhaustion. Yet these seasons produce the most spiritually mature leaders. Joseph's pit prepared him to lead Egypt; your pit prepares you to shepherd with purity, compassion, strength, and spiritual authority. Ministry built without pits is shallow. Ministry built through pits is unstaggering. This is where sermons become anchored in struggle, compassion deepens, ego dies, shepherding becomes authentic, and vision becomes God-sized rather than platform-sized. Jesus Himself passed through a pit-like moment (Gethsemane) before fulfilling His calling. God never wastes this kind of season.

For FAMILY DYNAMICS, THE PIT is about SURVIVING RELATIONAL EARTHQUAKES. Family pits take a different shape: betrayals, favoritism, rejection, silent treatment, emotional abandonment, scapegoating, sudden coldness, and competition or jealousy. Joseph endured all of these at once. But here's the truth Scripture teaches through Joseph's story: God will not allow family brokenness to sabotage a God-built identity. Sometimes God allows the fractures so He can free you from a system that could not hold your calling. Joseph never would have left Canaan if his brothers had embraced him. God used dysfunction as propulsion. Your pit may be the spiritual pathway out of a system that was too small for what God placed inside you.

For PEOPLE LEADING THEMSELVES, THE PIT is WHEN LIFE SHIFTS UNDER YOUR FEET. For those not leading teams, churches, or families, the pit often looks like losing a job, a breakup, a sudden move, unexpected financial hardship, the dream falling apart, or being forced into a restart. But the pit trains you in the discipline of internal leadership: how to talk to yourself biblically, how to regulate emotions through prayer, how to rebuild confidence through Scripture, how to cultivate resilience, how to make decisions from identity instead of insecurity, and how to walk with God without needing clarity from circumstances. You learn that God is enough. And you learn that you are more than you thought.

For ORGANIZATIONAL LEADERS, THE PIT is WHEN BETRAYAL MEETS RESPONSIBILITY. For executives, managers, and team leaders, pits look like political undercutting, unexpected resignations, toxic board members, sabotaged projects, quiet quitting inside your team, and loss of trust. God uses these pits to strengthen your emotional intelligence, sharpen your discernment of people, refine your communication, teach you to lead without applause, and anchor your leadership in values, not volatility. Leaders who survive pits emerge with clarity, courage, and conviction that cannot be purchased—only formed.

Driver Seat Quote: "Your pit is not the end—it is the excavation before the elevation."

Excavation is violent. It is messy. It is disruptive. It removes what cannot support the weight of what is coming. The pit excavates identity attachments, fragile confidence, people-pleasing tendencies, unprocessed trauma, pride masked as vision, roles you outgrew, relationships that were unhealthy, and dependencies that were dangerous. Elevation would crush you if excavation hadn't happened first.

What God Was Doing While Joseph Saw Nothing

What Joseph could not see from the bottom of the pit was that God had already arranged the next stage of his journey. That is the mystery and mercy of divine timing: God is working on chapters you haven't reached yet, using people you haven't met yet, in places you haven't imagined yet, to accomplish purposes you don't understand yet. While Joseph saw darkness, God saw direction. While Joseph felt abandoned, God was orchestrating alignment. What looked like a dead end was actually a divine handoff, moving Joseph from the field of favoritism to the furnace of formation.

The pit is where you learn that God doesn't need a spotlight to move. He often does His best work in silence. Just as the brothers sat down to eat, God was stirring the hearts of traders. Just as Joseph felt forgotten, God was scheduling a caravan of ishmaelites. Just as Joseph grappled with the trauma of betrayal, God was positioning him for a destiny that would feed nations.

Heaven's timeline is never disrupted by human cruelty.

How God Moves In Hidden Places

Biblically, God often secures the next chapter in the very moment you think the story is collapsing:

- Moses was rescued by Pharaoh's daughter *while* he floated helplessly.

- David was anointed as king *while* Saul was still reigning.

- Elijah heard God's whisper *after* the earthquake and fire subsided.

- Jesus secured resurrection *while* lying in a tomb sealed by Rome.

God's greatest reversals often begin in the lowest places. The pit is a womb, not a grave.

If the pit represents shock, the next chapter represents forced transition, a psychological phenomenon where you are moved into a new season before you feel ready. Joseph was not asked if he wanted to leave Canaan. He was taken.

Dragged. Displaced. Pulled into a future that felt like a violation of everything familiar. And as brutal as that sounds, Scripture makes it even clearer: Joseph wasn't simply carried away, he was about to be sold, transported, and trafficked by his own brothers into the hands of strangers. What he experienced was not a gentle divine nudge; it was a violent human transaction. The next steps of his journey were not chosen; they were forced upon him. Joseph's transition into Egypt was not the result of opportunity but of exploitation. He was moved like property, handled like cargo, and treated like he had no agency, no dignity, and no voice in his own story. This layer is essential because it underscores the severity of what Joseph survived and the depth of what God redeemed. Before he ever entered Potiphar's house, Joseph passed through the trauma of being human-trafficked, and yet even that could not interrupt God's plan for his life.

Prayer

Father, thank You that You are present even in the pits of life. When I fall into places I never expected, remind me that Your hand has not let go of my future. Strip away every identity, attachment, and dependency that cannot carry what You've placed inside me. Anchor me in who You say I am, not in the roles I've worn or the approval I've lost. Heal every fracture caused by betrayal, rejection, silence, or shock. Strengthen my heart to see that this pit is not punishment, it is preparation. Remind me that what others meant for harm, You are already bending toward healing. Teach me to trust Your process when I cannot see Your plan. Fill every empty place with Your presence. Rebuild me from the inside out until resilience rises, purpose clarifies, and Your voice becomes louder than every fear. Lord, let my pit become the womb of the leader You are forming me to be. I surrender the pain, the confusion, and the timing into Your hands. Write the next chapter according to Your will, and make me ready for it. In Jesus' name, Amen

Driver Seat Takeaways

- **The pit is sudden, disorienting, and emotionally violent, but never purposeless.** Joseph's fall happened without warning, mirroring the psychological shock we face when life collapses faster than our hearts can interpret. The pit is not a sign of abandonment; it is a classroom of identity.

- **Stripping seasons are holy seasons.** When Joseph's robe was torn away, God was removing external identity so internal identity could rise. The same is true for us. God strips what is fragile so He can strengthen what is eternal.

- **Identity must detach from applause, roles, and outcomes.** The robe represented validation, position, and belonging. Losing it revealed Joseph's true substance. You are not what you lost. You are what God placed within you.

- **Trauma does not cancel calling, it clarifies it.** Joseph's betrayal was brutal, but it purified motives and pruned attachments. The pit exposes who you are without the props and reveals who you are becoming under God's hand.

- **God uses pits to build psychological resilience and spiritual depth.** Self-concept shifts, agency deepens, attachment reorganizes around God, and meaning-making reframes suffering as formation. The pit breaks the false self and births the true self.

- **The pit is a womb, not a grave.** Joseph's darkest moment was also the birthplace of divine direction. Where people see an end, God sees a beginning. Where people abandon, God orchestrates.

- **People's cruelty cannot cancel God's authorship.** His brothers walked away and ate while he cried out, but God was already arranging the caravan. Destiny is never at the mercy of jealousy. The story belongs to God.

- **God works in silence, hiddenness, and transitions you didn't choose.** Joseph was dragged, displaced, and trafficked, not consulted. Yet heaven was in full control. Forced transition does not mean failed purpose.

- **Every great leader has a pit season.** David had caves, Moses had Midian, Daniel had lions, Jesus had Gethsemane. The pit is not punishment. The pit is preparation. The pit is necessary.

- **Your pit is not where you die, it is where God builds the version of you that will live out destiny.** Your pit is refining, excavating, strengthening, grounding, and aligning you for the place God is taking you.

***

There comes a moment in every story when the ground beneath you gives way and the fall becomes the bridge to the future. Joseph entered the pit as a son, but he would rise from it as a servant in the hands of strangers. Everything familiar had been stripped away, every illusion of safety had collapsed, and every voice he trusted had gone silent. Yet even in that darkness, heaven was already arranging the next step. What Joseph could not see from the bottom of that cistern was that God was still writing, still guiding, still aligning, and still preparing a path that would eventually lead to purpose.

The pit was not the destination. It was the passage. It was the rupture that broke him away from a system that could not carry his destiny, and it was the place where God detached him from what could not go with him into the future. Joseph's story turns here, not with comfort, but with movement. His transition will not feel gentle. It will not feel fair. It will not feel redemptive.

Not yet. He will be pulled out of the pit only to be handed over to traders. He will leave Canaan not by choice but by force. And in that moment, Joseph steps into a truth every leader must eventually face: destiny rarely begins in clarity, it begins in disruption.

Chapter 4 opens at the intersection of trauma and transition, where God moves a person into their next season before their heart has caught up with what has happened. This is where we watch Joseph shift from beloved son to bound traveler, from familiar soil to foreign ground, and from the safety of what he knew to the uncertainty of what God was building. The pit was the breaking. Egypt will be the shaping. And the next chapter of Joseph's life begins not with celebration but with chains, not with applause but with displacement, not with elevation but with a journey he did not choose.

Turn the page. The road to Egypt is beginning.

CHAPTER FOUR

THE ISHMAELITES: WHEN STRANGERS CARRY YOU INTO YOUR NEXT SEASON

Genesis 37:25–28 — "And they lifted up their eyes and looked, and, behold, a company of Ishmeelites came from Gilead... and Judah said unto his brethren, What profit is it if we slay our brother... Come, and let us sell him... Then there passed by Midianites merchantmen; and they drew and lifted up Joseph out of the pit, and sold Joseph... for twenty pieces of silver: and they brought Joseph into Egypt." Context: This passage captures the entire moment. A caravan of traders appears, the brothers negotiate the sale, and Joseph is pulled from the pit and carried toward Egypt. In a matter of moments, his life is redirected. This is the beginning of Joseph's displacement, the start of his adaptive formation, and the first movement of his destiny without his consent.

PART I: MOVEMENT WITHOUT CHOICE

When Strangers Carry You Into Your Next Season

Genesis 37:25–28. There are moments when the people closest to you fail you, and then there are moments when people who don't even know you take hold of your destiny. Joseph's pit was painful, but it was familiar pain, pain from brothers, pain from proximity, pain from people whose faces he recognized. But what happens when the next stage of your journey is orchestrated through complete strangers? What happens when people who know nothing about your calling, nothing about your value, and nothing about your history become the ones responsible for your next chapter? This is what makes Genesis 37:25–28 such a defining transition in Joseph's life. The text says that as his brothers sat down to eat, a chilling picture of casual cruelty, they looked up and saw a caravan of Ishmaelites coming from Gilead. They were traders, merchants, travelers passing through with spices, balm, and myrrh. They had no emotional connection to Joseph. They had no bias, no resentment, no jealousy. They were simply on their way to Egypt, minding their business, unaware that heaven had positioned them to be divine transportation for a dreamer. Sometimes the next stage of your assignment doesn't come wrapped in comfort. Sometimes it comes on the backs of camels led by strangers. Sometimes God moves you through people who don't recognize your value, only your usefulness for the journey. Driver Seat Quote: "Sometimes God moves you through people who don't know your value, only your assignment."

Unchosen Carriers

Unchosen Carriers. The Ishmaelites transport Joseph. Strangers. Foreign language. Foreign land. Leadership Principle: God often uses unfamiliar systems to move you forward. The Ishmaelites, When Strangers Carry You Into Your Next Season. The pit was not the end. It was a pause. **Genesis 37:25–28** "And they lifted up their eyes and looked, and, behold, a company of Ishmeelites came from Gilead... and Judah said unto his brethren, What profit is it if we slay our brother... Come, and let us sell him... Then there passed by Midianites merchantmen; and they drew and lifted up Joseph out of the pit, and sold Joseph... for twenty pieces of silver: and they brought Joseph into Egypt." Joseph goes from the bottom of a pit to the hands of strangers. No goodbye. No closure. No explanation. Just movement. And here is the leadership truth:

Sometimes your next season arrives through people who do not love you. This scene is not metaphor; it is exploitation. Joseph is being human-trafficked at the hands of his brothers, sold, transported, commodified, and carried by strangers into a future he did not choose.

The Moment Familiarity Replaced You With Profit

While Joseph was in the pit, his brothers made a decision. Greed spoke louder than guilt. Judah asked, "What profit is there if we kill him?" The brothers weren't simply trying to hide a crime, now they wanted to benefit from it. Betrayal deepens when people realize they can make something out of hurting you. They were no longer content to silence him; they wanted to gain from his disappearance. This is one of the hardest truths to swallow: sometimes people are willing to trade your destiny for their convenience. Joseph was sold for twenty pieces of silver. To the brothers, he was worth a price. To the Ishmaelites, he was merchandise. To God, he was a man in divine transition. And Joseph had no say in any of it.

The Psychology Of Being Sold

Twenty pieces of silver. That is what Joseph's life is valued at by his brothers. Not a conversation. Not reconciliation. A transaction. And this is another layer of trauma. He is not only betrayed. He is commodified. Reduced to currency. Psychologically, that does something to a person. When you are treated like a transaction, it tempts you to believe your worth is negotiable. Joseph is seventeen. He is still forming identity. And now he is learning this brutal lesson: Some people will reduce you to what benefits them. This is not just ancient history. This is corporate culture. This is politics. This is ministry. This is family dynamics. This is entrepreneurship. This is dating. This is leadership. People will use what you carry when it profits them. The question is: Will you internalize their valuation.

Here is the part we miss. Those twenty pieces of silver were not random. In Joseph's era, twenty pieces of silver was the standard market price for a teenage slave. Historical records and biblical law indicate that a male under twenty was valued at twenty shekels according to Leviticus 27:5, and commentaries note that this was the average slave price in the Ancient Near East, which is why Joseph was sold for that amount.

Economically, twenty pieces of silver equaled about 220 grams of silver, because a shekel weighed roughly 11 grams. Using modern silver prices, this would be approximately 176 dollars today if silver is valued at eighty cents per gram. Another analysis places the value at roughly 8.06 ounces of silver, which is a little over 216 dollars when calculated with the price of silver at twenty six dollars per ounce.

So the brothers sold Joseph for the modern equivalent of somewhere between 175 and 220 dollars. That is what his life was worth to them. Less than a car payment. Less than a pair of luxury sneakers. Less than a weekend trip. The cost of his destiny, his dreams, his identity, and his very existence came down to pocket change in the modern world.

And this is where the deeper point emerges. When people put a price on you, the number never reflects your value. It reflects their blindness. Their jealousy. Their insecurity. Their poverty of perspective. Joseph's brothers were not appraising his worth. They were revealing their wound. People who cannot see their own calling will always discount yours. People who refuse to grow will always minimize what God is growing in you. People who feel threatened by your future will always price you according to their fear, not according to heaven's intention.

The tragedy is not that Joseph was sold for so little. The tragedy is that his brothers believed so little. But the glory is this. God does not let human valuation decide divine destiny. Joseph may have been sold for the price of a teenage slave, but he would one day manage an empire. He may have been measured at twenty pieces of silver by men, but he was measured as invaluable by God. And the same is true for you. People may put a price on you, but heaven has already placed a calling inside you that no market can calculate.

The Ishmaelites: Unlikely Carriers

The text says Ishmaelites. Descendants of Ishmael. Abraham's other son. The line that was not chosen for covenant inheritance. Strangers to Joseph. Strangers to his father's house. Strangers to his story. And yet they become the vehicle of his relocation. This is where Driver Seat dismantles another myth: God does not only use people who understand your calling. Sometimes He uses people who don't even know your name. Joseph is not saved by family. He is transported by foreigners. And this is uncomfortable for many leaders. Because we prefer familiar hands. We prefer validation from people who already know our history. But sometimes destiny travels through unfamiliar systems.

When Strangers Become The Transportation Of Purpose

The Ishmaelites weren't rescuers, they were transporters. They didn't know they were helping fulfill a prophecy. They didn't know they were holding a future governor. They didn't know they were carrying a man whose leadership would shape nations. They simply saw a boy who could be sold. The beauty of God's sovereignty is that people don't need to know your purpose to participate in your destiny. God can use a stranger's decision, a trader's routine, a merchant's route, a caravan's schedule, and an enemy's intention to move you to the exact place He designed. The Ishmaelites were unknowingly part of Joseph's divine GPS. This is the difference between value and assignment: The Ishmaelites didn't value Joseph, but they were assigned to him. His brothers didn't value him, but they were instrumental in positioning him. Pharaoh wouldn't fully understand him, but he would elevate him. People do not have to understand your worth for God to use them in your journey.

Driver Seat Quote: "God will use the hands of strangers to carry you where jealousy tried to bury you."

Strangers As Strategic Tools

Here is what most people miss. If Joseph had never been sold, He would have never entered Egypt. If he never entered Egypt, He would never interpret Pharaoh's dream. If he never interpreted Pharaoh's dream, He would never lead during famine. The Ishmaelites are not kind. But they are critical. Driver Seat principle: Just because someone's role in your story was painful does not mean it was pointless. Strangers can become bridges. And bridges are rarely comfortable.

Reframing The Strangers

Let's say it clearly. The Ishmaelites did not rescue Joseph. They purchased him. But in purchasing him, They preserved him. If he stayed in the pit, He dies. If he stayed with his brothers, He is murdered. The strangers are not gentle. But they are directional. Driver Seat principle: Not every painful transition is a setback. Some are relocations disguised as losses.

Leadership Lesson: Purpose Without Permission

Joseph didn't volunteer for any of this, and yet he was being carried toward his calling. Real leadership often begins in seasons where you feel the least in control. Destiny isn't democratic. It doesn't ask for your permission. It asks for your participation, sometimes unwilling, sometimes unconscious, but always necessary. In leadership development: You must learn to pivot when transitions are forced, not requested. You must adapt even when the move feels unfair. You must learn detachment from origins, because origin cannot determine elevation. You must embrace leadership without consent, because calling often begins in captivity. Joseph was being moved from one chapter to another without understanding any of it. Leadership sometimes begins by surviving transitions you didn't choose.

The Driver Seat Reality

Here is the hard truth: Sometimes you are not walking into your next season. You are being carried into it. And it does not feel strategic. It feels traumatic. But forced movement is still movement. Joseph did not volunteer for Egypt. But Egypt becomes the platform of his purpose.

When You Are Moved Without Warning

The text doesn't tell us what Joseph said as they lifted him out of the pit. We don't know if he screamed, begged, or remained silent. What we do know is that no amount of pleading could have changed the brothers' minds. No amount of humanity could have softened their hearts. He was lifted out, not for restoration, but for sale. Transitions come in two forms: 1. Transitions you walk into 2. Transitions you are carried into. Joseph's transition was the second. This is often how God accelerates you. Not through the doors you plan, but through the ones you never imagined you'd have to walk through. Strangers became the bridge between Joseph's pit and his palace. This is divine irony: the people who hurt you push you down, but the people who don't even know you pick you up, pushing you forward. Sometimes God hides deliverance in places that don't look divine.

The Question Every Leader Faces

When strangers carry you somewhere you did not plan to go, you ask: "Is this punishment?" "Is this exile?" "Is this the end?" Joseph could not see the palace from the caravan. And you often cannot see the breakthrough from the relocation. Driver Seat requires this level of maturity: You do not need full clarity to maintain internal alignment. You do not need comfort to maintain discipline. You do not need familiarity to maintain faith.

What This Means For You

There will be seasons when you lose familiar support. You enter unfamiliar systems. You must learn new languages, literally or metaphorically. You feel outnumbered. You feel misunderstood. You feel underestimated. And it will feel like exile. But exile is not extinction. Joseph is not shrinking. He is expanding. He is being stretched beyond comfort so that later he can lead beyond limitation.

Movement, Mastery, And The Driver Seat

There are different ways to move through life, and not all movement comes from the same place of awareness. Some people are moving because something is pushing them. Others are moving because something is pulling them. A few are moving because they have learned how to sit behind the wheel of their own decisions, even when the road was not chosen for them. That distinction matters, because movement alone does not determine maturity. Motion does not equal mastery. Direction does not automatically mean discernment. The danger is assuming that motion automatically means direction. Many people are busy but not deliberate, active but not anchored, advancing but not grounded. They are in the car, but they are not driving. Life is happening to them faster than they are happening with it. Scripture is filled with examples of people in motion who were not yet intentional, people traveling physically while remaining internally unformed. Joseph's life forces us to confront this uncomfortable truth: there are moments when you are not asked where you want to go, but you are still responsible for how you show up while you are moving. That distinction separates different kinds of people and different kinds of futures. Joseph does not choose Egypt. Joseph does not choose the Ishmaelites. Joseph does not choose movement at all. His movement is imposed, not initiated. Genesis 37 makes this explicit. He is lifted out of a pit and sold. No consent. No preparation. No explanation. Yet the responsibility of who he becomes does not disappear simply because choice was removed. This is one of the hardest truths of leadership and adulthood: even when movement is forced, character is still formed.

Level One: Reactive Living

There are different ways that we talk about being intentional, and the first way, the most basic level, is reactive living. At this level, people live reactively. This is survival mode. Decisions are made based on urgency, fear, pressure, or circumstances. The road is chosen by necessity, not discernment. Emotions sit behind the wheel. Whatever feels loudest at the moment determines the next move. Reactive living is understandable, especially for people who grew up navigating instability. When environments are unpredictable, reaction becomes protection. When systems are unsafe, hesitation feels dangerous. Joseph's early movement fits this category. He is reacting because there is no other option. He is being moved by forces stronger than him. His nervous system is likely flooded with fear, confusion, shock, and grief. Psychologically, this is what happens when agency is removed abruptly. The brain prioritizes survival over strategy. Scripture does not record Joseph's emotions in detail, but the silence itself is consistent with trauma responses. Sometimes the body absorbs what the mouth cannot yet articulate. In reactive living, life feels exhausting. You are always adjusting, always bracing, always responding. You do not feel led; you feel driven. The destination is unclear because survival does not require vision, only endurance. Many people never leave this level, not because they are incapable, but because they mistake movement for mastery. They confuse resilience with readiness.

Level Two: Ambition-driven Living

The second level of intentional living is ambition-driven living. This level looks better on the outside. Here, people are not just reacting; they are striving. Goals are clear. Momentum is visible. Hunger is loud. Planning replaces panic. Structure replaces chaos. But ambition can still hijack the wheel. In this stage, achievement becomes the compass, progress becomes proof of worth, and speed feels like purpose. Joseph will encounter this later in Potiphar's house, but the seeds are already present. He is gifted. He is capable. He adapts quickly. Scripture shows that wherever Joseph lands, excellence follows. But ambition-driven living carries danger when internal healing has not caught up with external opportunity. You are driving, but you are speeding. And speed hides cracks until pressure exposes them. Ambition-driven living can take you far and fast, but it can also take you places your inner life is not prepared to manage. Many people arrive successful but fragmented, accomplished but unsettled, influential but internally unstable. They reach the destination, but they lost themselves along the way. Joseph's story warns us here. Giftedness accelerates exposure, but it does not guarantee stability.

Level Three: Humbling Awareness In Forced Routes

Here, you begin to recognize that not every road is self-selected. Some routes are imposed. Some turns are unexpected. Some movements are initiated without your consent. This is where Joseph truly lives during his transport to Egypt. The illusion of control is dismantled. You realize you are not always asked where you are going, but you are still accountable for who you become along the way. This kind of living humbles you. Being in the driver's seat does not mean choosing every road. It means choosing your posture on the road you are on. It means learning restraint when you would rather rush, awareness when you would rather numb out, discipline when you would rather disengage. This is where maturity begins, not when movement becomes comfortable, but when response becomes intentional.

Level Four: Governed Living

The fourth level of intentional living is governed living. This is where life starts to cohere. At this level, you are no longer driven by reactions, ambition, or resistance. You are guided by internal governance. Your values are clear. Your responses are measured. Your decisions are not rushed by emotion or fear. You understand timing. You no longer confuse movement with meaning. Joseph will eventually embody this posture. His later leadership in Egypt reflects a man who has learned restraint, discernment, and timing. He interprets crisis without panic. He manages resources without ego. He holds authority without impulsiveness. This did not appear suddenly. It was cultivated during seasons where movement was forced and silence was long. Governed living produces a different kind of confidence. Not loud. Not defensive. Not desperate. It is the confidence of someone who does not need to force outcomes, because they are becoming someone who can carry outcomes when they arrive. Integrity becomes intensive. You do not perform it; you live it. Your inner life and outer life begin telling the same story. You are in the driver's seat of your life, not gripping the wheel in panic, but holding it with awareness.

Level Five: Stewarded Living

Now here is the level that brings it all together, stewarded living. At the deepest level, life is not just driven; it is stewarded. You understand that your abilities, influence, and opportunities are not just for personal advancement. They are responsibilities. They affect other lives, other futures, and other outcomes. Here, patience replaces urgency. Wisdom replaces impulse. Care replaces ego. Joseph's later authority is stewarded, not self-serving. He does not weaponize power. He does not rush revenge. He does not exploit leverage. He moves carefully, not because he is afraid, but because he understands the weight of consequences. He does not just ask, "Can I?" He asks, "Should I?" He does not just ask, "Is this possible?" He asks, "Is this consistent with who I am becoming?" This is where Joseph eventually lives, not hurried, not reactive, not defensive, but aware. He learned how to sit still before he learned how to stand tall. He learned how to carry silence before he carried responsibility. He learned how to be moved without losing himself so that later, when he led, he would not misuse power. Knowing you are still going somewhere, this is the peace that comes when you realize you do not have to control the entire route to remain responsible for your life. You may not have chosen the road, but you can choose your awareness. You may not understand the timing, but you can choose how you live inside it. And this is where Joseph's story stops being ancient and starts being personal. Because some of us were moved without consent. Some of us were transferred by decisions we did not make. Some of us were carried by systems, people, or circumstances that did not ask our permission. But movement did not cancel responsibility. It clarified it. Joseph teaches us that leadership is not about choosing every road. It is about becoming someone who can steward the road you are on.

Cultural Displacement

Cultural displacement is the experience of being removed from the environment, language, customs, and systems that once defined your normal life. It happens when a person is forced to operate in a culture that is unfamiliar, where the rules, expectations, and structures are different from everything they once understood. Cultural displacement requires adaptation. It requires emotional regulation. It requires the ability to observe before reacting and to learn before leading.

Joseph's leadership timeline unfolds in stages. Stage 1 was the field. This is where Joseph lived as the favored son, where dreams were given but leadership had not yet been tested. Stage 2 was the pit. This is where betrayal, rejection, and humiliation introduced Joseph to suffering and stripped away the protection of family. But Stage 3 begins on the road to Egypt.

Egypt is a new political system, a new language, and a new economy. Joseph must now learn structure, hierarchy, and administrative flow. His life moves from familiar fields to foreign systems. The Ishmaelites do not take Joseph home. They take him to Egypt. Genesis 37:28 records it plainly: "...and they brought Joseph into Egypt." Egypt is not just geography. Egypt is culture. Egypt is language. Egypt is politics. Egypt is economy. Egypt is power. Egypt is structure. Joseph is about to learn that leadership is not formed in comfort; it is formed in adaptation. He does not know the language, the customs, the hierarchy, or the rules. This is forced transition. No orientation. No preparation. No mentorship. Just survival.

From age 17 to 30, Joseph will live inside systems that are not his own. Yet something powerful is being formed during this season: cross-cultural intelligence, systems awareness, administrative skill, emotional restraint, and situational awareness. Joseph is no longer the favored son in a field. He is property in a caravan of Ishmaelites. This is the kind of moment where identity can fracture, because when your environment changes suddenly, you are tempted to overcorrect. Some people become aggressive. Some become invisible. Some become defensive. Some become compliant just to survive. Scripture does not give us Joseph's internal monologue, but we see the fruit of what happened inside him later. He does not become hardened. He does not become chaotic. He does not lose composure. Which means something stabilized inside him on the road to Egypt.

Like Joseph, some of us were relocated without consent. A new city, a new economy, and new power dynamics surrounding us overnight. This is displacement trauma. For some of us, this moment can feel familiar. This is immigration without choice. This is foster care. This is a forced job transfer. This is relocation after divorce. This is military deployment. This is economic displacement. This is cultural assimilation under pressure. Sometimes you do not choose the road; the road chooses you. And in that moment you must decide whether you will learn or collapse.

When everything external changes, identity is either clarified or confused. Joseph loses his coat, his tribe, his language, his social position, and his safety. Yet he does not lose his discipline, his discernment, his awareness, or his internal dignity. We know this because Genesis 39:2 will soon declare, "And the LORD was with Joseph." That line reveals that something happened internally on the journey, because the presence of God is not geography dependent. Joseph does not leave his God in Canaan. He carries his conviction into Egypt.

Joseph's next chapter will unfold in Potiphar's house, but the foundation of that leadership begins here on the road, in chains, surrounded by strangers. The Ishmaelites are traders. They understand commerce. Joseph watches carefully. He learns how goods are transported, how negotiations happen, how markets function, and how value is assessed. What Joseph does not yet realize is that he is studying a system he will one day oversee. The same kind of caravans that now carry him as property will later come to Egypt carrying nations desperate for grain. The same trading systems he observes in chains will become the systems he administers in power. Leadership training does not always happen in classrooms. Sometimes it happens through observation while you are simply trying to survive. Sometimes the pain you endure becomes the preparation you steward. And when it is stewarded well, suffering can become purpose, and purpose can become power.

During this chapter Joseph is learning how to move without control, how to observe before speaking, how to survive displacement, and how to adapt without losing identity. He is no longer a boy with dreams; he is becoming a man with stamina. The Ishmaelites do not realize they are transporting a future Prime Minister. But destiny often travels quietly, and sometimes the people who carry you do not know what they are carrying.

PART II — WHEN MOVEMENT IS NOT RESCUE: LOSS OF AGENCY, TRAUMA, AND THE COST OF SURVIVAL

Part I revealed movement without choice, Joseph lifted from the pit, sold, carried, and repositioned by strangers. Part II names what that movement actually *was*: human trafficking, a loss of agency that wounds identity, fractures safety, and reshapes time. Movement moved the body; loss of choice wounded the soul.

Loss Of Agency: The Core Injury

When movement is not rescue, the soul experiences a different kind of injury. Human trafficking is not defined first by geography. It is defined by loss of agency. Psychiatrists are clear on this point: the core trauma of trafficking is not simply violence, confinement, or exploitation, it is the systemic removal of choice. When a human being is moved, sold, transferred, or relocated without consent, the injury penetrates deeper than the body. It fractures the mind's relationship with safety, identity, and time. This matters because Joseph's story includes all the psychological ingredients modern clinicians now recognize as trauma-producing conditions. He is moved without consent. He is sold. He is transferred between power holders. His autonomy is stripped, and his future is determined by forces outside of him. Scripture does not sanitize this. Genesis 37 tells us plainly that Joseph is taken. Movement happens to him. And that distinction, movement without choice, changes the way the mind adapts.

Complex Trauma: Adaptation Under Duress

Trafficking creates a specific psychological injury often described as complex trauma. It overlaps with post-traumatic stress but extends far beyond a single event. Survivors are not merely reacting to one moment of harm; they are adapting to a prolonged condition where autonomy was stripped and survival required psychological contortion. The mind does not break immediately. It adapts. And that adaptation is what makes the trauma so enduring. Joseph's endurance is not proof that the injury did not occur. It is evidence that adaptation took place. When freedom is taken, the brain can enter a state of hypervigilant survival. The nervous system begins to scan constantly for threat. This is not weakness; it is intelligence. It is the body learning how to stay alive in unsafe conditions. Over time, however, this recalibration can reshape how reality is experienced, even when danger has passed.

What Forced Movement Does Over Time

sychologists consistently observe several long-term impacts in individuals who have experienced forced movement or prolonged loss of agency. These include dissociation, where the mind separates from the present moment to endure it; learned helplessness, where repeated powerlessness trains the brain to stop attempting escape; identity fragmentation, where the self divides into who I was, who I had to become, and who I no longer recognize; chronic distrust, where relationships are perceived as inherently unsafe; temporal distortion, where the future becomes difficult to imagine beyond survival. Many survivors describe a haunting psychological reality: life can feel as though it paused at the moment their freedom was taken.[1] This matters deeply when we read Joseph's story.

Adaptive Containment: The Silence Of Survival

Joseph is silent for long stretches of the narrative. Scripture does not record him processing verbally. It does not describe emotional outbursts. This absence is often spiritualized, but psychologically it resembles what trauma specialists describe as adaptive containment, the mind's ability to suppress emotional expression in order to function under sustained threat. This is not weakness. It is survival intelligence. But survival intelligence comes at a cost. Individuals who endure prolonged loss of control often develop exceptional situational awareness, emotional restraint, and strategic thinking. These traits look like leadership strength. They look like maturity. They look like composure. But internally these traits can be rooted in vigilance, not peace. That tension matters.

Strengths Forged Under Pressure

Joseph's later capacity to manage systems, interpret crises, and remain emotionally composed reflects a mind trained under pressure. He reads rooms accurately. He interprets danger early. He responds without panic. These are strengths, but they are strengths forged under duress. Scripture never suggests that this process was painless or neutral. God's purpose unfolds, and trauma is still real. This is where theology must slow down. There is a dangerous tendency in faith spaces to rush toward redemption language without sitting in the injury. Psychology warns against this. Premature meaning-making, assigning purpose before acknowledging harm, can deepen trauma. Survivors often report feeling unseen when their suffering is reframed too quickly as "necessary," "worth it," or "part of God's plan." Healing requires truth before theology. Joseph's story does not glorify forced movement. It exposes it. The Bible does not deny the injury by celebrating the ending. It allows both truths to coexist. God redeems Joseph's future, and Joseph's trauma still mattered. God's sovereignty does not sanitize human cruelty. Divine purpose does not erase psychological cost. God redeems from trauma. He does not deny it. This distinction is holy.

Life After Being Taken: Not Linear

Life after being taken is rarely simple. Recovery from trafficking, or any prolonged loss of agency, is not linear. Psychiatrists emphasize that freedom does not automatically restore wholeness. Survivors often describe a paradox: they are physically free, yet internally restrained. Quality-of-life studies consistently show that survivors struggle with decision-making even in low-risk situations; they experience heightened anxiety around authority figures or systems; they carry a persistent sense of being out of place, even in safe environments; they feel shame disconnected from actual guilt; they oscillate between emotional numbing and emotional flooding. One longitudinal study noted that many survivors struggle not because they lack resilience, but because resilience was forged under conditions that required emotional shutdown. What once preserved life later complicates living. In other words, survival skills do not automatically convert into peace skills.

Complexity In Joseph's Later Life

Joseph's later life reflects this complexity. Even when elevated, he remains measured. Even when powerful, he is restrained. Even when reunited with his brothers, he tests before he trusts. This is not manipulation; it is discernment shaped by history. Trauma does not disappear when circumstances improve. It must be integrated. Trauma researchers such as Judith Herman and Bessel van der Kolk note that psychological healing often involves three critical elements: restoration of agency, narrative integration, and relational safety.[2] Joseph's story quietly reflects all three. He regains agency through wise decision-making rather than impulsive reaction. He integrates his narrative when he eventually names meaning without minimizing pain: "You meant it for evil, but God meant it for good." Notice, he does not deny evil. He does not rewrite history. He integrates it. And he forms relational safety, not everywhere, but intentionally. He builds stable bonds. He protects life. He steward's trust carefully. This is not accidental. It is evidence of slow internal restoration. Healing does not mean forgetting. It means no longer living as if control can be taken at any moment.

Why This Chapter Matters

This is why this chapter matters so deeply. It exists for readers who have been moved without consent, physically, emotionally, relationally, or spiritually. For those who lived under someone else's decision-making. For those who survived environments they never chose. Being taken does not make you broken, but it does change how you live afterward. Joseph's story reminds us of something sacred: God's alignment does not cancel human trauma, but it can outlast it. Redemption is not the eraser of injury. It is the slow reclamation of life after control. And that reclamation is holy work.

Joseph teaches us that being moved against your will does not disqualify you from becoming whole. But it does require gentleness with your story, patience with your healing, and truth about what survival demanded of you. Movement was not rescue for Joseph. Awareness was. Integration was. Stewardship was.

And for anyone who has lived through forced movement, loss of agency, or survival-based adaptation, this chapter stands as a witness: You are not weak because you adapted. You are not faithless because you needed time. You are not broken because survival shaped you. God is not in a hurry with your healing. He was not in a hurry with Joseph's. And the work of reclamation, slow, intentional, honest, is still sacred ground.

How Loss Of Agency Reshapes Faith

The reason this matters so deeply is because loss of agency reshapes how a person experiences God, not just how they experience life. When agency is repeatedly taken away, the inner framework through which a person understands authority, protection, and trust is altered. God is no longer encountered only as comfort or guidance; He is encountered through questions of safety, control, and survival. Prayer can feel different. Dependence can feel complicated. The language of surrender, which once sounded like faith, can begin to echo the memory of powerlessness. When choice is removed repeatedly, the mind learns to associate authority with danger and dependence with risk. That association does not disappear simply because circumstances change. Joseph's story forces us to confront this honestly. God's presence does not prevent trauma, and trauma does not negate God's presence. Both coexist in the narrative, and Scripture never rushes to resolve the tension.

Silence, Containment, And Wisdom

Joseph's silence in captivity is not spiritual apathy; it is adaptive restraint. Trauma clinicians explain that when autonomy is removed, expression becomes dangerous. The safest response is often containment, minimizing emotional exposure to preserve psychological energy.[3] Joseph is not emotionally absent; he is emotionally strategic. He learns when to speak and when silence protects him. That skill later becomes wisdom, but it was first survival.

This reframes how we read Joseph's emotional composure later in life. His calm is not naïveté. His measured responses are not detachment. They are the result of a nervous system trained under prolonged threat. Scripture does not criticize this adaptation. It contextualizes it. Joseph is neither romanticized nor pathologized; he is revealed.

Narrative Control: Agency Reclaimed

The theological mistake many readers make is assuming that because God later elevates Joseph, the earlier violations must have been inconsequential. Psychology strongly disagrees. Trauma does not disappear because outcomes improve. In fact, success often activates unresolved injury. When power is restored after powerlessness, unprocessed trauma can distort leadership, intimacy, and trust. Joseph's restraint, delay, and testing of his brothers before revealing himself reflect this reality. He does not rush reconciliation. He creates safety before vulnerability. This is not revenge; it is wisdom shaped by history. Psychologists refer to this as narrative control, the survivor's need to re-enter the story as an agent rather than a victim.[4] Joseph's structured engagement with his brothers allows him to reclaim agency without reenacting harm. He does not deny what happened. He does not collapse under it either. He integrates it.

"You Meant Evil... God Meant Good": Integration, Not Bypass

This is why Joseph's famous statement, "You meant it for evil, but God meant it for good"—must be read carefully. It is not spiritual bypassing. It is not denial. It is narrative integration. Joseph names intent accurately and names God's redemptive power without confusing the two. That distinction is psychologically healthy and theologically sound. Healing is not about erasing memory; it is about restoring the ability to choose again in the present. Joseph's later life demonstrates this restoration. He chooses restraint when he could retaliate. He chooses wisdom when he could dominate. He chooses stewardship when he could indulge power. These are not automatic virtues; they are practiced recoveries of agency.

From Survival Intelligence To Stewardship Intelligence

This is why survival intelligence must eventually be transformed into stewardship intelligence. Survival narrows focus to self-preservation. Stewardship expands focus to responsibility. Joseph learns this transition slowly. Scripture gives him time. God gives him space. Healing unfolds over years, not moments. For readers who have lived through loss of agency, whether through abuse, abandonment, systemic injustice, or relational control, this matters deeply. Your adaptations were not failures. They were intelligence under pressure. But what preserved you then may limit you now if it is never re-examined. God does not shame survival. He invites integration. The gospel does not demand that you forget what shaped you. It invites you to stop living as if you are still trapped inside it. Joseph's story reassures us that God does not rush reclamation. He does not demand instant peace. He does not force premature forgiveness. He walks with people through the long work of becoming whole. That work includes grief, truth-telling, and the slow rebuilding of trust. This is why redemption must be understood as process, not punctuation. God's alignment does not bypass trauma; it works through it. Purpose does not cancel pain; it redeems it over time. Joseph's life is not a shortcut story. It is a long obedience through fractured seasons. And that is good news.

If Movement Was Not Rescue

Because it means that if movement was not rescue for you, you are not behind. If survival shaped you more than peace, you are not disqualified. If silence protected you, God does not condemn you for it. He understands what it cost. Reclamation is holy work. Integration is holy work. And in case you forgot, holy work is the quiet rebuilding of a life after control was taken. Learning how to live without bracing for loss is holy work. Joseph did not just survive being taken. He learned how to live again without losing himself. And that is the deeper miracle of his story.

Scripture's Realism: Functioning With Unnamed Wounds

What makes Joseph's story so piercing is that Scripture does not give us a dramatic moment where trauma is named and resolved. There is no altar call scene in the pit. There is no prayer recorded where Joseph says he forgives his brothers. There is no divine interruption that explains the suffering in real time. Instead, the Bible gives us time. Long stretches of silence. Years where Joseph is functioning, contributing, interpreting dreams, managing systems, while carrying an unspoken history of being taken without consent. That absence of narration is not oversight. It is realism.

Continuity Before Meaning

Psychology helps us understand why. When agency is removed, the mind does not immediately process meaning; it prioritizes continuity. Survivors of prolonged control often move forward without language for what happened to them. They do not collapse; they compartmentalize. Joseph's life reflects this precisely. He does not spiral into chaos. He adapts. He learns systems.

He reads environments. He becomes exceptionally aware of power dynamics. These are not coincidences; they are survival adaptations refined into leadership tools. This is where theology must slow down and refuse to rush Joseph into inspiration. Because what looks like divine favor from the outside often feels like sustained vigilance on the inside. Trauma researchers consistently note that individuals who experienced forced movement develop heightened situational awareness, not because they are calm, but because unpredictability once cost them safety.[5] Joseph's discernment in Egypt is not just spiritual insight; it is a nervous system trained to anticipate shifts before they occur. That does not diminish God's hand. It deepens our understanding of it.

Power Before Peace; Responsibility Before Rest

God does not waste Joseph's adaptations, but He also does not confuse adaptation with healing. Joseph's ascent does not immediately restore his inner life. Power returns before peace does. Responsibility precedes reconciliation. This ordering matters.

Many people receive opportunity before integration, influence before rest, visibility before wholeness. A promotion may come while someone is still healing from what nearly broke them. A leadership role may arrive before a person has fully processed the seasons that shaped them. Scripture allows us to see that this is not failure; it is reality.

Joseph becomes responsible for the survival of nations while still carrying the memory of how his own life was taken from him. Grain passes through his hands before his story ever finds its voice. Power increases while peace is still forming.

Joseph's life reminds us that responsibility does not always wait for restoration. Sometimes God entrusts stewardship while the deeper work of healing is still unfolding.

This is the chilling reality of a Driver Seat leader. Like Joseph, you must learn how to function with excellence even while pain still exists in the background of your story. Leadership often requires the ability to steward responsibility while your own life is still being restored.

Boundaries, Safety, And Wisdom

Joseph's restraint when confronted with his brothers is one of the most psychologically honest moments in Scripture. He does not reveal himself immediately. He tests the environment. He observes behavior. He watches how power is handled now compared to before. Anyone who has lived through betrayal understands this instinctively. Vulnerability is rarely offered until safety is demonstrated consistently. Joseph's delay is not manipulation; it is discernment shaped by history.

Theologically, this challenges shallow interpretations of forgiveness. Forgiveness is not the absence of boundaries. Reconciliation is not the denial of memory. Joseph's process honors truth. He does not pretend nothing happened. He creates conditions where repentance, responsibility, and change can be observed. Only then does he move toward reunion. This is not hardness; it is wisdom.

Healing rarely happens by pretending the past did not occur. It happens when a person can re-enter relationships with restored choice. Joseph chooses the timing. Joseph chooses the disclosure. Joseph chooses the terms of engagement. That choice itself becomes part of the healing process.

This is why Scripture shows Joseph weeping privately before revealing himself. Tears emerge when safety finally exists. Emotion returns when vigilance begins to relax. The body releases what it could not afford to feel earlier. That detail matters. Joseph did not lack emotion; he delayed it until survival no longer required suppression.

Deferred Grief, Honored By God

This speaks directly to readers who have learned how to function without feeling, lead without resting, provide without processing. Your composure may not be denial; it may be deferred grief. And deferred grief does not disappear, it waits for safety. God does not punish waiting grief. He honors it by creating space where it can finally surface. This reframes silence again. Silence is not always spiritual distance. Sometimes silence is the only environment where the body feels safe enough to exhale. God works patiently with that pace. He does not demand instant emotional exposure. He works through years of stability before inviting vulnerability. That is deeply pastoral. It tells us that God is not intimidated by slow healing. He is not offended by measured trust. He is not threatened by boundaries formed through pain. He is committed to restoration that lasts, not restoration that performs well.

Don't Confuse Survival Identity With Permanent Identity

The danger, psychology warns, is when survivors confuse survival identity with permanent identity. Joseph could have remained only a manager, only a strategist, only a problem-solver. But God does not leave him there. The reunion with his family is not just narrative closure; it is identity expansion. Joseph integrates sonhood with leadership, vulnerability with authority, compassion with control. That integration is healing. Trauma narrows identity. Redemption expands it. This is why Joseph's later generosity is significant. He does not hoard power. He does not replicate scarcity. He does not punish dependence. He feeds nations. Trauma often produces either control or collapse. Joseph exhibits neither. He demonstrates stewardship. That is evidence of internal restoration, not just external success.

Redemption Without Romanticizing Suffering

Stewardship, psychologically, requires secure identity. It requires the ability to hold responsibility without fear of losing oneself. It requires the capacity to give without needing control. Joseph arrives there because his healing progressed alongside his calling, not after it. And this is where readers must be careful not to romanticize suffering. Joseph's pain was not necessary in the sense that evil was required for God to act. Scripture never calls betrayal good. It calls God faithful. That distinction matters. Trauma-informed theology refuses to justify harm while still affirming redemption. God does not orchestrate cruelty to build character. He redeems character in spite of cruelty. For those who were moved without consent, emotionally, relationally, systemically, this chapter exists to tell the truth gently and firmly: what happened to you mattered. It shaped how you move. It shaped how you trust. It shaped how you survive. And none of that disqualifies you from purpose.

Healing Is Not A Return—It's An Integration

But survival is not the end of the story. Healing is not about returning to who you were before. That person may not exist anymore. Healing is about becoming whole with who you are now. Joseph did not go back to being the boy with dreams and a coat. He became a man with wisdom and responsibility. Different, not diminished. That is hope rooted in reality. And that is why Joseph's story belongs not just in sermons, but in conversations about trauma, agency, leadership, and restoration. Because it refuses simplistic answers. It allows God to be sovereign without being cruel, purposeful without being dismissive, redemptive without being rushed. If you were taken, moved, controlled, or silenced, Joseph's life whispers something essential: you are not broken, you are unfinished. And God's work in you is not erasure; it is reclamation.

Part I + Part Ii: The Difference Between Moved And Free

What ultimately ties Part I and Part II together is this truth: movement alone is not healing, and freedom alone is not restoration. Joseph moves constantly throughout his story, sold, transported, placed, imprisoned, elevated, but movement does not immediately give him agency. Agency is rebuilt slowly, intentionally, and internally. This is where many readers misinterpret progress. They assume that because circumstances change, the inner life has caught up. Scripture never makes that assumption. Joseph's story forces us to confront the difference between being moved and becoming free.

Why Many Get Stuck Between Reactive And Ambition-driven

In Part I, we talked about levels of intentional living, reactive, ambition-driven, humbled, governed, and stewarded. What Part II exposes is why some people get stuck moving between the first two levels for years. Trauma interrupts the development of agency. When choice is repeatedly taken, the nervous system learns to survive without agency. Decisions become reactions. Ambition becomes armor. Speed becomes safety. Slowing down feels dangerous because stillness once meant vulnerability.

Restoring Executive Function: Pauses Return

Joseph experiences this directly. After being taken, his life is governed by external systems—slave markets, households, prisons, empires. Yet within those systems, Scripture shows him gradually reclaiming internal governance. He learns how to remain himself while being managed by others. That is not weakness. That is maturity forged under pressure.

Over time, Joseph begins to regain the ability to choose his responses instead of simply reacting for survival. The man who was once carried by other people's decisions slowly becomes someone who can pause, observe, and respond with intention.

Before anyone can make wise decisions, they must feel safe enough internally to pause. Joseph's pauses, his silence, his restraint, and his measured responses show this change taking place. They reveal that his inner life is stabilizing even while his external circumstances remain uncertain.

This reframes patience entirely. Patience is not passivity; it is regulated strength.

The Prison Matters As Much As The Palace

Joseph's capacity to wait, observe, and interpret rather than react marks a shift from survival-driven movement to stewarded living. He is no longer being dragged forward by circumstances; he is moving with awareness inside circumstances he did not choose. That distinction is the turning point of his life. Theologically, this shows us something vital: God does not merely relocate Joseph geographically; He re-educates his internal world. God is not just changing

Joseph's address; He is changing Joseph's posture. And posture determines how power is handled when it arrives. This is why the prison matters as much as the palace. In the prison, Joseph practices leadership without recognition. He interprets dreams without reward. He serves without visibility. Psychologically, this builds intrinsic identity, worth not dependent on outcome. Survivors of control often struggle here, because their value was once tied to usefulness. Joseph resists that trap. He remains faithful without becoming performative.

Stewardship Without Overcorrection

That restraint protects him later. When Joseph finally steps into authority, he does not overcorrect. He does not abuse power. He does not center himself. He moves carefully. He plans for famine. He distributes resources. He saves lives beyond his own story. That is stewarded living. Stewarded living does not mean perfection; it means awareness, restraint, and asking not just "What can I do?" but "What should I do?" Joseph's capacity to steward resources, relationships, and authority is directly tied to the years he spent without them. This reframes suffering without glorifying it. God did not need Joseph's trauma to accomplish His will, but He refused to waste it. That is not the same thing. The Bible never credits evil for God's goodness. It credits God for redeeming what evil intended to destroy. That distinction protects both theology and mental health.

For Those Still In The Middle

If you feel like you're still in the middle, still silent, still waiting, this chapter offers language for what you are experiencing: You are not inactive, you are integrating. You are not forgotten, you are stabilizing. You are not behind, you are being prepared for weight you cannot yet see. Joseph's story does not promise a palace for everyone. It promises something deeper: that your life is not reduced to the worst thing that happened to you, and your future is not limited by the season you didn't choose. Remember, God's alignment does not cancel trauma, but it outlasts it. Redemption is not the moment everything makes sense. It is the moment your life is no longer governed by what was taken from you.

The Invitation

And that is the invitation of Chapter 4. To move, not reactively, not defensively, not desperately, but deliberately. To live, not hurried, not numb, not fragmented, but stewarded. To trust, not because the road is clear, but because you are becoming someone who can walk it with integrity. Joseph did not rush into freedom. He grew into it. And so will you.

Driver Seat Truth

Before you lead a system, you must understand one. Joseph is carried by a system he did not choose (a caravan of men, a market, a house, a prison, an empire). He watches, learns, and adapts, commerce, chain-of-command, negotiation, risk, reward. Formation precedes elevation: the pit taught stillness; the caravan teaches steadiness. This is adaptive intelligence, the inner governance that lets you lead without losing yourself. This Driver Seat truth threads through everything you just read: movement can be forced, but maturity must be chosen. Joseph learns systems so that, in time, he can serve people inside them with wisdom and restraint.

Prayer

Lord, when I am moved by roads I did not choose, keep my identity anchored in You. Teach me the language of new systems, the wisdom of restraint, and the steadiness of governed living. Carry me without letting me lose myself. Give me grace to tell the truth about my story, patience to heal at Your pace, and courage to turn survival into stewardship. Amen.

Driver Seat Key Takeaways

- **Movement without choice can still be movement directed by God.** Joseph did not choose the caravan, the route, or the destination, yet heaven used strangers to move him toward purpose. Forced transitions do not cancel divine intention; they simply reveal it in unexpected ways.

- **Strangers can become the carriers of a destiny your own people resisted.** The Ishmaelites did not know Joseph, value Joseph, or understand Joseph, yet they transported him into the next phase of his calling. God often uses unfamiliar systems to accomplish what familiar environments refused to steward.

- **The price people place on you reveals their wound, not your worth.** Joseph was sold for twenty pieces of silver, the ancient price of a teenage slave. Their valuation exposed their jealousy and blindness, not Joseph's identity. Human pricing never determines divine purpose.

- **Being commodified attacks identity at its core, but God preserves what people cheapen.** When others treat you as currency, the temptation is to shrink your worth. Joseph's story teaches that being reduced by people does not reduce what God placed within you.

- **Exploitation can become the unlikely bridge to elevation.** Joseph's sale was sinful and traumatic, yet it became the hinge that moved him toward the palace. This does not justify harm, it reveals God's ability to redirect what was meant for destruction.

- **Painful transitions can be purposeful transitions.** Joseph was displaced, not promoted, yet the forced movement set the stage for the formation he would need in every future assignment. Not every painful shift is a setback; some are relocations disguised as loss.

- **Destiny often advances through people who do not understand you and systems you did not choose.** Joseph's journey shows that divine orchestration can work through strangers, traders, or even adversaries. People do not have to honor your identity to participate in your assignment.

- **Loss of agency is real trauma, yet it does not end God's involvement.** Joseph was taken, sold, stripped of choice, and relocated without consent. Still, God remained active in silence, arranging what Joseph could not see. Agency may be stolen, but destiny cannot be.

- **What carries you may not care about you, but God still uses it to shape you.** The caravan of men saw merchandise, not a minister. Their indifference did not hinder God's direction. God uses even careless hands to move chosen people into the right place at the right time.

- **Forced movement reveals a deeper leadership truth: character must travel even when control is taken.** Joseph could not govern circumstances, but he governed himself. He maintained dignity, discipline, and discernment under captivity. True leadership begins when you can steward who you are while life is carrying you where you did not plan to go

***

POTIPHAR'S HOUSE: SUCCESS THAT YOU'RE NOT READY FOR

The caravan of men delivers Joseph to Potiphar's house, movement becomes opportunity, and opportunity becomes visibility. But visibility can arrive faster than integration. What happens when doors open before the inner life is finished forming? Chapter 5 begins where many leaders stumble: success that you're not ready for, and how God uses it to finish what pain began.

SECTION TWO

THE TRANSITION YEARS

CHAPTER FIVE

POTIPHAR'S HOUSE: SUCCESS THAT YOU'RE NOT READY FOR

(**Genesis 39:2–3**): "The Lord was with Joseph... his master saw that the Lord was with him and that the Lord caused all that he did to succeed."

Entering Potiphar's House: The Illusion of Improvement

Joseph's life takes a sudden turn. Genesis tells us plainly what happens next: Joseph is taken to Egypt. He is carried there by the Ishmaelites. He arrives not as a visitor, not as a guest, but as property. He is sold. Genesis 39:1 says he is purchased by Potiphar, an officer of Pharaoh and captain of the guard. There is no transition scene, no recovery moment, no pause between trauma and responsibility. Joseph moves from the pit into a house, from emptiness into structure, from abandonment into responsibility. And on the surface, this looks like improvement. *But in hindsight, its not.*

He is no longer exposed. There are walls now. There is routine. There is order. There are expectations. There is food. There is shelter. There is a role to fill. But this transition is deceptive, because improvement in environment does not automatically equal healing of the soul. Potiphar's house introduces a dangerous illusion: things look better, so I must be better. Joseph has not been healed yet. He has been positioned. After acute trauma, the nervous system often "downshifts" when danger subsides (relief), but identity, grief, and meaning-making (resolution) lag behind. Hence, making relief feel like healing, but it isn't the same thing.

Favor Can Outpace Formation

That distinction matters, because this is where many people confuse progress with preparedness. God allows Joseph to succeed externally while still carrying internal fractures. Scripture is careful here. The Bible does not say Joseph healed before he was promoted. It says he was favored. Favor can outpace formation. Joseph goes from slave to leadership inside the same system that purchased him. He is trusted quickly. Responsibility expands rapidly. His competence is noticed. His work is effective. And soon, everything he touches prospers. But nothing in the text suggests that the pit has been processed. Nothing suggests that betrayal has been named. Nothing suggests that his inner life has been repaired.

Before we move into Joseph's internal world, I think there's something I need to point out to you. In Genesis 39, the Bible repeats a phrase with intentional precision: "The Lord was with Joseph." Genesis 39:2, 3, 21, 23. It's not mentioned once. It's not hinted at. It is announced as the defining reality of Joseph's life in Potiphar's house. And then Scripture goes even further: "The Lord blessed the Egyptian's house for Joseph's sake." Genesis 39:5. This is important: The text emphasizes God's presence and God's blessing, but it does not emphasize Joseph's emotional resolution. Joseph is still wounded, still processing betrayal, still piecing himself back together yet God is with him, and because God is with him, everything around him is experiencing overflow. Potiphar didn't know it, but the greatest asset in his entire estate was not his military status, his rank, his power, or his wealth. It was Joseph. Not because Joseph was perfect, healed, or whole, but because God's favor was sitting on Joseph. And here is the truth we often forget: Blessings flow through people. God's favor travels through vessels. His increase is often attached to an individual, not an environment. Scripture consistently shows this pattern: God blesses others because of someone He has chosen. Laban was blessed because of Jacob. "The Lord has blessed me because of you." Genesis 30:27. Nations were blessed because of Abraham. "All peoples on earth will be blessed through you." Genesis 12:3. Israel prospered because of Moses' intercession. Exodus 32 shows God sparing a nation because of one man's favor. Paul's ship survived because Paul was on board. "God has graciously given you the lives of all who sail with you." Acts 27:24. This is the pattern: God places favor on a person, and everyone connected to that person benefits. Which leads to the the point i am reaching for: Discernment matters because people often walk away from the very person God was using to bless them. Potiphar's house was blessed because Joseph was in it. Not because Potiphar was righteous. Not because Egypt was holy. Not because the environment was conducive. God blessed the house for Joseph's sake. And this happens today: People pass on, betray, overlook, or abandon the Joseph in their life, the very person carrying the favor that was blessing them. They don't realize: When you disconnect from someone God is using, you may be disconnecting from the blessing God was sending. Favor is not random. Favor is not abstract. Favor is not detached. Favor has a vessel. Favor has a carrier. Favor has an assignment. And if you don't have spiritual discernment, you can lose the blessing by losing the person through whom God intended to deliver it. Now that framework matters deeply, because Joseph is experiencing something complex: He is the vessel of blessing, but he is not emotionally healed. He is carrying favor, but he is carrying wounds. He is the source of increase for someone else, while still recovering from decrease himself. And that brings us right into what comes next.

Stable Outside, Unsettled Inside

The house does not ask Joseph how he is doing; it asks what he can handle. This is why the transition is deceptive. Because stability creates assumptions. When chaos ends, the body relaxes. The nervous system slows down. The mind stops bracing for impact. And when that happens, we rush to meaning: if my surroundings improved, then something inside me must have improved too. But that assumption is not faith. It is relief masquerading as wholeness.

Joseph's life looks stable before it feels settled, and this is where the danger lives. The most dangerous seasons are the ones that feel stable before you feel settled. Potiphar's house feels like relief, walls instead of exposure, routine instead of chaos, responsibility instead of abandonment. Relief slows the pulse. It convinces the body to unclench. But relief is not the same as resolution. Relief happens when threat subsides. Resolution happens when meaning is rebuilt.

Many of us mistake a calmer calendar for a healed heart. We assume that when the noise dies down, when the phone stops ringing, when the intensity of the crisis fades, we must be better. But a quiet season doesn't automatically mean an internal one. Stillness outside is not the same thing as stillness inside. A peaceful schedule can trick you into thinking you've reached emotional restoration, when all you've reached is a moment without pressure.

This is why "I'm finally okay" collapses the instant a new stressor hits. Because the statement wasn't coming from a settled soul, it was coming from a relaxed environment. The heart wasn't healed; it was simply unbothered. The nervous system wasn't regulated; it was simply unprovoked. The emotions weren't processed; they were simply dormant. What looked like recovery was really just the absence of disturbance.

When life is calm, unaddressed wounds go quiet. Trauma softens its voice. Old grief sits still. Pain behaves. Not because it has been resolved, but because nothing has awakened it yet. And the moment a new pressure enters the room, the moment a new conflict arises, the moment a new disappointment shows up, everything that was unprocessed gets activated again. The calm evaporates. The old patterns return. The same fears flare. The same insecurities react. The same emotions rush back to the surface as if they were never gone.

This is the signature of unhealed places. They hold together when nothing is touching them. They crumble when life applies weight.

A stress-free season is not the same as a restored soul. A lighter schedule is not the same as deep emotional work. Getting a break is not the same as getting breakthrough.

And this is exactly where Joseph is. His surroundings have stabilized, but his insides have not. His responsibilities have increased, but his soul has not been rebuilt. His environment is organized, but his identity is still rearranging itself. He looks functional because nothing is poking his wounds yet. But the unprocessed places are still living inside him, and the next chapter will prove it.

This is why Potiphar's house is so dangerous. It's not a place of chaos. It's a place of calm. And calm has fooled many people into believing they are whole.

When Usefulness Becomes a Hiding Place

And because he is functioning, no one interrupts the process. He learns systems. He observes expectations. He anticipates needs. He becomes reliable, and reliability is rewarded everywhere, corporate spaces, ministry settings, creative industries, leadership environments. The one who shows up consistently becomes indispensable. The one who produces becomes trusted. The one who does not complain becomes safe. But usefulness can become a hiding place. Joseph's competence organizes his outer life, but it does not interrogate his inner one. He becomes effective faster than he becomes settled. And when that happens, life does not slow down, it accelerates. More access. More trust. More responsibility. The system benefits from your discipline long before it notices your exhaustion. This is how favor outpaces formation. Trauma survivors often default to over-functioning (performing, people-pleasing, perfectionism) to maintain safety and control. It works, until it doesn't.

And this shows up so clearly in our modern world. Many of us live in rhythms where productivity is praised louder than emotional honesty, where performance is rewarded faster than self-awareness, and where burnout hides beneath excellence. We know how to meet deadlines but not how to acknowledge disappointment. We know how to be competent in public while feeling fragmented in private. Over-functioning becomes the armor we wear to survive environments that never stop asking. It shows up in the employee who never takes a day off because slowing down feels unsafe. It shows up in the parent who carries the entire household on their back because receiving help feels like weakness. It shows up in the leader who keeps producing because producing is the only place they feel valued. It shows up in the friend who is always the strong one because being vulnerable feels like losing control. We learn to outrun our inner world by mastering our outer responsibilities, but eventually the body keeps score, the soul sends signals, and life reveals that effectiveness without emotional integration is unsustainable.

Modern culture celebrates the version of you that performs but rarely creates space for the version of you that is hurting. That is why many people look successful while secretly feeling depleted. They are applauded for producing but unnoticed in their exhaustion. They are promoted for reliability but unseen in their fragility. They become everyone's solution while carrying unspoken burdens of their own. In a world that rewards doing over being, efficiency can become a mask, and excellence can turn into a hiding place for unaddressed pain. This is why favor can be dangerous when formation is incomplete. The very traits that elevate you on the outside can suffocate you on the inside when they are used to avoid healing.

Joseph's world and our world are not as different as we like to imagine. The systems around us often love our output but overlook our wounds. People will celebrate your competence long before they ever ask about your condition. And if we are not careful, we will confuse being needed with being known, being busy with being whole, and being productive with being healed. Over-functioning feels like control until it collapses. It feels like safety until it becomes suffocation. It feels like strength until a new stressor exposes how tired the heart really is. This is how many people live today—high-performing, highly trusted, highly exhausted, and highly unaware that their usefulness has become a hiding place where unprocessed wounds remain untouched.

Functioning ≠ Wholeness

And many of us recognize this moment. A job comes after loss. A promotion follows burnout. A platform grows after obscurity. Life starts working again, and because it's working, we assume we are healed. But functioning is not the same as being whole. Movement is not the same as maturity. Order is not the same as alignment. What makes this so deceptive is that outward progress feels like inward restoration. Bills get paid. Relationships stabilize. Opportunities open. People start affirming us again. The calendar fills with good things instead of painful ones, and without realizing it, we interpret activity as recovery. But often, all that has changed is circumstance, not condition. Life becomes manageable, but the heart remains untouched.

Potiphar's house feels like confirmation, but theologically, it is confrontation. Because better conditions do not fix the inner life they expose it. When life is chaotic, you react. When life stabilizes, you reflect. And if the inner life has not been addressed, stability becomes dangerous. This shows up every day in the modern world. Someone gets a new job and feels confident again, until one correction from a supervisor reopens old insecurity. Someone enters a healthy relationship and feels whole again, until one disagreement awakens old abandonment fears. Someone finally feels peace in a quiet season, until one unexpected stressor reveals how fragile that peace truly was. Stability does not heal us; it simply reveals what healing has not yet reached.

This is why Joseph's life does not turn with applause; it turns with procedure. No ceremony. No questions. No healing narrative. Just a quiet relocation into responsibility. And if this transition is misunderstood, an illusion settles in: things look better, so it is better. That illusion will shape every decision that follows unless it is confronted here. The modern believer faces the same temptation. We tell ourselves we are fine because nothing is falling apart. We tell ourselves we are strong because we are no longer crying. We tell ourselves we are healed because life is behaving. But God uses stable seasons as mirrors, not medals. They reflect what is real; they do not reward what is complete.

Psalm 105:17–19 pulls back the curtain on Joseph's story and shows us what was happening beneath the surface. Scripture says Joseph was "sent ahead." That means none of what he walked through was random. Not the betrayal. Not the pit. Not the caravan. Not the sale. Not Potiphar's house. God was using every step to send Joseph into position long before Joseph understood the assignment he was being shaped for.

And then the psalm says something even more revealing: "the word of the Lord tested him" (Psalm 105:19). That phrase means that the promise spoken over Joseph's life did not just guide him, it pressed him. It measured him. It refined him. The word tested him by bringing him into situations that revealed who he was and who he was becoming. Before the word could be fulfilled *through* Joseph, it had to be fulfilled *in* Joseph. God never allows a promise to rest on a character that cannot carry it.

This is where the connection becomes powerful: Favor opens doors; God's word refines what walks through them. Joseph's favor opened the door to Potiphar's house. But the word of the Lord tested him inside that door. Favor can place you in rooms you didn't prepare for. But the word will prepare you for the weight of those rooms. Favor accelerates you. The word stabilizes you. Favor elevates you. The word purifies you. Favor positions you quickly. The word shapes you slowly. Favor brings opportunity. The word builds capacity.

This is why many people misunderstand seasons of success that feel uncomfortable. They assume that if favor is present, everything should feel easy. But Psalm 105 tells us the opposite. Sometimes the very season that looks like promotion is actually a proving ground. God will let favor open a door and then let His word test your motives, your identity, your integrity, your endurance, and your inner life. The door is confirmation. But the testing inside the door is formation.

Joseph walked into Potiphar's house because of favor. But he grew inside Potiphar's house because of testing. And the same happens in our lives. God may open a door for you because of His favor, but once you step through, He begins the deeper work. He starts addressing the parts of you that the blessing will demand. He begins refining the insecurities, healing the fractures, strengthening the discipline, and shaping the maturity necessary to stand in what He is giving you. Favor gets you in. Formation keeps you there.

Psalm 105:19 says Joseph remained in that testing season "until the word of the Lord proved him true." In other words, the promise was still alive, but Joseph needed to be made ready for the weight of fulfillment. God loved Joseph too much to let the dream come to pass before the man was strong enough to carry it.

So when I say "Favor opens doors; God's word refines what walks through them," I'm naming a kingdom pattern: God uses blessing to bring you forward, and He uses testing to build you deeper.

Both are part of His goodness. Both are part of His process.

And Joseph is living in that exact tension in Potiphar's house. He is favored enough to rise, and tested enough to grow.

Favor, Promotion, and the First Leadership Laboratory

Like we talked about earlier, scripture makes something unmistakably clear in Genesis 39:2–3: the Lord is with Joseph. We already know that Joseph prospers in Potiphar's house not because the system is fair and not because his trauma has resolved, but because God's presence is active. We've covered how deliberately the Bible repeats it. The Lord is with Joseph. God's favor is evident in his work. Everything Joseph does succeeds. But here is the part I want to highlight now: Potiphar notices (Genesis 39:3). That is the shift in the story. That is the entire reason we revisit the theme of favor right here. We are not circling back for repetition; we are circling back for revelation. Favor becomes visible before healing becomes internal, and the moment favor becomes visible, people begin to respond to you differently. Joseph is still recovering on the inside, but the exterior evidence of God's hand is already undeniable, and Potiphar sees it. And once someone in power notices favor, the dynamics in the story begin to shift.

This is the first moment Scripture tells us Potiphar notices something supernatural. He does not notice Joseph's trauma. He does not notice Joseph's wounds. He does not notice Joseph's story. He notices the results. He sees that the Lord is with Joseph. He sees that everything Joseph touches prospers. He sees that prosperity follows Joseph, not the system. Potiphar is not discerning Joseph's heart; he is observing Joseph's fruit.

And because Potiphar notices the favor, he elevates Joseph. Genesis 39:4 says, "So Joseph found favor in his sight, and served him. Then he made him overseer of his house, and all that he had he put under his authority." What triggers the promotion? Potiphar seeing the favor. Joseph's elevation is not based on his résumé. Not based on his healing. Not based on his emotional stability. Not based on his background. Not based on his comfort level. His promotion is based purely on Potiphar recognizing God's hand.

But promotion is not proof of readiness. It is proof of trust. And trust often arrives before understanding. This is where Potiphar's house becomes Joseph's first leadership laboratory, not the throne, not the palace, not the position he dreamed about as a boy, but a house. A space small enough to watch him closely, quiet enough to shape him slowly, and close enough to test what was still unsettled inside him. Before Joseph ever leads a nation, he must learn how to lead himself. That's a vital, important message, because the hardest person to lead in life is yourself. And that lesson does not happen in public. It happens in private. Leadership does not begin with authority; it begins with formation. And formation rarely announces itself as important while it is happening. Potiphar's house is not glamorous or prophetic in appearance, but it is intentional.

It becomes the first place where Joseph learns how power feels in his hands, how trust is extended, how access works, and how proximity can either mature you or undo you. This house teaches him systems, order, routine, expectation. It teaches him how to manage resources, how to steward responsibilities, how to move with authority without possessing it. But more dangerously, it teaches him how easily it is to look healed when you're simply functioning. Leader's Mirror: God often grows private integrity before public influence (1 Pet 5:6; Col 3:23).

The Subtle Temptation of "I Must Be Better"

Things look better now, and the mind quietly draws a conclusion it has not earned yet: if life looks better, I must be better, right? That assumption has undone, more leaders than failure ever has. Every person has a Potiphar's house, not a building, but a season, a moment early in life where responsibilities arrive before understanding, when trust comes before self-awareness, and when influence appears before identity is fully formed.

For some, it was a first job where someone believed in you. For others, it was a first ministry assignment, a first leadership role, a first platform, a first time being seen. It was that place where you realized people were watching you now, where expectations quietly increased, where you learned how to carry weight before you knew how to carry yourself. This is where imposter feelings meet real responsibility. The temptation isn't drama; it's a drift into performance as identity.

Joseph steps into Potiphar's house still carrying the residue of the pit.

Betrayal has not evaporated. Loss has not been explained. His sense of self is still rearranging itself after being stripped, sold, and silenced. But remember, no one in the house asks about the pit. They only care if he can perform. And that is how leadership laboratories work. They do not ask where you've been. They ask what can you handle. They reward competence, not processing. They celebrate reliability, not reflection.

Structure begins to feel like safety. Predictability feels like peace. But structure is not the same as safety. Structure tells you what to do. Safety allows you to feel. Many of us were taught to perform long before we were taught to process. We learned how to filter our feelings more than feeling them. We learned how to show up, how to be dependable, how to carry responsibilities. But we never learned how to sit with disappointment and name grief.

And to this day, many of us still don't realize that grief is a natural emotion. And if you don't let it out the right way, you will act it out the wrong way. So we become strong early, capable early, reliable early. And no one notices that strength is covering sorrow, that excellence is hiding overextension, and that consistency is masking unresolved pain. And if you are reading this and feel like this describes where you are right now, and you feel like you need healing, let me guide you toward healing God's way.

Real Healing Often Begins With Lament. Name the grief. Lament is biblical courage, not weakness. Scripture never teaches us to swallow sorrow; it teaches us to bring it to God. The book of Psalms is full of people who refused to let pain harden their hearts. Instead, they opened their wounds before God so healing could begin. But for many believers, the word "lament" sounds too heavy or too unfamiliar, so let me show you what lament actually looks like and how you can practice it in a way that leads to real healing. Lament begins with honesty (Psalm 62:8): "Pour out your heart before Him." Not your filtered heart. Not your polished heart. Your real heart. Lament is the permission to say, "I'm not okay, but I'm still coming to You." Healing begins with refusing to hide what God can heal. God cannot transform what we keep pretending does not hurt. Lament also names what hurts (Psalm 142:2): "I pour out my complaint before Him; I declare my trouble before Him." Healing requires specificity. You cannot heal from what you refuse to name. This may sound like, "God, I'm grieving what they took from me." "God, I'm hurting from what I never received." "God, I'm still wounded by what happened to me." Naming the wound is not bitterness. Naming the wound gives God access to it. It opens the door for God to touch what life damaged. Lament allows you to feel without falling apart (Psalm 34:18): "The Lord is close to the brokenhearted." God is not threatened by your emotions. He draws closer to them. This means you can cry and be spiritual. You can hurt and be holy. You can feel deeply and still walk in faith. Grief does not disqualify you; it positions you for God's nearness. God meets you in the cracks, not the performance. Lament turns your pain into prayer (Psalm 13). David begins Psalm 13 with, "How long, O Lord?" but he ends with, "I will sing of Your goodness." The shift from sorrow to trust happens inside the prayer, not after it. This teaches us something transformative: Healing does not require you to feel better first. It requires you to face God with the truth of where you are. God does not wait for you to feel hopeful; He meets you in the lament and grows hope inside the honesty. Lament creates space for God to heal what life damaged (Psalm 147:3): "He heals the brokenhearted and binds up their wounds." Some wounds God heals immediately. Others He heals gradually. But all wounds require exposure before they can be restored. This means you move toward healing by sitting with God more than sitting with your performance, allowing silence to touch what busyness has been covering, giving God permission to address pain you've hidden, and returning to the places you rushed past emotionally. Lament is not dwelling on pain; lament is inviting God into it. It is choosing presence over pretense. Lament prepares you for strength (Nehemiah 8:10): "The joy of the Lord is your strength." Notice the order: Lament comes first. Joy comes after. God heals you into strength, not around sorrow. You do not bypass grief to become strong; you become strong because you let God walk with you through it. The practical steps for you are simple, actionable, and scriptural: Sit in stillness for five minutes daily and invite God into the emotions you usually outrun (Psalm 46:10). Write down one thing you are grieving and bring that specific grief to God in prayer (Psalm 142:2). Speak truth over yourself: "God is near to me in this" (Psalm 34:18). End each lament with trust, even if it's one sentence: "But Lord, I trust You will heal me" (Psalm 13:5–6). This is what biblical healing looks like. Not denial. Not numbing. Not pretending. But turning grief into a meeting place with God.

Proximity, Temptation, and the Identity Test

Potiphar's house teaches Joseph something else. Leadership brings proximity, not just proximity to power, but proximity to temptation. And temptation does not arrive loudly or violently. It arrives familiar, close, repetitive. It does not announce destruction. It suggests relief. This is where leadership laboratories become dangerous, because they introduce access before identity is settled. They place you near influence before your inner life has matured, and unresolved places begin to whisper.

After everything you've been through, after how hard you've worked, after how faithful you've been, Joseph's test is not desire. It is entitlement. Will he let access rewrite identity? Will he let proximity blur conviction? Will he let comfort justify compromise? Genesis 39:6 contains a seemingly simple detail: *"Now Joseph was handsome in form and appearance."* At first glance, it reads like a side note, almost an unnecessary description. But in biblical narrative, physical descriptions are never random. Scripture rarely pauses to comment on someone's appearance unless that appearance plays a role in what comes next. This verse functions as literary foreshadowing. It signals to the reader that Joseph's rising favor and visibility are about to attract the wrong kind of attention.

This is the Bible's way of setting the stage. Joseph's success has made him noticeable. His competence has made him trusted. And now, his appearance will make him vulnerable. The text is quietly preparing us for the next turn in the story. Immediately after the narrator mentions Joseph's appearance, the very next verse begins, *"And after some time his master's wife cast her eyes on Joseph."* That "after some time" is intentional. It indicates that temptation does not come when Joseph is weakest and wounded from the pit; it comes later, when his life finally feels structured, stable, and successful.

This is an important spiritual pattern. Temptation often emerges not in the chaos but in the calm, not in the pain but in the progress, not when we are fighting to survive but when we begin to flourish. Joseph is no longer in the pit. He is no longer being sold. He is no longer wandering. He is functioning well, trusted deeply, and living in a season of visible favor. It is *precisely* then that temptation walks into the room.

Genesis is showing us something: stability creates opportunity, not just for blessing, but for testing. Potiphar's house becomes a place of prosperity, but prosperity also creates proximity. And proximity exposes vulnerability. The higher Joseph rises, the more noticeable he becomes. The more noticeable he becomes, the more targetable he becomes. The detail about his appearance is not vanity; it is vulnerability.

In other words, Scripture is whispering to us: Pay attention. What comes next is connected to the favor that was just made visible.

Joseph's physical attractiveness is the narrative bridge that connects his public success to his private testing. It tells us that what happens with Potiphar's wife is not accidental, random, or disconnected. It is the next logical tension in a story where God's favor lifts Joseph, and that same favor draws both admiration and attack.

So when I say, "after some time, temptation arrives, right when life finally feels stable," I am naming a biblical pattern. The test comes in the season where Joseph might have been tempted to think he was safe, settled, or secure. Stability is not the absence of danger; sometimes it is the setup for the assignment. And just as favor drew Potiphar's attention, it now draws the attention of someone whose motives are not pure.

This is the hinge in Joseph's story. One set of eyes saw favor and promoted him. Another set of eyes saw favor and targeted him. And Scripture wants us to understand that both are part of the journey to destiny.

And this is where the story turns from simple foreshadowing to soul-level formation. Joseph's visibility has increased, his favor has become undeniable, and the eyes on him are no longer neutral. Potiphar's attention brought promotion, but Potiphar's wife's attention will bring pressure. And it's right here, in this shift from being noticed for favor to being targeted because of it, that the deeper work of leadership begins. Because before temptation ever touches the body, it exposes the heart. Before accusation ever enters the room, it reveals what has been hidden beneath responsibility. Favor put Joseph in the spotlight, but the spotlight now reveals the internal world he has carried quietly until this moment.

And that is where many of us find ourselves. The same environments that elevate us are often the first places that expose what we have never processed. When you rise, you carry two things with you: your gift and your grief. Your competency and your cracks. Your favor and your fractures. And the pressure of visibility tends to reveal what stability had managed to hide.

Which brings us here: For many of us, our first leadership laboratory was also the first place we learned how to hide. We learned how to hide fatigue behind productivity, confusion behind confidence, and pain behind respon-sibility. Being needed felt safer than being known. And something in us quietly learned to survive rather than settle.

Joseph refuses. Not dramatically. Not loudly. Not impulsively. He refuses because somewhere in that house, he learns a truth that costs him everything and saves him at the same time: if I lose myself here, I will never survive what comes next. Leadership is not proven by how much you can carry. It is revealed by what you refuse to carry. Joseph loses position, reputation, and safety. And it looks like failure. But it is actually graduation. The laboratory did its work. It exposed what could not follow him forward.

Your First Laboratory Isn't Meant to Impress You

Your first leadership laboratory was never meant to make you impressive. It was meant to make you honest. It was meant to teach you restraint before reach, depth before influence, integrity before access. Some of us are still grieving who we were before responsibilities made us guarded. Some of us miss the version of ourselves that had not yet learned how to perform. And God is not trying to take us back to that version, He's trying to take us deeper.

Potiphar's house is the place where leaders learn that character must outgrow opportunity, that identity must outlast access, and that obedience must become internal before authority can ever be external. Joseph leaves that house not with status, but with self. And that is why when he finally stands in power, it does not destroy him, because leadership that is learned in private can be trusted in public.

When God's Hand Rests on You in Strange Places

Joseph's rise in Potiphar's house wasn't the result of circumstance or skill alone; it was the unmistakable evidence of God's hand at work in an unlikely place. Joseph prospered in a context where he had no rights, no language mastery, no social standing, and no natural advantage. This alone reveals a foundational truth of spiritual leadership: success is not location-dependent; it is presence-dependent.

Even though Joseph had been stripped of his robe, God clothed him with something greater, credibility. Joseph didn't walk into Potiphar's house with a title; he earned influence through consistency. Favor opened the opportunity. Excellence sustained it. Joseph's work ethic became the language his new environment understood.

In a foreign land, excellence became his translator. Integrity became his reputation. And stewardship became his pathway to authority.

The Discipline of Excellence When You Don't Feel Exceptional

Joseph prospered because "the Lord made everything he did succeed." But God wasn't doing the work for him, He was blessing the work Joseph was doing. That distinction matters. Joseph wasn't passive in Potiphar's house. He wasn't sulking, complaining, or sabotaging his own opportunity because his circumstances were unfair.

Trauma could have turned him bitter. Grief could have made him disengaged. Disappointment could have produced apathy. But Joseph chose discipline. He chose stewardship even though no one celebrated him. He chose excellence even though he didn't choose the environment. He chose responsibility even though he didn't get recognition for it.

The deepest form of leadership training happens when you serve faithfully in environments that do not reflect your calling. When your surroundings do not match your purpose, yet you choose purpose anyway.

Driver Seat Quote: "Excellence is not a mood; it's a discipline. And discipline builds destiny."

Stewardship Under Authority

Joseph's success in Potiphar's house was not leadership the way we often imagine it. He wasn't leading from the top, he was leading from underneath someone else's authority. This is where leadership development becomes uncomfortable. True leaders must first become excellent followers.

God was training Joseph to handle responsibility without recognition, to manage systems he did not design, to align under authority he did not choose, and to build trust through consistency. He was developing Joseph's administrative skill long before anyone acknowledged it and teaching him to operate with excellence even when he was overlooked. All of this formation was happening quietly, internally, and intentionally, shaping Joseph into a leader who could carry weight long before he ever stepped into visibility.

This season was building competencies Joseph would need later in the palace. Before Joseph could manage a nation, he had to manage a household. Before he could oversee grain during a famine, he had to oversee operations in Potiphar's estate. Before he could interpret Pharaoh's dreams, he had to interpret the needs of his immediate environment.

Potiphar's house was a leadership school for the palace.

Identity Stabilization After Trauma

Joseph was prospering, but he was still healing. As we saw earlier, success doesn't erase trauma; it simply creates a new context where trauma must be managed. One of the most psychologically complex aspects of this chapter is the tension Joseph experienced internally: he was functioning well externally but still recovering internally.

Identity stabilization is the process of reconstructing your sense of self after everything familiar has been stripped away. Joseph had to discover who he was without his father's affirmation, without his robe, without the security of home, and without the familiarity of his language or culture.

Success in Potiphar's house wasn't just professional success, it was personal reconstruction. Each task completed well rebuilt his confidence. Each moment of trust from Potiphar rebuilt his sense of competence. Each responsibility assigned rebuilt a portion of his identity. He was finding fragments of himself in the work he performed.

This is often how leaders are developed. Leadership is rarely discovered in theory; it is uncovered through experience. As Joseph performed the work placed before him, he began to recognize the abilities that had always been within him. Competence revealed capacity. Responsibility revealed strength. The more he managed, the more he learned what he was capable of managing.

Leadership formation often happens this way. People discover their strengths while carrying responsibility, not before it. Joseph did not arrive in Potiphar's house fully aware of the leader he would become. He discovered it through the assignments placed in his hands. Every task completed well revealed another layer of ability. Every responsibility entrusted to him confirmed that he could be trusted with more.

Long before Joseph ever governed Egypt, he was learning how to govern small things well. Each responsibility entrusted to him was more than a task; it was training. In God's kingdom, leadership is rarely revealed in grand moments first. It is formed in the quiet stewardship of small assignments. Joseph's management of Potiphar's household was preparing him for something far greater. Scripture teaches this principle clearly: "Whoever is faithful in very little is also faithful in much" (Luke 16:10). The palace did not make Joseph a leader. His faithfulness with small things did.

Driver Seat leaders are not formed by big moments; they are formed by how faithfully they steward small ones.

Controlled Ambition: The Quiet Strength of Slow Rising

Joseph had the gift of leadership, but he didn't rush it. There is a kind of ambition that destroys people when success comes too quickly. He understood, whether consciously or by necessity, that unchecked ambition can consume a person when opportunities arrive faster than character is ready for. His was a restrained ambition, refined by hardship, softened by humility, and anchored by responsibility. Joseph wasn't chasing a position; he was honoring the work in front of him. He wasn't striving to prove himself; he was choosing to be faithful where he stood. This is the kind of ambition that grows in the shadows, ambition that does not demand elevation but develops endurance. It is ambition purified by adversity, ambition that knows how to rise without rushing, lead without forcing, and influence without stepping over others. Joseph's ascent did not happen because he was loud or self-promoting; it happened because he was steady. Success came looking for him because faithfulness had already shaped him. Scripture frames this truth clearly: "Humble yourselves... that he may exalt you in due time" (1 Pet 5:6). God raises what humility secures, and in Joseph, humility became the quiet strength that carried him upward at the right time.

Success That Comes Too Soon

This chapter's Driver Seat truth is this: When Success arrives early, maturity must catch up fast.

Joseph stepped into influence before his inner world fully caught up. He carried responsibility while still learning resilience, and he carried respect while still discovering who he was becoming. God did not wait until Joseph was completely formed to advance him; instead, He used advancement as the environment where formation would accelerate. Growth happens differently under pressure, and Potiphar's house became the place where Joseph's character was stretched to meet the weight of his calling.

Potiphar's house was not just a promotion; it was a proving ground. It was both elevation and education, a space where favor opened doors and formation shaped the person who walked through them. Opportunity arrived, and with it came the kind of stretching that develops strength. God increased Joseph's influence so that his inner life would mature to match the assignment resting on him. In this season, God wasn't simply moving Joseph forward; He was growing Joseph deeper, ensuring that the leader emerging in private could withstand the influence he would eventually carry in public.

Maybe you recognize this dynamic in your own life. Sometimes opportunities show up before you feel completely ready. Doors open while you're still sorting through old wounds. People start trusting you while you're still learning to trust yourself. And you wonder why God would let success arrive before you feel fully settled. But this is often how God grows us. He places us in spaces that stretch us, not to expose weakness, but to strengthen what is still developing. Many of us are living in our own version of Potiphar's house, stepping into roles, responsibilities, or seasons that feel bigger than where our maturity currently stands. And just like Joseph, you may discover that God is using the pressure you didn't ask for to produce the maturity you didn't know you needed.

Driver Seat Quote: "God will give you a taste of the future to force you to grow into it."

PRAYER

Father, thank You for opportunities that come before I feel fully ready. Give me the discipline to steward well what You place in my hands. Strengthen my identity as I move through unfamiliar places. Mature me quickly where success requires growth. Protect me from pride and help me lead with humility, integrity, and consistency. Prepare my character for what my calling requires. *And when relief feels like healing, teach me to seek resolution with You.* Amen.

Driver Seat Key Takeaways

- **External improvement does not equal internal healing.** Joseph's circumstances changed from pit to house, from exposure to structure, yet the shift in environment did not address the wounds in his soul. Relief is not the same as restoration, and many mistake calmer surroundings for a restored inner life.

- **Favor can outpace formation.** Joseph succeeds quickly in Potiphar's house, but his success does not mean his trauma has been processed. God allowed favor to operate even while Joseph was still healing, reminding us that external promotion often arrives while internal maturity is still developing.

- **God's presence is the true source of Joseph's success.** Four times Genesis 39 repeats the phrase that the Lord was with Joseph, signaling that prosperity flowed not from Joseph's position but from God's supernatural presence within him. Favor is not geographic; it is relational.

- **God often blesses environments because of a person, not because of the environment.** Potiphar's entire household prospers because Joseph is in it, carrying the blessing of the Lord. Scripture shows this pattern with Jacob, Abraham, Moses, and Paul, demonstrating that favor has a vessel and blessings flow through people, not places.

- **Usefulness can become a hiding place for unhealed pain.** Joseph's reliability, competence, and excellence made him indispensable, yet these same traits allowed his wounds to stay hidden. Many high functioning people operate effectively in public while carrying unresolved heartbreak in private.

- **Stability can deceive you into believing you are whole.** Potiphar's house offered Joseph structure, food, and routine, which created the illusion of progress. But calm seasons do not automatically heal the fractures created by betrayal; they simply stop triggering them. Quiet does not equal closure.

- **Performance can outrun identity if the inner life is not addressed.** Joseph became productive faster than he became settled. Without intentional reflection, leaders can build systems, fulfill roles, and manage responsibilities while remaining disconnected from their own emotional condition.

- **Favor opens doors while God's word refines what walks through them.** Psalm 105 teaches that Joseph was sent ahead and that the word of the Lord tested him. Potiphar's house became Joseph's proving ground where favor provided opportunity, but God's testing shaped character that could sustain that opportunity.

- **Potiphar's house becomes Joseph's first leadership laboratory.** Joseph learns responsibility, stewardship, administration, and trustworthiness long before he steps into national leadership. God uses private spaces and unseen seasons to shape the leader before revealing the leader.

- **Promotion is not evidence of readiness; it is evidence of divine trust.** Joseph rose in Potiphar's house not because he was fully healed, but because God trusted the trajectory of his character. Promotion becomes an invitation to formation, not a confirmation of completion.

***

Joseph's rise in Potiphar's house was only the beginning. Just when success seemed to stabilize his life, a new test waited for him, a test not of leadership, but of integrity. "After some time" (Gen 39:7), proximity invited temptation, and a false accusation from Potiphar's wife would threaten everything favor had built. In the next chapter, we'll face that moment, how integrity stands when lies advance.

CHAPTER SIX

FALSE ACCUSATIONS

When Your Character Is Tested by Lies

Genesis 39:7–20

False accusations do not begin by attacking your future, they begin by invading your mind. Long before anything external changes, something internal starts to shift. The accusations enter, and suddenly your inner world becomes unstable. You replay conversations. You rehearse explanations no one asks for. You imagine how others are now seeing you, and without realizing it, you are no longer living from your center. You are orbiting, orbiting around a story you did not write. This is how agency is threatened, not by force, but by distortion. The moment an accusation lands, the psychological pressure is not simply to prove innocence, but to surrender authorship. You begin to ask, Who am I allowed to be now. What version of me will survive this. And the mind, desperate for relief, considers shrinking, hardening, or reshaping itself just to escape the discomfort of being misunderstood. The most dangerous part of an accusation is not that it is believed by others, but that it is rehearsed by you.

False accusations attempt to steal the driver's seat of your inner life. They want to decide how you respond, how you think, how you see yourself, and eventually how you move forward. They try to make reactions feel inevitable. And once reaction becomes your default, intention disappears. You stop choosing who you are becoming and start managing how you are perceived. Joseph does not control the accusation, but psychologically, that is not the battle. The real battle is whether the accusation will become his internal narrative. Will it explain his worth to him. Will it redefine his identity. Will it set the emotional temperature for the rest of his life. Because even when a person is externally restrained, the mind still has choices. And the most important choice is not what happens next, but who gets to decide who I am in the middle of this.

Here is where many people lose themselves, not because they did something wrong, but because they begin responding as if they did. The mind subtly shifts from grounded confidence to hypervigilant. You become careful with your words, guarded with tones, strategic with your presence. You start performing stability instead of inhabiting it. And performance over time erodes authenticity. When you live to correct a false story, you slowly abandon your true one. Psychologically, accusations fracture identity by introducing doubt into places that were once settled. You may still know the truth, but now the truth feels like it needs defended. And the moment truth feels fragile, anxiety grows. The mind begins scanning constantly, Who believes this. Who does not. Who is watching me now. That constant scanning drains emotional energy and fractures focus. You are present, but not fully. You are functioning, but internally split.

Joseph's power is not that he ignores the accusation. It is that he refuses to internalize it. He does not allow it to become a mirror. He does not use it to explain himself to himself. This is maturity: the ability to say, "This is happening to me, but it is not who I am." That separation between experiences and identity is the difference between resilience and collapse. You lose agency the moment you confuse what happens to you with who you are. Being in the driver's seat does not mean preventing injustice. That belief alone creates unnecessary self blame. If you think being strong means avoiding harm, then every unjust moment will feel like personal failure. But strength is not about control over circumstances. It is about control over alignment. It is the refusal to let external events dictate your internal direction.

Psychologically, the driver's seat is about authorship. Who is writing the meaning of this moment. Is it the voices outside of you or the value within you.

Is your identity being shaped by reaction or by intention. When accusations arrive, the mind wants to rush toward explanation. But explanation is not always healing. Sometimes restraint is. Sometimes silence is not avoidance, it is preservation. Silence is not weakness when it protects your inner coherence.

False accusations also tempt people to abandon posture. You may feel the urge to harden, to retaliate, to become sharp where you were once soft. That shift feels empowering at first, but it comes at a cost, because when you change who you are to survive an accusation, the accusation wins. Even if your name is later cleared, you survive externally but lose internally. Joseph refuses that trade because injustice always comes with an offer. It says, I am going to hurt you, and in exchange, you are going to become someone you never intended to be. False accusations do not just try to take your position, they try to purchase your posture. They do not simply aim at your reputation, they aim at your internal alignment. The offer is subtle: let this make you colder. Let this make you harder. Let this make you suspicious of everyone. Let this make you stop trusting. Let this make you stop serving. Let this make you protect yourself at all costs. That is the trade, you survive the moment, but you lose yourself in the process. Joseph refuses it. Not because it does not hurt, not because he does not feel the sting of betrayal, but because he will not allow pain to choose his personality.

He does not allow injustice to tutor him in bitterness. Bitterness is what happens when pain becomes your teacher and resentment becomes your language. When something unfair happens, the mind scrambles to make meaning of it, and if you are not careful, the meaning becomes distorted: people cannot be trusted. Doing right does not matter. Kindness makes you vulnerable. Integrity is naive. If you do not strike first, you will be struck. Bitterness feels like strength because it builds emotional armor, convincing you that if you harden your heart and lower your expectations, you will not be hurt again. But armor restricts movement. It protects you and imprisons you at the same time. Psychologically, bitterness is often the mind's attempt to regain control after helplessness. If I could not control what happened, I will control how I feel. If I could not stop the accusation, I will stop caring. If I could not prevent betrayal, I will never be vulnerable again. Joseph refuses that internal shift. He does not let unfairness educate him into becoming unsafe.

He does not let confinement train him in resentment. Confinement is not only physical, it is psychological. It is the feeling of being stuck, misrepresented, limited, silenced, delayed. Those conditions grow resentment quickly because resentment is the protest of the unheard. When you are falsely accused, something inside you wants to ask: Why should I keep giving? Why should I keep trying? Why should I stay faithful when it cost me this? That is the emotional crossroads. Joseph loses external power but keeps internal posture. He loses freedom, public credibility, control of his narrative, and protection within the system, but he keeps integrity, self restraint, alignment with God, and stewardship of what is in front of him. That is psychological strength at its highest level, the ability to remain internally consistent under external constraint. It means the state of your heart is not dictated by the state of your environment. External pressure may tighten, but your core does not have to fall through with it. Circumstances may confine your body, but they do not have to command your identity.

Resilience is not pretending it did not hurt. It is not spiritual bypassing or silence rooted in fear. Resilience is alignment under pressure, the refusal to let external events determine internal direction. And this is where it shows up in our lives today. It appears when you are lied on at work and feel the temptation to withdraw from every new relationship. It appears when you are misjudged in a friendship and decide you will never open up again. It appears when you are falsely accused in ministry and begin leading from defensiveness instead of conviction. It appears when family members distort your words and you slowly start believing you are too much or too difficult. It appears when a system labels you unfairly and you begin adjusting your personality to survive rather than leading from your calling. That is when the outside starts trying to reshape the inside. That is when identity begins reacting instead of choosing. And that is the danger, not just the accusation itself, but the internal drift that follows it.

Ask yourself this: Who am I becoming in response to what I cannot control? Are you becoming smaller, quieter, harder, colder, or are you becoming clearer, steadier, more grounded? Because every unjust moment carries a hidden curriculum. It is teaching you something about how you see yourself, how you relate to power, and how you define victory. Injustice always asks a question, Will you abandon yourself to survive, or preserve yourself to endure. Being in the driver's seat means refusing to let injustice decide your emotional posture. It means choosing not to live reactively. It means slowing down when everything in you wants to speed up. It means holding on to your values when reputation feels unstable. It means understanding that your future is not just about where you end up, but about who arrives there.

Joseph's story reminds us that agency is not loud. It does not argue its case. It does not demand validation. It quietly chooses alignment again and again, and that choice repeated over time becomes identity reinforced. The mind stabilizes not because circumstances improve, but because inner authorship is reclaimed. You are not healed when an accusation disappears. You are healed when it no longer explains you. So here is the final question, and it is one only you can answer: Who is driving your inner life right now? Is it fear? Is it the need to be understood? Is it the pressure to correct perception? Or is it a grounded sense of self that knows injustice can touch your environment without owning your identity?Being in the driver's seat does not mean the road is fair. It means you decide the direction anyway. And that decision, quiet, unseen, deeply internal, is the most powerful leadership move a person can make.

Now let's dive into how the accusation unfolds Biblically.

How Scripture Records the Accusation

The Setup

Genesis 39:6 — "And Joseph was a goodly person, and well favoured." Joseph was competent, and he was noticeable. Leadership principle, visibility increases vulnerability. The higher you rise in trust, the more exposed you become to scrutiny, jealousy, projection, and desire. Joseph was no longer operating in the shadows. He was in a position of influence. And influence always attracts attention, not all of it healthy. What this means internally is that Joseph is now living with the weight of being watched. Excellence has lifted him into rooms where motives mix, and the human heart does not always greet favor with celebration. Psychologically, visibility increases self monitoring and raises the stakes of every interaction. Spiritually, favor carries a stewardship, not a spotlight, which requires boundaries, humility, and vigilance. Joseph's competence made him reliable, but his favor made him recognizable, and recognizable people often become screens for other people's projections. He must learn to navigate admiration without absorbing entitlement, proximity without losing purity, trust without naivety. The text's brief note about his appearance signals a layered reality, he is gifted, he is responsible, and now he is appealing. That combination will require more than skill. It will require a settled conscience and a guarded inner life.

And this is where the betrayal quietly begins again. The pit was public betrayal. This is intimate betrayal. In the pit, Joseph was stripped because he was hated. In the house, he will be targeted because he is favored and attractive. Both moments share a common thread: his distinction makes him vulnerable. Scripture does not exaggerate his appearance; it simply notes it. But that note becomes narrative ignition. What makes him admirable becomes the excuse for what is about to happen to him. This is the systemic pattern of projection: when someone carries favor, discipline, and difference, their visibility becomes a canvas for others to paint upon. Joseph's rise did not eliminate betrayal; it repositioned it.

And in many ways, this echoes the coat of many colors that once marked his life. That coat symbolized a life layered with distinction. Joseph carried many dimensions at once. He was capable. He was disciplined. He was favored. He was attractive. He was gifted. In other words, Joseph carried many "colors." And people who carry many colors often experience the same dynamic in today's world. When someone is competent, attractive, talented, and responsible all at the same time, they draw attention in ways that are not always safe. Their gifts attract opportunity, but they also attract projection. Their presence can inspire admiration in some people and insecurity in others. The same qualities that open doors can also create tension, jealousy, or desire. Many multi-gifted people experience this quietly: their excellence becomes the reason they are watched, talked about, misinterpreted, or pursued. Joseph's life reflects a reality that still exists today, sometimes the very qualities that make a person remarkable are the same qualities that make them an easy target.

The Temptation Begins

Genesis 39:7 — "And it came to pass after these things, that his master's wife cast her eyes upon Joseph." This was the opening move. The language is slow and deliberate. After these things. The gaze arrives after trust has been earned, after responsibility has grown, after favor has become visible. The temptation is not merely sensual, it is strategic. Being cast upon by a gaze is the experience of becoming an object of someone else's desire and design. Psychologically, objectification detaches a person's value from their character and reassigns it to the beholder's appetite. Spiritually, this is the moment when Joseph's integrity must be anchored in Someone (God) beyond the room, because the room itself is beginning to reshape the moral weather. Leadership wise, the opening move tests whether Joseph's identity rests in God's presence or in human approval. The lure is not only pleasure, it is power, access, and the illusion of consequence free secrecy. This first look is the quiet beginning of a long campaign.

But notice the power dynamic. She is not merely a woman attracted to a man. She is the wife of his master. She lives in the house he manages but does not own. She possesses social authority he does not have. The temptation is layered with hierarchy. This is not equal footing. This is leverage to her advantage. The gaze is not passive; it is positional. When Scripture says she cast her eyes, it signals intent, not accident. Joseph is again in a system where someone above him is attempting to define him. Betrayal here is not emotional; it is structural.

He is vulnerable not because he is weak, but because he is under authority in a foreign land, under the authority of someone who holds power over his environment, his reputation, and his future. What Potiphar's wife is doing is not simply attraction; it is coercion wrapped in privilege. She is using proximity, status, and power to pursue what she wants, knowing Joseph's ability to refuse is complicated by the system he lives inside.

This is how abuse of authority often works. It rarely begins with open force.

It begins with pressure, suggestion, and the quiet assumption that the person with less power will eventually comply. The person in authority controls the environment, the narrative, and often the consequences. Refusing them does not simply mean rejecting a person; it means risking position, reputation, and security.

Many people today recognize this dynamic. It happens in workplaces where a supervisor uses influence to pursue someone beneath them. It happens in organizations where the person with status assumes access to the person with less protection. It happens when someone's authority becomes the very tool they use to test another person's boundaries. What Potiphar's wife is doing is an abuse of power disguised as desire.

Joseph is not navigating a simple moral temptation; he is navigating a system where saying no carries real cost. That is what makes his integrity remarkable. He is resisting not only attraction but coercion. He is refusing to let someone else's authority redefine his character.

In other words, Joseph is facing a moment where power is being used to pressure him, but he refuses to surrender the authority of his own soul.

Joseph's refusal, internal leadership before external consequences

Genesis 39:8–9 — "How then can I do this great wickedness, and sin against God." Joseph names four things in his refusal: his master's trust, his access, his responsibility, and his loyalty to God. Notice what he does not say: "What if we get caught?" This will ruin my reputation. He frames it morally before he frames it socially. That is internal leadership. True leadership begins in private restraint. Joseph was not just resisting temptation. He was protecting his relationship with God and his future capacity. This refusal shows a well-ordered conscience. He interprets the opportunity through covenant, not convenience. Psychologically, this is the power of a pre-decision.Because he has already decided who he is before the pressure peaks, he can answer without bargaining with himself. Spiritually, he names sin as sin and places God at the center of the frame. Social calculations will always wobble under pressure, but reverence stabilizes conviction. There is also executive maturity here, impulse control, boundary clarity, and the ability to honor trust without witnesses present.

And yet this refusal sets the stage for betrayal. Because when power is denied what it expects to access, it often retaliates. Joseph's no is not just moral; it is disruptive. It interrupts entitlement. It rejects misuse of proximity and power. It exposes that access does not equal consent. His integrity works, and because it works, it destabilizes the environment. Some betrayals happen not because you failed someone, but because you would not cooperate with their distortion.

Driver Seat Quote: "Integrity is proved not by what you avoid once, but by what you refuse repeatedly."

The Sustained Pressure, Not Sudden Failure

Genesis 39:10 — "She spake to Joseph day by day." This was not a moment, it was a campaign. Some tests are not dramatic explosions. They are repetitive whispers. This is where leaders get worn down, not by one catastrophic choice, but by sustained pressure that slowly erodes boundaries. The enemy rarely begins with destruction, he begins with erosion. He does not always attack your integrity head on. He leans against it. Repeatedly. Subtly. Patiently. The pressure was persistent. The enemy studies patterns. He watches for exhaustion. He waits for loneliness. He times his approach for when you are isolated, overworked, uncelebrated, or emotionally depleted. Sustained pressure distorts perception. Repetition normalizes what once felt extreme. That is why sustained pressure is more dangerous than sudden temptation. It does not shock you. It reshapes you. And Joseph's strength is not just that he said no once. It is that he said no repeatedly, over and over again, when no one was affirming him, when no one was protecting him, when no one would have known. That is spiritual stamina. And leadership requires it. Psychologically, this is decision fatigue and habituation at work, which is why Joseph's boundaries are both moral and practical; he refuses the proposition and limits the access. Spiritually, daily refusal becomes worship in motion, an unseen liturgy of faithfulness that fortifies the soul for the inevitable escalation.

And this repetition intensifies betrayal. Each no compounds rejection. Each refusal increases the likelihood of retaliation. The campaign reveals that when integrity is consistent, manipulation must escalate. Betrayal is not impulsive here; it is building.

The Empty House

Genesis 39:11 — "There was none of the men of the house there within." The space is clear. The hallway is quiet. The environment is controlled. The setup is complete. Joseph had been doing what he had done every day, managing, overseeing, stewarding what belonged to another man. Scripture tells us Joseph found grace in Potiphar's sight and was placed over his house, Genesis 39:4. It tells us that everything Potiphar owned was under Joseph's supervision, and the Lord blessed the Egyptian's house because of Joseph, Genesis 39:5–6. He was thriving. Visible. Trusted. Effective. And now more vulnerable, because no one is around—it's just him and her in the house. Interiorly, this is a collision of routine and risk. He is simply doing his work, which lowers vigilance, while the absence of witnesses heightens danger. Isolation is often the final ingredient temptation waits for. Psychologically, isolation reduces external accountability and increases the plausibility of secrecy. Spiritually, it becomes a crucible where integrity stands without the social scaffolding of support. Theologically, providence can allow an empty house because God is forming a heart that can be trusted in any house. Joseph's task is ordinary, the room is not. The setup is complete because the conditions of compromise are present, fatigue, familiarity, and privacy. What happens next will reveal who has been winning the inner war during the quiet days.

And here betrayal tightens. The house that once symbolized stability now becomes the stage for accusation. The environment that elevated him now surrounds him in silence. The same walls that witnessed his faithfulness will soon echo with a lie.

The Lie and The Narrative Manipulation

Genesis 39:13–18: *And it came to pass, when she saw that he had
left his garment in her hand, and was fled forth,*
That she called unto the men of her house, and spake unto them,
saying, See, he hath brought in an Hebrew unto us to mock us; he
came in unto me to lie with me, and I cried with a loud voice:
And it came to pass, when he heard that I lifted up my voice and
cried, that he left his garment with me, and fled, and got him out.□
And she laid up his garment by her, until his lord came home.□
And she spake unto him according to these words, saying, The
Hebrew servant, which thou hast brought unto us, came in unto me
to mock me:
And it came to pass, as I lifted up my voice and cried, that he left
his garment with me, and fled out.

Genesis 39:13–18 — She builds a story: he came in unto me. He mocked us. She tells her husband, See, he hath brought in a Hebrew. She moves from personal rejection to ethnic framing. She calls him a Hebrew. This weaponizes cultural difference and shifts blame upward to Potiphar, You brought this Hebrew here. It reframes a private encounter as a collective threat. Identity becomes evidence. This is how false accusation cuts, it turns righteousness into evidence against you.

Here is where systemic modeling becomes explicit. She does not merely accuse Joseph of misconduct; she racializes the accusation. Hebrew is not neutral here. It signals foreigner. Outsider. Other. She leverages ethnicity to give her story credibility. She converts difference into danger. The narrative shifts from "I was rejected" to "we are threatened." This is how systems preserve themselves. They amplify difference to justify removal. Joseph is betrayed not only as a man, but as an outsider within the structure.

We still see this dynamic in today's world. When a person is already marked as different by race, culture, language, or background—the accusation does not need as much proof. Difference itself becomes suspicion. Black men, for example, have often been accused or feared not because of evidence, but because their presence was framed as a threat. A misunderstanding becomes aggression. A refusal becomes defiance. A boundary becomes hostility. History has shown this pattern repeatedly: someone's identity is used to make a story believable before the facts are even examined. What happens to Joseph reflects a reality that many people still experience today, when systems feel threatened, they do not always confront the truth; they sometimes magnify difference to justify removing the person who exposed it.

Driver Seat Quote: "When people cannot reach your character,
they will reach for your clothing."

Theologically, injustice often recruits whatever labels are available to carry the lie, ethnicity, status, outsider language. Psychologically, this is moral injury and shame displacement, the guilty assigns guilt to the innocent to preserve control. For Joseph, the cost is cognitive dissonance, he did right and is named wrong, which is why narratives like this drain resilience and tempt the soul toward bitterness. Spiritually, his task is to refuse ownership of a story he did not author while refusing animosity toward the people who are wielding it. That is exceedingly difficult. It is also the path of maturity and leadership.

The Sentence, No trial, No defense

Genesis 39:19–20 — "And Joseph's master took him, and put him into the prison." There is no recorded investigation. No cross examination. No defense speech. Integrity did not shield him from consequence. Let me be honest here, righteousness does not eliminate injustice. Joseph did right and still went to prison. Sometimes obedience costs you, access, promotion, comfort, relationships, reputation.

And here betrayal is complete. First betrayed by brothers. Now betrayed by power. The pit was family betrayal. The prison is institutional betrayal. In both cases, Joseph is displaced without defense. His silence is not weakness; it is evidence that he trusts a court higher than the one in front of him.

Driver Seat Quote: "Doing the right thing does not protect you from being misunderstood."

Internally, this is where many leaders fracture, not at the moment of refusal, but at the moment when refusal is punished, when doing what is right and being ethical is punished. Psychologically, the soul wrestles with helplessness and the mind strains to reconcile a good God with a broken outcome. Spiritually, this is the altar where vindication is surrendered and trust is chosen. Joseph's agency is not in the verdict, it is in his alignment. He cannot control the system, but he can control the story he tells himself about who he is inside the system. The prison will become the next classroom precisely because God refuses to let lies write the last word over a faithful life. The timeline closes with chains, yet what God is forming in Joseph is a freedom deeper than circumstance, the liberty of a conscience that stayed clear when the room went empty and the narrative turned hostile.

Leadership Under Suspicion

Great leaders must develop reputation loss resilience, the ability to keep leading when the commentary about them is untrue and unkind. Reputation is external and fragile, character is internal and fortified. Joseph had lost reputation in Potiphar's network, but he had not lost the core that God was building. He had been trusted with authority and stripped of it in a single day, and the whiplash between elevation and accusation can twist identity into knots. The temptation now was not to sin, but to surrender to cynicism, to decide that doing the right thing is a fool's errand, and to replace devotion with bitterness. Many destinies die on that altar. Joseph refused it. He let the loss burn away entitlement but not expectation. He laid down the need to be believed and held on to the need to be faithful. Leadership without the right to defend yourself becomes a purifying fire. It cleans the motives, clarifies the audience, and re-teaches the heart to work for the applause of One. Joseph's world had shrunk to iron and stone, but his calling had not shrunk at all. If anything, the constriction was concentrating him. His gift would speak again, in the darkness, not despite it.

The Psychology of Injustice

To pretend that Joseph could glide through this season untouched would be to deny the humanity that God created and honors. False accusation creates moral injury, that interior wound that forms when your ethical framework is punished instead of affirmed. Joseph did right and suffered wrong, and the human spirit reels under that contradiction. Injustice shock follows, a mental disorientation in which the order of the world seems inverted and unsafe. Shame displacement then hovers, where someone else's sin slips its coat onto your shoulders, and you carry the heat of what you refused. Finally, faith strain pulls every thread of trust tight, not because God has failed, but because His method refuses our schedule and contradicts our instincts.

Many who read this have lived some version of that disorientation. Some have experienced it systemically, where policies, power structures, or cultural currents quietly penalized integrity and rewarded manipulation. You worked twice as hard only to discover that merit was not the metric. You watched doors close without explanation and narratives form without your consent. In those moments, injustice does not feel theoretical. It feels architectural. It feels built into the walls. And the temptation is not merely to grieve but to harden.

Others have encountered it in church spaces, where spiritual language was used to silence legitimate pain, or where loyalty was valued above truth. You told the truth and were labeled divisive. You set boundaries and were called rebellious. You endured leadership failure and were advised to pray more rather than process honestly. When sacred environments mishandle justice, faith strain intensifies because the place meant to reflect God begins to distort Him. The injury is not only relational. It is theological.

Still others have faced injustice in personal or entrepreneurial arenas. A partnership dissolved dishonorably. Credit was taken for your labor. Contracts shifted after trust was extended. You built something with clean hands and watched it be undermined by hidden agendas. In those spaces, moral injury can tempt you to adopt the very tactics that wounded you. You begin to ask whether integrity is naïve and whether softness is weakness. The contradiction presses on identity.

Acknowledging these layers does not weaken faith, it anchors it. Authentic spirituality does not skip grief in order to perform resilience. Joseph's strength was not a stoic denial of pain, it was an honest walk through it with God. Lament is holy. Tears are not treason. The psalmist's question, "How long?" (Psalm 13:1), is allowed to sit beside the patriarch's destiny. In that mingling, character is not merely preserved, it is deepened. And when the reader recognizes that injustice did not make Joseph corrupt, only clarified him, something stabilizes internally. You realize that suffering wrong does not require becoming wrong.

Driver Seat Quote: "The wound of a lie can heal without infecting your soul when truth remains your physician."

Holding Faith When Truth Seems Powerless

There is a particular pressure that arises when the truth cannot defend you. It is the suffocating tension of knowing you are right and still being rendered powerless. Leaders who rely on vindication as fuel will run out of energy in long seasons of silence, because vindication is unpredictable, but faith must be steady. When the applause disappears and the narrative is hijacked, something deeper is exposed: were you standing on being understood, or were you standing on being aligned?

Joseph had to learn to live without the dopamine of being understood. He had to learn to breathe without the relief of being exonerated. He had to learn to worship without the clarity of resolution. That kind of worship is stripped of theatrics. It is not the worship of outcomes. It is the worship of surrender. It is choosing to believe that God's silence is not His absence, and that delay is not denial.

These are not advanced electives in the school of destiny; they are the core courses. If you will carry authority later, you must carry ambiguity now. If you will hold the trust of many, you must first learn to be trusted by God in the dark. The dark is not where your calling dies; it is where your motives are purified. When truth seems powerless, faith must detach itself from optics and attach itself to eternity.

Faith in this season becomes less like a victory shout and more like a steady pulse. It does not spike emotionally; it stabilizes spiritually. It is the quiet insistence that God is not mocked by human courts, not intimidated by human lies, and not delayed by human systems. It is the refusal to let injustice rewrite your theology. It is the discipline of believing that heaven is not confused by what earth has misrepresented.

The prison door swung shut, but heaven's door did not. The narrative in the house belonged to Potiphar's wife, but the narrative in eternity belonged to God. Joseph's future did not depend on a rumor's half-life; it depended on a promise that never decays. Human stories expire. Divine promises do not.

And this is where faith matures. Not when you are celebrated, but when you are mischaracterized. Not when truth wins publicly, but when it survives privately. Joseph's integrity did not protect him from confinement, but it protected him from corrosion. His environment changed, but his alignment did not. His reputation was attacked, but his relationship with God remained intact.

There is a difference between being defended and being preserved. Joseph was not defended in that moment, but he was preserved. And preservation is often quieter than vindication, but far more powerful in the long run. Vindication corrects perception. Preservation secures destiny.

Driver Seat Quote: "*When the story told about you is false, keep living the life that will outlast it*".

Driver Seat Thesis in Motion

This chapter crystallizes a Driver Seat reality that every rising leader must accept, doing the right thing does not protect you from being misunderstood. Obedience is not a shield from rumor, purity is not a vaccine against slander, excellence is not a contract guaranteeing applause. But righteousness is still the road, because God writes the ending. Joseph learned that integrity's first reward is integrity itself, unfragmented soul, untangled motives, unbroken allegiance. Everything else, reputation, position, platform, must be held loosely, ready to be stripped without subtracting the person. Joseph's punishment for something he did not do did not interrupt his trajectory, it rerouted him to the next training ground. The palace was always the destination, but the path demanded a prison because a palace entrusted to an unbroken heart becomes a throne of self. God loves nations too much to put an immature soul in charge of their famine. The cell was not a detour, it was an anvil.

Modern Application: How This Shows Up Today

Leaders get lied on. Parents get misrepresented in custody battles. Pastors get accused without process. Entrepreneurs get blamed for systemic failure. Women leaders get scrutinized unfairly. Men leaders get mischaracterized emotionally. False accusations still happen. In fact, studies of wrongful convictions in the United States estimate that at least 4 to 6 percent of incarcerated individuals may be innocent, with false testimony and misidentification listed among the leading contributors. That is not a small number. That is thousands of lives shaped by accusations that should never have stood. The question is not, will you be misunderstood. The question is, will you stay behind the wheel when your reputation is attacked.

Scripture does not ignore this reality. Joseph was falsely accused and imprisoned. David was slandered and hunted though he had served faithfully. Psalm 35 records David praying, "Let those who accuse me falsely be put to shame and confusion." In Psalm 37 we are told, "Commit your way to the Lord, trust also in Him, and He shall bring it to pass. He shall bring forth your righteousness as the light, and your justice as the noonday." Isaiah 54:17 declares, "No weapon formed against you shall prosper, and every tongue that rises against you in judgment you shall condemn." Even Jesus stood silent before false witnesses, entrusting Himself to the Father who judges justly. The biblical pattern is clear. God does not deny that accusations come. He promises that they do not have final authority.

Some have asked me a question: How do you combat false accusations without losing yourself? Here is my answer. **First,** anchor your identity internally. Like Joseph, define yourself by God's opinion and your values, not public opinion. When accusations come, the first battle is not external, it is internal. If you do not already know who you are, the pressure will try to tell you. Build your identity on convictions, not compliments. Let your character be rooted deeper than your reputation. Public perception shifts. Personal alignment must not. And pray accordingly. Father, You are my defender. Establish my steps in truth. Guard my heart from distortion. Let my righteousness be revealed in Your timing.

Second, document, do not explode. In modern systems, keep records. Protect yourself structurally. Integrity does not mean gullibility. Wisdom says preserve emails, clarify conversations in writing, and maintain boundaries. Emotional outbursts feel relieving in the moment but weaken your credibility in the long term. Calm documentation is strength. It protects truth without compromising dignity. Proverbs reminds us that the prudent see danger and take refuge (Proverbs 27:12). Structural wisdom is not fear. It is stewardship.

Third, choose strategic silence, not reactive speech. Not every accusation requires immediate emotional defense. There is a difference between silence that preserves strength and silence that surrenders ground. Reactive speech is driven by panic. Strategic silence is driven by clarity. Sometimes restraint keeps you aligned while the system reveals itself. Speak when it serves truth, not when it soothes ego. Psalm 62 says, "My soul waits silently for God alone, for my expectation is from Him" (Psalm 62:5). Silence before God strengthens speech before men.

Fourth, seek safe counsel. Isolation magnifies distortion. When you are falsely accused, your thoughts can spiral. You replay conversations. You question yourself. You begin to internalize what was never yours to carry. Wise voices stabilize perspective. Safe counsel reminds you of who you are when pressure tries to redefine you. Leadership was never meant to be processed alone. Scripture reminds us: "Where no counsel is, the people fall, but in the multitude of counsellors there is safety" (Proverbs 11:14). Safety is not just physical, it is psychological.

Fifth, refuse bitterness as fuel. Bitterness corrodes decision making capacity. It feels powerful, but it narrows vision. It turns discernment into suspicion and strength into hardness. You can lead wounded for a season, but you cannot lead well if resentment becomes your compass. Protect your heart. Your future leadership depends on it. Pray as David prayed in Psalm 51: "Create in me a clean heart, O God." Ask God to purge what the accusation tried to plant.

Sometimes accusations, betrayal, or injustice plant seeds inside us that we do not immediately notice. At first it feels like survival, protecting yourself, staying guarded, holding onto the memory of what happened. But over time those seeds can grow into resentment, and resentment slowly begins to shape how you see people, how you make decisions, and how you lead. You may still function, but the lens of your leadership becomes clouded.

If you sense that happening in you, bring it honestly before God. Ask the Holy Spirit to uproot whatever the wound tried to plant and to heal the place where the hurt settled. Healing does not mean the injustice did not occur. It means you refuse to let that injustice determine the kind of leader you become. When God restores the heart, He restores clarity, compassion, and strength, so that you can lead well.

And **finally,** remember, integrity is long term capital. Reputation may dip temporarily. Character compounds over time. False accusations can delay promotion, but they cannot erase consistency. Systems may misunderstand you, but sustained integrity builds credibility in rooms you have not yet entered. Do not trade long term authority for short term vindication. Fighting false accusations is not about winning the moment. It is about keeping yourself intact while the moment passes. Stay in the driver's seat of your identity. Let truth unfold in time. Do not let someone else's distortion determine who you become.

And remember this from a biblical standpoint. God is not passive in the face of injustice. He calls Himself a defender of the innocent. He declares that He loves justice. Romans 8:33 asks, "Who shall bring a charge against God's elect?" It is God who justifies. When God justifies, accusation loses its ultimate power. Joseph went from prison to palace without rewriting his story. God addressed it. God overturned it. God elevated him in the very system that confined him.

I want you to remember this. Integrity does not always protect your position. But it protects your person. Your environment may strip your title. But lies cannot strip your character unless you surrender it. And when God stands at the end of your story, no accusation has the final word.

Prison Was Not Punishment. It Was Protection

Genesis 39:20 notes that Joseph is placed in the king's prison. This is not random incarceration. This prison housed political offenders, including Pharaoh's officials, Genesis 40:1–3. This was not a common dungeon for petty criminals. It was a controlled environment connected to the highest levels of government. Even in confinement, Joseph was placed within reach of destiny. Had Joseph stayed in Potiphar's house, he would have remained a successful servant. His influence would have stayed local. He never would have met the butler. Genesis 40 only happens because Genesis 39 hurt him. Leadership lens, sometimes God does not stop the lie. He redirects the outcome. Your demotion may be divine repositioning.

We cannot skip how even in jail Joseph is elevated. Genesis 39:21–22 shows that the keeper of the prison entrusted everything into Joseph's hand. In other words, confinement did not cancel competence. When God's hand is on you, favor does not disappear because the address changes. It follows assignment. Even in prison God is preparing him and proving him, proving that he will lead well no matter where he is dropped. The environment shifts, but the excellence remains. That is leadership integrity. Joseph was not promoted because of location. He was promoted because of consistency.

Genesis 39:21 repeats, But the Lord was with Joseph. The same phrase used in prosperity, Genesis 39:2, is repeated in prison. God's presence did not fluctuate with Joseph's status. Scripture declares in Psalm 37:23, "The steps of a good man are ordered by the Lord." Ordered does not always mean comfortable. It means intentional. A Godly man's footsteps are ordered by God, even when those steps echo through iron gates. The prison was not evidence that God had withdrawn. It was evidence that God was arranging.

This positioning placed him beside the butler so that his gift is proven and used to elevate him. The gift did not expire in confinement. It matured. It gained credibility. It gained timing. Potiphar's wife thought she won. Her accusation looked final. But her plot was used to elevate him. What was meant to discredit him became the corridor to the palace. Genesis 50:20 would later give language to what Genesis 39 demonstrated in seed form. You meant evil against me, but God meant it for good.

And here is where I need you to lean in. What people do to hurt you does not ultimately harm you when you are walking with God. It may wound. It may delay. It may confuse. But it cannot cancel what God has ordered. Romans 8:28 reminds us, "All things work together for good to those who love God and are called according to His purpose." All things includes false accusation. All things includes confinement. All things includes misrepresentation. All things includes lies told about you when you are not in the room to defend yourself. All things includes backstabbing from people you trusted. All things includes heartbreak from relationships that did not end the way you hoped. All things includes rejection from places you believed were part of your future. All things includes mistakes you regret and wish you could undo. All things includes seasons when your character is questioned, your motives are misunderstood, and your name is spoken in ways that do not reflect who you really are.

All things includes the quiet disappointments people carry in today's world, lost opportunities, broken partnerships, betrayal in workplaces, family conflicts, and moments where doing the right thing seemed to cost more than doing the wrong thing. All things includes the pain that comes when you are overlooked, misjudged, or treated unfairly because of who you are, where you come from, or how others perceive you.

And yet Scripture insists that all things, not some things, not the comfortable things, not only the victories, but all things are capable of being gathered into God's redemptive work.

Identity stability is leadership stability. Your location may change. Your value does not. When God is with you, even prison becomes preparation. Even limitation becomes leverage. Even what was designed to bury you becomes the soil that grows you. Prison was not punishment. It was protection. It was positioning. It was proof that wherever you land, favor can still find you.

And sometimes God does something even more astonishing. He makes the very circumstances meant to harm you become the environment where your future begins to grow. The people who misunderstood you become the witnesses of your integrity. The places that tried to contain you become the places where your gifts are discovered. The doors that closed in rejection redirect you to rooms you never would have entered otherwise.

There are people who can testify to this in today's world. Someone loses a job unfairly, only to discover a calling they never would have pursued if the job had remained comfortable. Someone is betrayed in business, and the separation forces them to build something healthier and stronger than what they left behind. Someone is overlooked for a promotion, and the disappointment becomes the motivation to develop skills that later open a much greater opportunity. What looked like loss becomes leverage.

Even enemies can become instruments in the process. A false accusation can refine your character in ways success never could. A critic can expose weaknesses you needed to strengthen. A person who tried to block your progress can unintentionally push you into the path God was already preparing for you. Scripture repeatedly shows that God is capable of making even opposition serve His purpose.

This does not mean the hardship was good. Betrayal is still betrayal. Injustice is still injustice. Pain is still pain. But God's ability to redeem circumstances means that the story does not end where the harm began. What was meant to bury you can become the soil where something stronger grows. What looked like restriction can become refinement. What felt like rejection can become redirection.

Joseph's prison proves something powerful about leadership. Your environment can change overnight. Your title can disappear. Your reputation can be attacked. But if your identity is stable in God, your future is not determined by the room you are placed in. Grace can still locate you there. Purpose can still develop you there. And sometimes the place that looked like the end of your story becomes the beginning of the part God intended all along.

Prayer

Father, You see the moments when truth is ignored and lies are loud. You know the weight of being misunderstood and the ache of being unable to defend myself. Guard my heart from bitterness, my mind from despair, and my identity from the residue of accusation. Teach me to love righteousness for Your sake, not for reward. Strengthen my spine for seasons when obedience costs me position. Heal the moral wounds I cannot name and the shocks I cannot shake. Let Your presence be my vindication and Your timing my relief. Keep me faithful in the dark and gentle when I could become hard. I trust You to shepherd my name and steer my path. Amen.

Driver Seat Key Takeaways

- **False accusations attack identity long before they touch reputation.** The first battlefield is the mind. Accusations destabilize your inner world by trying to rewrite who you believe yourself to be. Before anything external shifts, something internal is pressured to collapse.

- **The most dangerous part of an accusation is not that others believe it, but that you begin rehearsing it.** Accusations gain power when you subconsciously adopt their narrative. The true harm occurs when you internalize what was never true about you.

- **Accusations try to steal authorship of your inner life.** The enemy's strategy is not just to distort your story publicly but to become the one writing your story internally. Staying in the driver seat means refusing to surrender internal authorship.

- **Identity fractures when you start performing stability instead of inhabiting it.** When you become hypervigilant, guarded, and self monitored, you begin living from reaction rather than alignment. Performance replaces authenticity, and the soul splits under the weight.

- **Resilience begins where internal definition is reclaimed.** Joseph's strength is not that he ignores injustice, but that he refuses to let it define him. He separates experience from identity. That separation is the foundation of resilience.

- **Injustice always offers a dangerous trade: survive externally but lose yourself internally.** Accusations tempt you to become smaller, colder, harder, or suspicious in order to protect yourself. But when you let pain choose your personality, the accusation has already won.

- **Bitterness feels like control, but it becomes a prison.** Bitterness is the mind's attempt to reclaim power after helplessness, yet it restricts movement, hardens the heart, and distorts identity. It protects you and imprisons you at the same time.

- **Integrity is proven not by avoiding injustice but by staying aligned through it.** Being in the driver seat does not mean preventing lies or controlling outcomes. It means refusing to let external distortion dictate internal direction and identity.

- **The soul collapses when reaction replaces intention.** Accusations push you toward reactive living, constantly scanning who believes what, adjusting behavior to manage perception. Intentional identity stabilizes the inner life; reactive identity fractures it.

- **You are healed not when the accusation disappears, but when it no longer explains you.** Freedom is not the clearing of your name, but the reclaiming of your narrative. Healing comes when you decide who you are in the presence of lies, not in the absence of them.

***

Joseph is now in chains again. No apology. No vindication. No public correction. Just confinement. If we are honest, that is the part that unsettles us. We want resolution. We want the record cleared. We want the truth announced publicly. But Joseph does not get closure, he gets custody. He does not get affirmation, he gets incarceration. The narrative does not reward him immediately for doing right. It places him in a cell. Because sometimes the reward for integrity is not promotion. It is protection you do not yet recognize. Joseph is not just being punished. He is being repositioned. He is moved from a private house into the king's prison. The butler and the baker are coming. The next door is forming. The platform is incubating. What looks like setback is actually staging. The clang of the prison gate did not cancel Joseph's calling, it concentrated it. In the dim corridors of confinement, his gift would not wither, it would ripen. What looks like a dead end becomes a doorway, and what feels like punishment becomes placement. The next chapter opens in the shadows, where Joseph learns that even behind bars, the favor of God finds him, his competence makes room for him, and his interpretations begin to align him with the palace he cannot yet see. Now we turn to Chapter 7, The Prison, Gifted, Called, and Confined.

CHAPTER SEVEN

GIFTED, CALLED, AND CONFINED

By the time Genesis 39:20 arrives, the damage is already done. The accusation has already been spoken. The trust has already been broken. The sentence has already been decided. Scripture does not circle back. It moves forward. "And Joseph's master took him, and put him into the prison..." (Genesis 39:20) Now Joseph is not fighting for truth. He is living inside the outcome. "And he was there in the prison." (Genesis 39:20)

Some transitions are not chosen. They are imposed. Some confinements are not consequences. They are collisions with power. And this chapter is not primarily about what Joseph does in prison, that comes next. This chapter is about what prison does to a leader. Because prison does not only lock doors. It applies pressure.

The Psychology of "Stuck"

Confinement does not only restrict movement. When movement is restricted long enough, it compresses identity. That sentence is not poetry. It is diagnosis. The first thing confinement takes is not your schedule, it is your sense of self. Your world narrows. Your options shrink. Your future feels farther away. Your name starts to feel smaller than it used to. What once felt expansive now feels contained. What once felt possible now feels postponed.

In a literal prison, the body is contained. In modern confinement, it may not be bars, but it feels the same. You can survive the restriction and still lose the person you used to be behind it. The deeper damage happens when the mind begins to shrink to match the size of the space. You start adjusting your expectations to fit the walls around you.

When Genesis says, "he was there in the prison," that line speaks to every reader who feels "there." There in a job you have outgrown but cannot leave. There in a season that will not end. There under a label you did not earn. There in legal limbo. There in custody conflict. There in immigration delay. There in financial restriction. There in ministry pause. There in trauma recovery. There in public misunderstanding you cannot correct. There in a marriage that feels frozen. There in a diagnosis that changed your timeline. There in a leadership role where your authority shrank but your responsibility did not.

Confinement triggers predictable psychological battles. Learned helplessness whispers that nothing you do matters. Hypervigilance scans the room for who is against you now. Rumination replays the injustice on a loop. Moral injury asks how you can be punished for doing right. Identity diffusion makes you forget who you were before the walls closed in. Bitterness tempts you to let injustice rewrite your personality.

This is where many leaders break down internally, not because they were weak, but because confinement rearranges the terrain of the mind. It reduces your field of vision until survival replaces strategy. It narrows your thinking until endurance replaces imagination.

Here is the brutal part. Confinement does not just keep you from going somewhere. It keeps you from becoming someone. It interrupts the normal storyline of life, work, family, growth, and repair, and replaces it with a single repeated message: wait. Waiting under punishment does not feel like patience. It feels like erasing. Days blend. Time turns thick. You stop tracking progress and start tracking survival.

When identity is compressed long enough, people begin to accept a smaller version of themselves just to make the day bearable. That is not weakness. That is what human beings do when the environment refuses to let them expand.

You lower your voice. You reduce your vision. You shrink your expectations. You stop introducing yourself with conviction. You begin to live inside the limitation as if it were definition.

Some cages are made of steel. Others are made of conclusions you start believing about yourself.

Now step into the specific conflict that makes confinement spiritually dangerous. If I did everything right, why am I still here? That question is not simple frustration. It is a moral injury to the soul. It is the collision between effort and outcome. It is what happens when your inner narrative says integrity should protect me, but your reality says integrity still got you punished.

When those two realities collide, the mind begins to split. Either it starts believing nothing matters because doing right did not change the result, or it starts believing something is wrong with you because you did it right and still ended up here. Both paths are lethal to hope. One erodes motivation. The other erodes identity.

Watch someone sit in confinement long enough and you can see the compression unfold. It starts with anger. Then confusion. Then numbness. Then a quiet dread settles in. When your external world is controlled, your internal world becomes the only territory you can still govern. If that inner territory is filled with unanswered questions and unresolved pain, it becomes a war zone.

What do you do when your body is stuck but your mind will not stop running? What do you do when your conscience is clear but your circumstances are cruel? What do you do when your past is complicated but your punishment feels absolute?

Theologically, this is where faith fractures, not because people stop believing in God's existence, but because they start questioning God's fairness. They may never say it out loud, but the whisper forms. If God is good, why does my good not matter? Confinement turns whisper questions into daily companions. You are forced to live with your thoughts. You cannot outrun them with work, noise, or distraction. The silence becomes interrogation.

And this is also why confinement has devastating effects beyond the person inside. The United States holds hundreds of thousands of people in local jails at any given time. According to the Bureau of Justice Statistics, approximately 664,200 people were held in local jails at mid-year 2023. These are not just individuals. These are missing parents, missing paychecks, missing stability, and missing presence at the dinner table.

The Bureau of Justice Statistics has also documented how common parenthood is among incarcerated people. In 2016, an estimated 684,500 state and federal prisoners were parents of minor children, representing about 1,473,700 minor children. When we say confinement compresses identity, we also have to say it compresses family, because the family begins to contort around an absence it did not choose.

So what happens to the family? The financial strain is obvious. The emotional strain is quieter and often worse. Research consistently highlights how incarceration strains family finances, contributes to instability such as homelessness, especially for Black children, and how maternal incarceration can increase the likelihood of children entering foster care. This is not a statistic to skim. That is a child learning to sleep while their world shifts. That is a caregiver learning to answer questions they do not have the emotional permission to answer. That is a household learning how to celebrate birthdays with a missing chair.

The sentence is not only served by the person inside. It is absorbed by everyone who loves them.

Now consider national reform efforts and why this conversation matters. The Second Chance Act, passed in 2008 and reauthorized later, funds reentry services and systems reform aimed at improving the transition from incarceration back to the community. When people ask whether any of this works, there are data points that suggest progress is possible.

The Council of State Governments Justice Center has reported that the three-year reincarceration rate declined from 35 percent for people released from prison in 2008 to 27 percent for people released in 2019. That represents a 23 percent national decrease since the passage of the Second Chance Act. That means thousands of people are not cycling back. Thousands of families are not being fractured again. Thousands of children are spared another round of absence.

But here is the hard truth. Programs can reduce reincarceration and still not address the deepest compression of identity. Programs can help with housing, employment, supervision, and services, and still not touch the internal war a person fights when they return home carrying shame, hypervigilance, and grief. The system can say, you are released, while the mind says, I am still trapped. It is possible to be physically out and psychologically confined. That is why the phrase confinement compresses identity is not only about what happens inside, it is about what follows people home.

Now we must step carefully into the suicidal perspective, not in a sensational way, but in a truthful one. Unjust confinement, perceived unjust confinement, or simply the experience of being trapped can create a particular kind of internal conflict. It threatens the mind's ability to make meaning. The question, "If I did everything right, why am I still here?" can begin to mutate when it goes unanswered. It can become, maybe doing right is pointless. Then maybe I am pointless. Then maybe it would be easier if I were not here at all.

That progression does not happen because someone wants to die. It often happens because someone wants the pain to stop and cannot see another exit.

This is what we are talking about in Joseph's story. Prison was not just an experience. It was confinement. The mind in confinement is exposed to repetitive stressors, loss of autonomy, humiliation, isolation, disrupted sleep, fear, uncertainty, and sometimes violence or neglect. Those conditions are linked to elevated suicide risk in custody.

The Bureau of Justice Statistics has documented patterns in jail and prison suicides over time, including that between 2000 and 2019, unconvicted inmates in local jails accounted for nearly 77 percent of those who died by suicide. That detail highlights how confinement can be an especially volatile period. Research also consistently shows that suicide rates in jails exceed those of the general population, underscoring the urgency of prevention and care.

But beyond the numbers is the inner script. Confinement compresses identity by forcing a person to reduce themselves to a case number, a charge, a rumor, or labor. Once the label becomes the loudest name you hear, you begin to forget your other names: father, mother, artist, provider, mentor, friend, believer, human. You begin to question whether you are still allowed to be those things.

That is where despair becomes spiritual. Not simply I am hurting, but I am no longer myself. Despair is not only pain. It is pain that cannot find a future.

This is where theology must be precise, because people often hear simplistic faith statements that backfire in confinement. Just trust God. It will be okay. Everything happens for a reason. Those lines can feel like abandonment when you are living inside consequences you did not choose or consequences that feel disproportionate.

Biblical faith is not pretending the cell is a sanctuary. Biblical faith is refusing to let the cell become the final word about who you are. It is the stubborn insistence that circumstances are allowed, but not ultimate. Joseph is not in confinement because he was careless. He is there because he resisted corruption and was punished for it. He could have asked, what is the point of integrity if it lands me here? I did it right and it did not protect me, so right must not matter.

But Joseph's faith is not that integrity prevents suffering. His faith becomes that integrity preserves him through it. He learns that the environment can restrict movement without dictating identity. That is not inspirational fluff. That is survival theology.

So let me ask you a question that presses into self-examination. What if the most damaging part of confinement is not the locked door, but the locked narrative? What if the true compression happens when you begin summarizing your entire life by your worst day? What if the cell did not destroy you, but convinced you to abandon yourself? What if the greatest injustice is not only what happened to you, but what it tried to make you believe about you?

And if you are listening from outside, as a spouse, child, parent, or friend, what if you have been carrying your own compressed identity too? What if you have been reduced to the strong one, the responsible one, the one who has to make it work? Who told you that you had to become a machine to survive a loss you never asked for? When did your grief become a job description?

Driver Seat Quote: "Some families do not fall apart. They get forced into a shape that hurts to live in."

This is why reform programs matter. Reentry services matter. Reducing reincarceration matters. But the deeper reform has to include the restoration of identity for the incarcerated person and for the family, because if confinement compresses identity, then healing has to re-expand it. Healing has to reintroduce a person to themselves again, not the version of them that the system recognizes, but the version of them that God still calls by name. Healing must reach beyond housing, beyond employment, beyond compliance, and speak to the fractured sense of self that confinement quietly reshaped. It must address not only behavior, but belief. Not only circumstance, but self-concept.

This is why reform programs matter. Reentry services matter. Reducing reincarceration matters. But the deeper reform has to include the restoration of identity for the incarcerated person and for the family, because if confinement compresses identity, then healing has to re-expand it. Healing has to reintroduce a person to themselves again, not the version of them that the system recognizes, but the version of them that God still calls by name. Healing must reach beyond housing, beyond employment, beyond compliance, and speak to the fractured sense of self that confinement quietly reshaped. It must address not only behavior, but belief. Not only circumstance, but self-concept.

Confinement does not only happen to the body; it also happens to the mind. When a person is incarcerated for long periods of time, the environment begins to reshape how they see themselves, how they interpret authority, and how they respond to the world around them. Survival in confinement often requires emotional restraint, constant awareness, and the suppression of vulnerability. Those adaptations help someone survive inside the system, but they can make it difficult to transition once the walls are removed. The routines, the rules, and the identity assigned to them can linger long after release.

This is why the transition back into society can feel overwhelming for many people leaving incarceration. Freedom requires new decisions, new relationships, and new ways of seeing oneself. Without intentional healing, a person may leave the physical structure of confinement while still carrying its psychological weight. That is why true restoration must go deeper than external support. It must help a person recover their sense of identity, dignity, and purpose. Because when identity has been compressed by confinement, healing must slowly teach a person how to expand again, how to live not as the label they were given, but as the person God created them to be.

And this is where the deeper work of restoration begins. Identity restoration is not automatic when a door opens. Release papers do not automatically rebuild self-worth. Employment assistance does not automatically restore dignity. Supervision does not automatically restore purpose. Freedom of movement does not automatically produce freedom of mind. If confinement has taught a person to see themselves as a number, a charge, a problem, or a burden, then healing must deliberately reintroduce them to their fuller humanity. It must patiently untangle the internal narrative that says this is all you are. It must remind them that before they were a case, they were a calling. Before they were a file, they were a future. Before they were reduced, they were named.

That is why the suicidal conflict is so serious. It is often the moment when a person stops believing they can ever return to themselves. They do not just feel trapped. They feel erased. They feel as though the version of them that once hoped, dreamed, and imagined has been permanently overwritten. And when a person feels erased, death can begin to feel like an agreement with the eraser, a tragic surrender to the label, a way of saying the story is already over because the self they knew no longer feels reachable.

That is why we must speak life with specificity, not generic hope, but concrete reminders. Vague encouragement cannot repair specific damage. You are more than this place. You are more than this file. You are more than this delay. You are more than this accusation. You are more than this worst season. You are still a person with a future, even if the future is currently blurry. You are still a bearer of purpose, even if the path is unclear.

Driver Seat Quote: "Hope is not a mood. Hope is a decision to keep your name."

To keep your name is to refuse reduction. It is to resist letting the worst chapter become the title of the book. It is to reject the idea that confinement has final authority over identity. It is to insist that your life cannot be summarized by a sentence handed down by a court, a rumor, a system, or even a mistake. It is to stand in the tension between what happened and who you are, and refuse to collapse them into one thing.

So here is the deeper understanding of confined, compressed identity. Confinement does not create identity. It reveals what identity was built on. It exposes the foundation. If identity was built on freedom alone, confinement will crush it. If identity was built on reputation alone, accusation will crush it. If identity was built on success alone, limitation will crush it. If identity was built on applause alone, silence will crush it. Confinement does not invent fragility, it uncovers it.

But if identity is anchored in something deeper, faithfulness to a God who sees the truth when others do not, then confinement becomes pressure that cannot rewrite your essence. It can test your endurance. It can stretch your patience. It can expose your fears. It can confront your pride. It can purify your motives. But it cannot rename you. It cannot revoke what heaven has spoken. It cannot cancel what God has called.

And that brings us back to the haunting question, if I did everything right, why am I still here? Sometimes there is no satisfying answer inside the walls. Sometimes the answer is delayed. Sometimes the answer is complicated. Sometimes the answer is that systems are imperfect and justice can be slow. Sometimes the answer is that faithfulness does not always shield you from fallout.

But here is what can be answered immediately. Being here does not mean you are nothing. Being here does not mean your life is over. Being here does not mean your integrity was wasted. Being here does not mean God stopped seeing you. Being here does not mean the calling expired. The conflict is real, but it does not get to become your conclusion. Circumstances may speak loudly, but they do not get the final word.

Joseph embodies that tension. He does not become a new person just because he entered a new place. He does not let a locked door become an internal collapse. He does not allow confinement to dictate character. He stays internally consistent under external constraint. His inside does not become a slave to what is happening outside. He refuses to let restriction rewrite identity.

That is Driver Seat leadership. It is the discipline of guarding identity when circumstances shrink. It is the refusal to let environment define essence. It is the decision to remain who you are, even when where you are makes no sense. It is the quiet strength of integrity that survives injustice without becoming it.

Joseph's body is confined. His calling is not. His movement is restricted. His maturity is not. His location changes. His identity does not.

That is the difference between being imprisoned and being possessed by the prison.

God Was With Him, But God Did Not Free Him Yet

Right in the middle of confinement, Scripture inserts a sentence: "But the LORD was with Joseph..." (Genesis 39:21). That language should sound familiar. "The LORD was with Joseph" in Potiphar's house (Genesis 39:2). "The LORD was with Joseph" in prison (Genesis 39:21). His location changed. God's presence did not.

Leadership truth: God's presence is not seasonal. Your location changes. His covering does not.

Here is the lie this chapter must confront: "If God is with me, I will not be restricted." Joseph proves the opposite. God can be with you and you can still be confined. Not confined because you are forgotten. Confined because you are being formed.

Genesis 39:21 goes further. God "shewed him mercy, and gave him favour in the sight of the keeper of the prison." Mercy. Favor. In prison. We move too quickly past that word mercy. Mercy is not an escape. Mercy is restraint. Mercy is God not allowing the full weight of injustice to crush you. Mercy is God softening what should have hardened. Joseph could have been executed. He could have disappeared into a dungeon with no oversight. Instead, he is placed in a royal prison and shown mercy in the eyes of the keeper.

Mercy means the system did not have the final say. Mercy means the lie did not escalate to death. Mercy means God's hand limited what the accusation could do.

This is a critical leadership revelation: favor can function in confinement. God's presence is not proven by escape. It is proven by sustaining grace, by internal stability, by mercy that keeps you alive and favor that keeps you useful. Sometimes God does not remove the place. He redeems you inside the place.

Favor Granted in Prison

Even in confinement, Joseph's competence was visible. The prison keeper recognized in him the same integrity Potiphar had seen. Joseph did not promote himself. Excellence revealed him. This proves the Scripture that says promotion comes from the Lord. "For promotion cometh neither from the east, nor from the west, nor from the south. But God is the judge. He putteth down one, and setteth up another" (Psalm 75:6–7). Joseph had no platform to campaign from. He had no reputation to defend. He had no audience to impress. Yet elevation found him in a prison. That is not a coincidence. That is covenant.

The keeper placed Joseph in charge of the prisoners, trusting him to manage responsibilities and maintain order. The text says the keeper "paid no attention to anything under Joseph's care," proving that trust was earned through consistency, not title. God caused what Joseph did to prosper, even in the lowest place of his life. The same God who prospered him in Potiphar's estate prospered him in the dungeon. Favor was not environmental. It was covenantal. It was not tied to comfort. It was tied to calling. Mercy kept him alive. Favor kept him advancing.

This is a leadership principle. Focus on doing right. Focus on being excellent. Focus on being competent. Let integrity become your strategy. Let stewardship become your language. When you are committed to excellence in hidden places, you remove the desperation to self-promote in visible ones. Joseph did not manipulate his environment to rise. He managed his responsibilities well. He did not network his way out. He nurtured what was placed in his hands. He did not force recognition. He embodied reliability. And over time, reliability becomes undeniable.

Leadership is not about announcing capacity. It is about demonstrating consistency. Promotion that comes from people can be political. Promotion that comes from platforms can be temporary. But promotion that comes from the Lord is purposeful. When God promotes, it is not merely to elevate status.

It is to expand assignment. It is to position you where your character can carry what your calling requires.

Joseph's life teaches this clearly. The same excellence that functioned in Potiphar's house functioned in prison. His environment changed. His standard did not. His title shifted. His integrity did not. That consistency is what made him promotable. This is why competence matters. Spirituality without skill is incomplete. Integrity without excellence limits impact. Joseph prayed, but Joseph also performed. He trusted God, but he also managed systems well. He interpreted dreams, but he also organized people. He was both faithful and functional. That combination is powerful.

If you focus on doing right, being excellent, and remaining competent, you position yourself for God's timing. You may not control when the door opens, but you can control how you steward the room you are currently in. You may not control the recognition, but you can control the reliability. Joseph did not chase promotion. He prepared for it. And when promotion finally came, it did not surprise him. It revealed him.

Promotion comes from the Lord. So do not exhaust yourself trying to manufacture what only God can authorize. Do the work. Guard your integrity. Strengthen your skill. Serve where you are placed. Because when God decides to set you up, no confinement can keep you down.

Responsibility Restored

Joseph had lost family, reputation, status, and security. He had lost position. He had lost public trust. He had lost the visible markers of leadership. Yet prison became the place where responsibility re-entered his hands. That detail matters. Joseph did not remain idle in confinement. He did not remain sidelined. The same man who once managed Potiphar's house is now entrusted with managing prisoners. Responsibility was restored before freedom was restored. Authority was rebuilt before his name was cleared.

Responsibility is often the evidence that your identity is intact even when your circumstances are not. Being trusted in confinement validates character. It proves that what was stripped externally was not destroyed internally. Leadership in low places builds the muscles required for leadership in high places. What Joseph stewarded behind bars became the foundation for what he would later steward before kings. His administrative skill sharpened. His emotional intelligence matured. His discernment deepened. His discipline hardened into resilience. Prison did not erase his leadership capacity. It reactivated it in a smaller room.

This is where many people miss the mercy of God. We think restoration begins when the door opens. Sometimes restoration begins when responsibility returns. Joseph's responsibilities were restored in layers. First trust. Then oversight. Then influence. Before the palace ever appeared, stewardship reappeared.

And here is the encouragement for the reader. If you have lost position, lost visibility, or lost momentum, do not assume you have lost purpose. If God begins placing responsibility back in your hands, even in a restricted place, that is not random. That is restoration in motion.

Do not grow weary in well doing. Galatians 6:9 says, "And let us not be weary in well doing, for in due season we shall reap, if we faint not." That verse is not motivational language. It is leadership endurance. It acknowledges that weariness is real. It assumes the season may be long. It implies that doing well does not always produce immediate results. But it anchors the promise in due season. Not your season. Due season. The kind appointed by God.

Joseph lived that Scripture before it was written. He kept doing well in a place that did not reward him publicly. He kept managing well when no one was applauding. He kept leading well when his name was damaged. He did not faint. And because he did not faint, he reaped. Responsibility returning is often the first sign that promotion is coming. God will test what you do with small oversight before He entrusts you with large outcomes. He will restore stewardship before He restores spotlight.

What the enemy meant as confinement, God used as concentration. Concentration is not punishment. It is focus. It is the narrowing of environment so that your development intensifies. In concentration, distractions are removed. Applause is removed. Options are removed. And what remains is formation.

God often isolates before He elevates. Moses spent forty years in Midian tending sheep before leading a nation. David was hidden in fields and caves before sitting on a throne. Elijah was sustained by a brook before confronting kings. Paul spent years in obscurity after conversion before stepping fully into apostolic influence. Even Jesus was led into the wilderness before public ministry began.

Isolation clarifies voice. It strengthens conviction. It purifies motive. In isolation, you learn who you are without affirmation. In concentration, you learn self-governance before public governance. Joseph's prison was concentration. His gift sharpened. His discernment deepened. His leadership was distilled. He learned to manage complexity in confinement. He learned patience under delay. He learned to steward without recognition.

Concentration develops what promotion will later expose. Without it, elevation can crush you. With it, elevation can rest on you. God was with him, but God did not free him yet. And sometimes that is the greater miracle. Because when God restores responsibility before He restores freedom, He is proving that your calling survived the season.

Joseph's body was confined, but his capacity was being rebuilt. And the same God who restored responsibility to Joseph will restore it to you. Stay faithful in the smaller assignment. Steward what reappears. Guard what is placed back in your hands. Responsibility restored is evidence that your story is not over.

Leadership Doesn't Pause Just Because Life Does

The Bible tells us that Joseph is entrusted again. That matters. Leadership is portable. Titles are not. Joseph does not wait for better conditions to start leading again. He leads from the bottom. Again. That is not regression. That is repetition as training. The same leadership muscle used in Potiphar's house now has to function in prison. Stewardship did not pause just because freedom did.

Joseph keeps getting trusted because he keeps being trustworthy. That is the Driver Seat principle: leadership is not a position you hold. It is a posture you carry. There is a lesson here for every leader. If your leadership only works in ideal conditions, it is not leadership. If your influence disappears when your title disappears, it was never influence, it was access. Joseph proves that when leadership is internal, it travels with you. When it is external, it collapses with the platform.

Leadership is easy when freedom is abundant, when opportunities are visible, and when recognition flows naturally. But Joseph learned leadership in the most restricted environment of his life. He did not confuse restriction with irrelevance. He did not assume that because the stage was smaller, the standard should be lower. Leading in limitation requires a special form of character, the kind that does not need applause or visible progress in order to stay faithful.

Joseph led with excellence even when there was no clear reward for doing so. He functioned not out of ambition, but out of identity. He discovered that true leadership is not about climbing. It is about carrying. Carrying responsibility. Carrying integrity. Carrying hope for people who have lost theirs. Leadership in limitation forces a person to develop internal authority when external authority has been stripped away. It demands self-governance before public governance. It trains discipline without supervision and consistency without recognition.

Joseph learned to lead hearts, not systems. To manage people, not platforms. To steward purpose, not position. He learned that leadership is proven in pressure, not preference. It is refined in repetition, not spotlight. It is measured by consistency, not comfort. And because he led well in limitation, God prepared him to lead well in liberation. The prison did not interrupt his leadership development. It intensified it. When freedom finally returned, Joseph was not becoming a leader. He already was one.

The Ego Test of Leadership

Prison did more than confine Joseph. It exposed him. Demotion is one of the clearest tests of ego a leader will ever face. When position is removed, visibility reduced, and influence minimized, something internal surfaces. Not talent. Not gifting. Ego. Joseph had every reason to shut down. He had done the right thing and was punished for it. He had resisted temptation and lost position. He had been promoted once and then publicly dropped into confinement. If anyone had a case for disengagement, it was him.

But he did not withdraw. He did not become bitter. He did not reduce his excellence to match his environment. Why? Because his identity was never built on the title he held. It was built on the integrity he carried. Ego ties worth to position. Calling ties worth to obedience. When ego leads, demotion feels like erasure. When calling leads, demotion becomes refinement. This is the ego test of leadership: who are you when your platform shrinks?

Many leaders unravel here, not because they lack skill, but because they lack internal anchoring. When the spotlight fades, they disengage. When recognition disappears, so does their effort. When authority is removed, so is their consistency. Ego reacts in predictable ways. It withdraws, thinking, if I am not in charge, I am not participating. It turns bitter, deciding, they do not deserve my best. It minimizes effort, settling for just enough since I am not valued. It even sabotages, reasoning, if I cannot lead it, I will let it fail.

Joseph does none of it. He keeps leading. He keeps stewarding. He keeps showing up. He does not punish the assignment because it does not reflect his capacity. That is maturity. Staying faithful when it looks like you failed is one of the highest forms of leadership development. Failure of circumstance is not failure of character. Joseph's demotion was not evidence of incompetence. It was evidence of injustice. But ego does not distinguish between the two. Ego hears demotion and translates it as you are less.

Joseph refused that translation. He understood something most leaders never learn: God measures obedience, not optics. If demotion makes you disengage, promotion would have destroyed you. If you cannot remain consistent without applause, you cannot be trusted with influence. If you need visibility to validate you, power will eventually expose you. Joseph passed the ego test in prison. That is why the palace did not corrupt him later.

Ego drives for recognition. Calling drives for faithfulness. Ego needs visibility. Calling needs obedience. Ego falters when demoted. Calling continues when misunderstood. When your platform shrinks, your posture is revealed. Joseph's posture did not change when his platform disappeared. That is why God could trust him again. Leadership is not proven when you rise. It is proven when you remain.

Leadership Development: Faithfulness Without Platform

Faithfulness without platform is one of the rarest traits in leadership. Many are excellent when the spotlight is warm, the applause is loud, and the opportunities are abundant. But Joseph's excellence remained consistent even in darkness, even in confinement, even in obscurity. He did not wait to be promoted to act like a leader. He did not wait to be recognized in order to excel. He did not wait for a stage to start walking in character.

Prison taught him that faithfulness has nothing to do with visibility. It is a heart posture, not a situation. It is a commitment, not a condition. Joseph mastered the art of doing big things in small places because God was preparing him to do small things in big places, quietly, humbly, consistently. That is the foundation of trustworthy leadership. Joseph influenced people without needing positional power.

Influence is not the ability to command. It is the ability to shift atmosphere, redirect behavior, and inspire trust. And all of this Joseph did while wearing chains. The warden trusted him because he carried influence the way others carry weapons, quietly, steadily, intentionally. Influence grows when character is tested, not when circumstances are ideal. Joseph learned to influence through example, reliability, excellence, and humility. His character preached louder than his resume. His work ethic spoke louder than his title. His consistency became the culture the prison understood.

And by the time Joseph finished this season, he had learned how to lead people who were broken, bitter, disappointed, and dangerous, the same people he would later govern during famine.

Leadership Development: Service Under Confinement

Service under confinement is service purified of ego. In Potiphar's house, Joseph still had visibility. In prison, he had none. And yet he served. He served God. He served the warden. He served the prisoners. He served purpose itself. Confinement taught Joseph the difference between serving for validation and serving from identity. It purified his motives. It cleared his intentions. It refined his posture.

Service is the language of true leadership, and confinement made that language fluent in Joseph's soul. When God needed someone to manage a famine, He chose a man who learned how to serve in restriction, because dominance cannot solve famine. Service can.

The Prison as Protection from a Different Perspective

Genesis 39:20 specifies this was "a place where the king's prisoners were bound." We know that detail is strategic. We know that Joseph is not thrown just anywhere. There is another layer here that must be said carefully. The prison was protection in more than one way, not merely protection from temptation, but protection from premature elevation. While prison is not Joseph's reward, it is Joseph's route.

Joseph is confined because a system punished what it could not control. But Joseph is also confined because God is moving him into proximity with what comes next. Genesis 40:1–4 tells us that Pharaoh's officials will soon enter this same prison. We will not unpack that yet. But understand this. Prison is not only a place of restraint. It is a place of positioning.

This tension exists in the real world as well. Systems often remove people who expose their weakness, challenge their authority, or refuse to conform to what is convenient. Sometimes integrity places a person in environments they never would have chosen. Sometimes doing what is right leads to confinement rather than promotion. But God's movements are often hidden inside moments that look like setbacks.

God trains drivers in restricted spaces because unrestricted influence requires internal stability. Confinement is not the opposite of calling. It is often the classroom of calling. Another question presses even harder. If your capacity were suddenly matched by your environment, would your inner life survive the exposure, or has limitation been the very thing protecting you? The protection of prison is not comfort. It is calibration.

The Leadership Psychology of Delay

Earlier we touched on the idea that delay is not denial. We introduced it briefly, but this moment in Joseph's story invites us to sit with it more carefully. If you do not mind going a little deeper with me, this is where that truth becomes more demanding. It is one thing to say delay is not denial when the delay is short. It is another thing entirely when the delay stretches long enough to test your identity, your patience, and your hope.

Prison also forces a deeper reckoning: the difference between being delayed and being denied. Denial ends the story. Delay intensifies it. Delay is waking up in the same place, under the same restrictions, with the same questions, and choosing not to abandon yourself. Joseph is gifted and limited at the same time. Called and constrained at the same time. Prepared and paused at the same time. And that conflict is where leaders are formed.

What makes confinement dangerous is not only what it takes. It is what it tries to give. It offers new identities: inmate, failure, forgotten, behind, disqualified. It offers new conclusions: nothing matters, why try, it is over. But Joseph refuses to let prison interpret him. He is confined, but not conquered. Restricted, but not rewritten. Delayed, but not denied.

And this is where delay begins to press on the reader as well. Delay can make you question your timing, your calling, and sometimes even your worth. It can make you wonder if the opportunity passed you by, if the promise was misunderstood, or if the season you are in will ever change. Delay has a way of whispering that everyone else is moving forward while you remain in place. But delay is not always a sign that something has gone wrong. Sometimes delay is the space where character is deepened, where endurance is strengthened, and where identity is tested until it becomes stable enough to carry what comes next.

Learned Endurance

The prison season demanded a type of endurance Joseph had never experienced before. The pit was sudden trauma. Potiphar's house was steady responsibility.

But prison required endurance, slow, daily, grinding strength of spirit. And Scripture quietly reveals something we often overlook.

Joseph was not in that prison for a few weeks. He was there long enough for the chief butler to forget him for two full years (Genesis 41:1). Two years after interpreting dreams. Two years after helping someone else. Two years of silence. That detail matters. Endurance that lasts days is one thing. Endurance that lasts years is another.

Prison required endurance that survives repetition. Endurance that wakes up to the same walls, the same routines, and the same unanswered questions. Endurance that remains steady when no progress is visible and no timeline is provided. Endurance that resists despair when breakthrough feels delayed.

Two years is long enough to question yourself. Long enough to wonder if you were forgotten. Long enough to replay the injustice until it tries to rewrite your narrative. Confinement builds spiritual stamina the way resistance builds muscle. You do not gain strength by lifting something once. You gain strength by lifting it repeatedly.

Joseph lifted disappointment daily. He lifted obscurity daily. He lifted delay daily. The pit tested his shock response. Potiphar's house tested his integrity. Prison tested his endurance. Joseph learned not to unravel under monotony, not to surrender under injustice, and not to drown under disappointment. He learned how to live faithfully in seasons that did not move quickly. He learned how to keep showing up when nothing was changing.

That is a different level of maturity. Anyone can be strong in crisis for a moment. Few can be steady in obscurity for years. Endurance is not dramatic. It is repetitive obedience. It is doing the right thing again when the reward has not arrived. It is trusting God again when the door has not opened. It is interpreting dreams for others while your own remain suspended.

Joseph learned endurance as a skill, not just survival, but resilience. Not emotional numbness, but disciplined hope. He learned how to hold onto calling without holding onto a clock. Two years in prison did not shrink him. It strengthened him. Endurance developed in silence prepares you for responsibility in public. The prison season did not simply delay Joseph. It deepened him.

Hope Management

One of the most complex psychological tasks Joseph faced in prison was managing hope. Hope is dangerous in confinement because it must be held delicately, not too tightly or it becomes desperation, and not too loosely or it becomes apathy. When you are in a waiting season, hope can either steady you or shatter you. If you grip it too tightly, every passing day feels like betrayal. If you loosen it too much, you begin to numb yourself just to survive. Waiting exposes how fragile and how powerful hope really is.

Joseph learned the art of keeping hope alive but not idolized, active but not credulous, present but not consuming. He had dreams from God. He had seen glimpses of destiny. Yet he remained in prison long enough for the chief butler to be restored and forget him completely (Genesis 41:1). Time passed. Seasons shifted. Life outside moved forward. Inside, nothing changed.

And here is the part we often rush past. Joseph was imprisoned for something he did not do. The chief butler was imprisoned for something he did do. Yet the butler was restored. Joseph remained confined. That was an opportunity for jealousy.

He could have watched another man walk out free while he stayed behind and allowed comparison to poison him. He could have interpreted the butler's restoration as personal rejection. He could have concluded that injustice had won twice. First the accusation. Then the delay.

Instead, Joseph interpreted the butler's dream accurately and served him faithfully, even knowing that another man's breakthrough would not immediately become his own. That is emotional maturity.

It takes strength to celebrate someone else's release while you are still restrained. It takes depth to help someone step into restoration when you are still waiting for yours. It takes discipline to guard your heart when someone else is lifted during your season of limitation.

Time passed. Seasons shifted. Life outside moved forward. Inside, nothing changed. He had every reason to assume that hope had expired. He had every reason to resent the timing. He had every reason to let jealousy whisper that

God was unfair. Instead, he learned how to carry hope quietly, not as entitlement, but as anchor.

Joseph understood something powerful. Someone else's elevation is not your elimination. Another person's restoration does not cancel your calling. God lifting someone near you does not mean He has forgotten you.

In waiting seasons, comparison is more dangerous than confinement. Jealousy can shrink your soul faster than prison can shrink your space. But Joseph refused to let another man's breakthrough distort his own belief.

He kept hope alive without making it competitive. He kept faith without making it fragile. He served without turning bitter.

Hope management is the process of believing God without dictating timelines, trusting the future without despising the present, and expecting change without abandoning steadiness. It is holding onto promise without demanding immediacy. It is remembering what God said without telling God when He must do it.

Scripture gives language for this kind of hope. "But they that wait upon the LORD shall renew their strength" (Isaiah 40:31). Waiting is not passive. It renews strength. "For I know the thoughts that I think toward you... thoughts of peace, and not of evil, to give you an expected end" (Jeremiah 29:11). The expected end may not arrive when expected, but it is still secured. "Let us hold fast the profession of our faith without wavering; for he is faithful that promised" (Hebrews 10:23). Hope is not confidence in the timeline. It is confidence in the Promiser.

When you are in a waiting season, the hardest part is not the delay. It is the silence. It is waking up and nothing has changed. It is praying and not seeing movement. It is serving faithfully and feeling unseen. In those moments, hope can start to ache. Proverbs 13:12 says, "Hope deferred maketh the heart sick." That is real. Deferred hope can wound you if you do not manage it wisely.

Joseph did not allow deferred hope to become diseased hope. He did not allow delay to turn into doubt. He continued stewarding the present while believing in the future. He stayed steady when no progress was visible. That is hope under discipline.

Joseph mastered this balance, and that emotional intelligence would later empower him to lead a nation, forgive his brothers, and provide for the very people who betrayed him. A man who has learned how to wait without unraveling can lead others through scarcity without panicking. A man who has learned how to hope without desperation can guide others through crisis without fear.

If you are in a waiting season right now, hear this clearly. Waiting is not wasting. Silence is not abandonment. Romans 15:13 says, "Now the God of hope fill you with all joy and peace in believing." God is not just the giver of outcomes. He is the God of hope itself.

Hope is not pretending everything is fine. It is choosing to believe that everything is not finished. It is whispering to your own heart, God has not forgotten me. It is deciding that the story is still unfolding, even if the page has been quiet for a while.

Joseph's prison did not erase his dreams. It refined how he held them. And in your waiting season, God may be doing the same, teaching you to hold hope without breaking under it. Teaching you to trust without controlling. Teaching you to wait without quitting.

Remember, hope is not a mood. It is a disciplined decision to believe that the God who spoke will also fulfill.

Emotional Containment

Prison is full of emotions that swell without warning. Anger, sadness, fear, confusion, regret, isolation, longing, these emotions are loud in confinement.

Joseph had to learn emotional containment, which is not suppression but stewardship. He learned to hold his emotions without letting them hold him. He learned to feel deeply without being ruled by the depth. He learned to process pain without projecting it. Emotional containment is what makes leaders safe for others. Because Joseph learned emotional discipline in prison, he later became a ruler who could cry freely, forgive fully, and govern wisely.

Identity Preservation

Identity preservation is perhaps the most profound psychological battle of Joseph's prison. His name was damaged. His reputation was destroyed. His freedom stripped. His accomplishments erased. Yet he preserved his identity, not the external identity of coats and titles, but the internal identity of calling and purpose.

Joseph did not allow confinement to redefine him. He refused to internalize the false narrative assigned to him. Identity preservation is the ability to remember who God says you are when everything around you suggests otherwise. Joseph held onto identity like a lifeline, and because he did, prison could not break him. It could only build him.

This battle is not limited to prison walls. It happens in the real world every day. It happens when a person loses a job and begins to question their worth. It happens when a false accusation damages someone's reputation and people begin to treat them differently. It happens when a business fails, a relationship collapses, or a dream is delayed long enough that doubt begins to whisper that maybe the calling was never real. It happens when a person is reduced to their worst moment, their worst decision, or someone else's version of their story.

Modern systems do this quietly. A person becomes a performance review. A social media mistake becomes a permanent label. A season of unemployment becomes a personal identity. A divorce becomes a definition. A charge becomes a character judgment. Over time the world begins to speak a new narrative about who you are.

And that is where the battle Joseph fought becomes the battle many people face today. The real struggle is not only what happens to you; it is whether you begin to believe what the situation says about you. Identity preservation is refusing to let circumstances write the final sentence of your story. It is remembering that the place you are in is not the person you are.

Joseph shows us something powerful: environments can change your location, but they do not have the authority to redefine your identity. When a person holds onto that truth, hardship may test them, but it cannot erase them.

Driver Seat Thesis

Confinement does not cancel calling, it concentrates it. Joseph's prison season condensed him, strengthened him, clarified him, matured him, and prepared him. Calling is not hindered by confinement. It is heightened. Prison was not the end. It was the intensification. It was the pressure that brewed power. The tightening that birthed transformation.

When you outgrow a season but cannot leave it, the real test becomes who you are while you wait. One of the most painful tensions in personal development is growth without mobility. It is the experience of becoming more while remaining in the same place, of gaining clarity while your environment remains unchanged, of feeling your inner world stretch forward while your outer world feels frozen.

This tension is not dramatic. It is quiet, grinding, and deeply personal. It does not announce itself as a crisis. It settles in as frustration, relentlessness, and low-grade grief that cannot fully explain. Joseph lived here. He has matured, but his environment has not moved. His capacity has expanded, but his position has not followed.

And this kind of delay has a way of pressing on the soul. Psychologically, this is one of the hardest places for the human mind to remain healthy. We are wired to associate growth with movement, learning with progression, effort with advancement. When those patterns break, the mind starts asking dangerous questions. If I've changed, why hasn't anything else? If I'm thinking differently, why am I still here? If I've learned the lesson, why hasn't the chapter ended? These questions are not signs of arrogance. They are signs of awareness colliding with limitations.

Joseph is no longer the same person who entered Potiphar's house. He has learned restraint, discernment, and self-governance. He has learned how to manage responsibility without owning it, how to operate with integrity in spaces that would reward compromise. Internally, he is not who he was, yet externally nothing has changed. The walls are the same. The routines are the same. The boundaries are the same.

And this created a psychological dissonance that many people experience but few can name, the pain of internal expansion without external permission.

The tension shows up everywhere. It shows up in professionals who have outgrown their role but cannot leave because of finances, family, retirement. It shows up in leaders who have matured beyond the culture they serve but feel trapped by loyalty or obligation. It shows up in creatives whose vision has evolved beyond their current platform. It shows up in public servants, executives, educators, parents, pastors, entrepreneurs who sense that they are operating below their present capacity but cannot yet move on.

And the danger of this season is not stagnation. It is misperception. When growth has no outlet, it turns inward. It becomes impatient. It becomes resentment. It becomes quiet arrogance or quiet despair. You begin to notice everything that is insufficient, everything that is small, everything that feels beneath you. Not because you are superior, but because you are no longer aligned.

And this misalignment tempts the mind to rationalize. If I'm still here, maybe it doesn't matter how I show up. If the environment hasn't caught up with me, maybe I'm justifying disengaging. Maybe I'm allowed to loosen my standards. This is where many people begin to lose what they gained internally.

Joseph's environment does not validate his growth. It does not reward it. It does not even acknowledge it. And this is psychologically significant because humans often rely on external feedback to confirm the internal change. When that feedback is absent, we begin to doubt ourselves. Did I really grow, or am I just impatient? Am I truly ready, or am I simply tired? These questions can either refine us or fracture us, depending on how we answer them.

There is a quiet grief in realizing that you have outgrown a season that still holds you. It is the grief of knowing you cannot go back to who you were, but you also cannot step fully into who you are becoming.

This in-between state is uncomfortable because it strips away illusion. You can no longer claim ignorance. You see too clearly now, but you also cannot act freely. You are still constrained. This is the space where integrity is tested, not by temptation, but by boredom, repetition, and delay.

Delay challenges our sense of agency. It confronts the belief that growth guarantees movement. It forces another deeper question: Who am I when my development outpaces my environment? This is not a question about ambition. It is a question about identity. Will I allow frustration to erode character? Will I let waiting distort my values? Will I become cynical, careless, or detached simply because the season did not end when I expected it to?

Joseph does something rare here. He continues to live as though his inner growth matters, even when it produces no immediate change in his circumstances. He does not downshift his integrity to match his environment. He does not numb himself to make the wait any easier. He does not sabotage the season to force an exit.

This restraint is not passive. It is discipline. It is the discipline to remain in alignment when advancement is delayed.

Here is a Driver Seat quote worth sitting with: "The season that cannot hold you anymore will still shape you if you stay honest inside it." Joseph's honesty is not emotional exposure. It is repeated faithfulness. He does not allow disappointment to make him careless. He does not allow delay to make him resentful. He treats the season as formative, not as punishment.

Across professions, this is where growth either matures or corrodes. For leaders, this is the season where you learn whether your discipline was dependent on recognition. For creatives, it reveals whether your vision is anchored in calling or applause. For executives, it tests whether your ethics were tied to ambition or conviction. For caregivers, teachers, and public servants, it exposes whether your compassion can survive monotony.

The question is not whether you will leave eventually. The question is who you will be by the time you do.

Joseph's maturity without mobility forces a deeper psychological reckoning. Can I respect a season that no longer reflects my capacity? Respect does not mean agreement. It means stewardship. It means refusing to treat the present moment as disposable simply because it feels too small or undeserved.

Many people damage their future by dishonoring the space they're still in. They rush mentally, detach emotionally, and begin living as though their current responsibility no longer matters. But inner growth is fragile. It can be undone not only by temptation, but by neglect.

Here's a thought that lingers: Delay is not defeat. It is direction without movement. It is like being in an airport with your bags packed, your ticket confirmed, your destination assigned, and the gate announced, but the plane has not boarded yet. You are not denied. You are not canceled. You are not forgotten. You are cleared for travel. You are simply waiting for departure. Joseph's delay is shaping his internal compass. It is teaching him patience that is not passive, humility that is not performative, and discipline that does not rely on applause.

These qualities cannot be learned quickly. They are formed under the weight of repetition, restraint, and unresolved longing. The mind resists this kind of formation. We want clarity without waiting, purpose without delay, and growth with visible reward. But psychology reminds us that the deepest transformation often occurs when external reinforcement is absent.

When no one is clapping, no one is promoting, no one is affirming, and you must decide whether your values are intrinsic or transactional. Do I live this way because it works, or because it is who I am? You have to decide who you are before your circumstances try to decide for you.

Joseph's environments keep changing, yet he does not. That mismatch is painful, yet it is also revealing. It reveals whether growth was about preparation or escape, whether maturity was about influence or integrity, whether development was about becoming someone or going somewhere. These questions are uncomfortable, but they are necessary.

Let me leave you with another Driver Seat quote to reflect on: "If you rush out of a season you've outgrown, you may carry unfinished parts of yourself into the next one."

Joseph does not give up. He remains present, and because of that, when movement finally comes again, he is not merely relocated. He is ready.

This is the invitation of the tension, to stay awake in seasons that feel too small, to stay honest when you feel overlooked, to stay aligned when your growth seems unrecognized, because who you become while waiting may matter more than where you go next.

Modern Driver Seat Reframes

This chapter gives you language for your own confinement. When you're restricted, don't let restriction turn into identity. Don't let delay turn into doubt. Don't let being unseen convince you you're unneeded. Don't let locked doors teach you you're unloved.

You can be called and constrained at the same time. You can be gifted and limited at the same time. You can be prepared while you feel paused. Prison does not prove you are disqualified. It proves you are being developed.

Loneliness as Formation

Loneliness teaches Joseph how to lead without affirmation. That single reality reframes his entire story. Before Joseph ever stands before a crowd, before authority rests in his hands, before his voice carries weight beyond himself, he is trained in the discipline of being misused. He is not surrounded by encouragement. He is not sustained by applause. He is not affirmed by people who understand his calling. Instead, he is shaped in loneliness.

And loneliness, when it is endured rather than escaped, becomes a tutor.

Scripture does not romanticize Joseph's isolation. It simply states it, so displaced, removed from familiarity, placed in foreign systems with no emotional safety net. What is striking is not that Joseph is alone, but that God allows his aloneness to last long enough to form him.

The text resists urgency. God does not rush Joseph into visibility. He lets him live where no one is clapping, where no one is confirming his worth, and where no one is reinforcing his sense of self.

And in that space, Joseph learns something most leaders never master, how to exist without being mirrored back to himself by others. Loneliness has a way of stripping us of borrowing identity. When affirmation is absent, you are forced to ask quieter, more honest questions. Who am I when no one notices me? Who am I when my work is unseen? Who am I when my obedience produces no immediate reward? These are not comfortable questions, but they are essential ones.

Scripture consistently shows that God asks these questions before He entrusts influence. Moses spent decades in obscurity before Pharaoh even heard his name again. David is anointed in private long before he is acknowledged in public. Elijah learns God's voice in isolation before confronting kings. And Joseph, perhaps more than all of them, is taught to lead himself when no one is validating him.

There's a deep psychological truth embedded here. Leaders who require constant validation often crumble when authority arrives. If you need affirmation to feel valuable, power will become a trap. Authority amplifies insecurities if insecurity has not been confronted.

When affirmation fuels identity, leadership becomes addictive rather than anchored. Decisions are shaped by applause rather than conviction. Silence feels threatening. Criticism feels annihilating, and loneliness, rather than being formative, becomes unbearable.

Joseph's loneliness does something different. It teaches him how to survive without emotional reinforcement. It trains him to locate his identity somewhere deeper than response. He learned to hear God without the noise of agreement. He learned to obey without witnesses. He learned to remain consistent without being celebrated.

This is not stoicism. This is spiritual maturity. Joseph is not desensitized. He is grounded. He does not deny pain. He refuses to let pain define him.

There's a reason temptation finds Joseph after he has proven himself reliable, but before he is given authority. Temptation often appears to the part of us that longs to be seen. It whispers to the unaffirmed places, offering recognition, intimacy, or validation in exchange for compromise.

But Joseph has already been trained in lack. He has already survived being unwanted. He has already learned that the absence of affirmation does not mean the absence of God. And that training gives him clarity and confidence to remain. Many people unconsciously believe that God's nearness is proven by recognition, but Joseph's story proves otherwise.

Prayer

Lord, when life feels small and my world feels confined, steady my identity in You. Teach me to steward what I cannot escape, to lead where I cannot move, and to stay whole in places that feel too narrow for who I'm becoming. Remind me that Your presence fills every room, that delay is not denial, and that nothing can imprison the calling You placed within me. Give me endurance without bitterness, consistency without applause, and hope that refuses to let this season rename me. Amen

Driver Seat Key Takeaways:

- Confinement compresses identity if you don't fight for authorship. Restriction does not just shrink movement; it shrinks the mind unless you actively resist internal collapse. Prison is external, but hopelessness is internal.

- God's presence does not prevent restriction, it sustains you inside it. "The LORD was with Joseph" in the house and in the prison. Location changed; proximity didn't. Divine presence is not proven by escape but by endurance.

- You can be gifted, called, and still confined. Calling does not exempt you from seasons where your outer world is smaller than your inner world. Maturity without mobility is not punishment, it is preparation.

- Leadership remains portable even when freedom isn't. Joseph is trusted in Potiphar's house. He is trusted in prison. He leads wherever he is placed because leadership is a posture, not a platform.

- Delay is not denial, it is formation. When you outgrow a season but cannot leave it, inner expansion is tested against outer limitation. The question becomes: Who are you when your development outpaces your environment?

- Restriction can protect you from premature elevation. Prison is not detour; it is divine engineering. God placed Joseph in proximity to Pharaoh's officials. Confinement positions him for calling.

- Identity must be anchored deeper than seasons, systems, or stories. If identity rests on freedom, accusation, or recognition, confinement will crush it. When identity rests in God, confinement cannot rewrite it.

- Silence, loneliness, and invisibility are part of leadership formation. Joseph's silent years train him to exist without applause, to remain consistent without witnesses, and to serve faithfully without reward.

- You are more than the season that holds you. You are more than the label, the file, the delay, the accusation, the worst moment. Confined does not mean erased; waiting does not mean wasted.

- How you handle the season too small for you determines whether you can be trusted with the one that's waiting for you.

***

Joseph is still confined. The walls have not moved. The door has not opened. The sentence has not changed. But something else has changed: Joseph has not collapsed. He is confined, but he is coherent. Restricted, but still responsible. Invisible, but internally intact.

And Scripture ends Chapter 39 with a quiet miracle: "That which he did, the LORD made it to prosper" (Genesis 39:23). Prosperity in a prison. Favor in a facility. Leadership in a locked place.

This is the paradox of divine formation: God will let the environment confine you while He refuses to let the confinement define you.

And now the stage is set. Because the next move in Joseph's story will not come from a throne, or a dream of his own, or a door he can open. It comes from two strangers with two dreams on two ordinary nights in the same confined place where Joseph has been faithfully serving.

Joseph does not know it yet, but the next chapter of his destiny is walking toward him in the form of other people's problems.

This is the part many leaders miss: your gift will often be required before your circumstances are repaired. Your calling will wake up before your situation changes. Your assignment will knock while you are still asking God for an exit.

The prison is not the interruption of Joseph's gift. It is the stage where his gift becomes necessary. And sometimes God hides you long enough for the right people to reach the same room.

Chapter 8 opens with this truth: when life feels stuck, your gift is still moving. When your story feels paused, your purpose is not.

Next: CHAPTER 8: The Baker and the Butler. Your Gift Works Even When Life Doesn't.

CHAPTER EIGHT

THE BAKER & THE BUTLER: YOUR GIFT WORKS EVEN WHEN LIFE DOESN'T

Your Gift Works Even When Life Doesn't

Genesis 40 opens without ceremony: Genesis 40:1–3 "And it came to pass after these things, that the butler of the king of Egypt and his baker had offended their lord the king of Egypt... and Pharaoh was wroth... and he put them in ward in the house of the captain of the guard, into the prison, the place where Joseph was bound." The text is sparse on theatrics and rich in implication. Power's servants have fallen; providence has not. The same prison. The same confinement. But new assignments. Life didn't change. Location didn't change. His case didn't get reviewed.

That detail matters more than we often realize. There is no dramatic music in the background. No angel unlocking the door. No public apology. Just routine incarceration. Just another day in a place Joseph did not choose. Scripture does not even slow down to dramatize it. It simply moves forward, as if to teach us that some of the most defining seasons of your life will arrive without spectacle. They will not feel historic while you are inside them. They will feel repetitive.

That is how many seasons in our lives feel. No announcement. No warning. No visible shift. You wake up in the same marital problems, the same workplace pressure, the same financial strain, the same misunderstood situation. You pray, but the walls look the same. You fast, but the environment feels unchanged. You try to adjust your attitude, yet the external facts remain unmoved. The scenery does not change. The confinement feels familiar. Your case still has not been reviewed.

And what makes that space dangerous is not the restriction itself, but the stagnation of it. Crisis at least gives adrenaline. Injustice at least gives clarity because it is clear that it is an injustice. But routine confinement produces questions. Why does this keep happening? Did I miss something? What did I do to deserve this? Has God moved on? Genesis 40 answers quietly by continuing the story. The absence of visible movement does not equal the absence of divine orchestration. God is not required to create spectacle to prove His presence. Sometimes He works most deliberately when nothing appears to be happening at all.

But something entered his environment. When nothing around you moves, God often moves toward you through people, opportunities disguised as burdens, connections disguised as inconveniences, conversations you did not ask for but cannot ignore. In everyday life this may look like a difficult client placed on your calendar, a struggling team assigned under your supervision, a neighbor who needs more than you feel prepared to give, a coworker who tests your patience but stretches your capacity. It may not feel like destiny. It may feel like disruption.

And notice something critical, these are not random inmates. These are high ranking officials. The cupbearer and the baker served Pharaoh directly. This is political proximity. These men worked near power. They had access to influence. They were trusted in the highest room in Egypt. Now they are disgraced. Now they are confined. Just like Joseph is still confined. But little does Joseph know that destiny just walked into his cell wearing chains.

In our world, destiny often walks in looking ordinary. It may sit beside you in the form of a partnership that does not yet have status, a mentorship that begins casually, a project that seems beneath your résumé, a volunteer opportunity that feels small. Destiny rarely knocks from the outside; it often sits beside you in limitation, waiting to be recognized through service. That is how transition works. It rarely announces itself as a promotion. It usually arrives disguised as responsibility.

Genesis 40:4 "And the captain of the guard charged Joseph with them, and he served them: and they continued a season in ward." Assignment precedes advancement. Before doors open, duties clarify.

Joseph is assigned to serve. Yet, again. Not promoted. Not released. Not vindicated. Assigned. And this is where the leadership tension sharpens. He is gifted. But still serving. He is capable. But still overlooked. He is ready. But still confined.

Many readers know this tension intimately. You have the degree but not the title. You have the vision but not the funding. You have the wisdom but not the microphone. You have the anointing but not the audience. You are doing the work without the recognition. You are carrying responsibility without the reward. That space can either refine you or exhaust you.

That is the first leadership truth of this chapter. Your gift does not wait for your freedom. Gifts withered by delay were never rooted in stewardship; they were fueled by applause. Joseph's gift survives because it serves, not because it shines. And if your gift only functions when it is seen, it was never anchored in purpose. But when your gift is anchored in service, it works in boardrooms and back rooms, on platforms and in prisons, in public and in private.

Emotional Intelligence Under Pressure

Genesis 40:6–7 "And Joseph came in unto them in the morning, and looked upon them, and, behold, they were sad. And he asked Pharaoh's officers... Wherefore look ye so sadly today?" Empathy is leadership's early warning system, seeing storms in faces before words provide forecasts. Joseph notices. That may seem small. It is not. Joseph is in prison. Falsely accused. Unjustly confined. Delayed. Restricted.

And he still sees other people's pain. Most people in confinement are consumed by self-preservation. Most people in delay are consumed by self-analysis.

Most people in injustice are consumed by defense. But Joseph is attentive. He walks in and reads the room. He sees sadness before it is explained. Most leaders in pain often turn inward. When you are wounded, it is easy to become self-absorbed. Trauma narrows vision. Confinement can make you hypersensitive to your own survival. When life squeezes you, empathy often shrinks. But Joseph's emotional intelligence remains intact. He does not say, "I have my own problems, so I do not have time for their issues." He does not say, "At least you will get out before me." He asks, "Why are you sad?" That is leadership.

Leadership is not proven by platform. It is proven by perception. Joseph models something profound here. You can be hurting and still be present. That is emotional regulation under stress. That is trauma-informed empathy. This is the mark of a leader who is truly in the Driver Seat. Many leaders fail here. Pain makes them reactive. Delay makes them detached. Injustice makes them cynical. Joseph does not allow confinement to erode compassion. Your gift is not just what you do. It is how you see.

And this is where you must examine your own maturity. Empathy is not softness. It is not agreement. It is not emotional indulgence. Empathy is the disciplined capacity to perceive, understand, and appropriately respond to the emotional state of another person without losing your own stability. It is entering someone else's experience without surrendering your discernment. It is awareness without absorption. It is compassion governed by wisdom.

Scripture does not treat empathy as optional. Romans 12:15 instructs us, "Rejoice with them that do rejoice, and weep with them that weep." That is emotional alignment. Proverbs 20:5 says, "Counsel in the heart of man is like deep water; but a man of understanding will draw it out." That is perceptive leadership. Philippians 2:4 commands, "Look not every man on his own things, but every man also on the things of others." That is intentional attention. Even Hebrews 4:15 reveals Christ as a High Priest who is touched with the feeling of our infirmities. If Christ leads with empathetic awareness, and we are supposed to model Christ, then empathy should be a part of our driving kit as a leader. Christ, as our example, proves that empathy is not weakness. It is a divine reflection.

Empathy shows up in how quickly you notice shifts in tone and body language. It shows up in whether you ask questions before offering conclusions. It shows up in whether people feel safer after speaking with you. For leaders, this is not optional. Empathy is strategic awareness. It allows you to detect discouragement before performance drops. It allows you to sense burnout before resignation letters are written. It allows you to perceive fear behind resistance and insecurity behind aggression. Leaders who lack empathy misdiagnose people. They treat symptoms but miss causes. They correct behavior without understanding the burden. They demand output without discerning capacity.

Immature leadership needs attention. It needs validation. It needs to be heard first. Mature leadership gives attention. It studies the room. It reads what is not being said. It understands that morale is as measurable as metrics. Immature leadership centers its own discomfort. When tension rises, it reacts. When challenged, it defends. When misunderstood, it escalates. Mature leadership can hold space for someone else's discomfort without being consumed by it. It can absorb emotion without absorbing identity. It can listen without losing authority.

Empathy also reveals how regulated you are. If someone else's frustration immediately triggers yours, your leadership is still reactive. If someone else's disappointment destabilizes you, your identity is still externally anchored. But if you can remain steady while someone else is unsteady, if you can remain curious instead of combative, if you can remain compassionate without becoming permissive, that is evidence of internal formation. This is evidence of a Driver Seat leader.

Joseph demonstrates this in prison. He is confined, yet observant. Restricted, yet responsive. Pressured, yet perceptive. He does not allow his own pain to eclipse someone else's humanity. That is rare. And that rarity is what distinguished him long before Pharaoh recognized him.

Empathy is the difference between managing people and leading them. Management controls tasks. Leadership shepherds hearts. People will tolerate authority, but they will trust empathy. And trust is the currency of sustained influence. When people know you see them, they will follow you even through uncertainty. When people feel unseen, they will comply temporarily but operate from duty, not devotion.

So examine yourself honestly. Do people leave conversations with you feeling understood or corrected? Do you listen to respond or listen to learn? Do you rush to fix, or do you first seek to understand? Scripture says in James 1:19, "Let every man be swift to hear, slow to speak, slow to wrath." That is empathy at work. Your answers reveal more about your leadership maturity than your résumé ever will.

How do you know if you are growing? You begin to respond instead of react. You begin to listen without preparing your defense. You begin to discern emotional undercurrents without being threatened by them. You do not weaponize vulnerability. You steward it. When pressure increases and your compassion decreases, that is a signal. When pressure increases and your awareness remains steady, that is growth.

If leadership is influential, then emotional awareness is its foundation. The capacity to perceive others while pressured yourself is not natural, it is practiced. Joseph practiced it long before Pharaoh ever heard his name. And that practice, developed in prison, became the reason he could later govern a nation without losing his humanity.

The Gift Is Portable

Joseph sees them sad. He asks what is wrong. He notices what others would ignore. That moment is not accidental. His concern becomes the doorway. His empathy becomes the bridge. The question he asks in confinement becomes the corridor to his elevation. What begins as awareness becomes access. What looks like simple compassion becomes strategic positioning. His sensitivity becomes the gateway to his deliverance, to his lifting. The very thing most leaders neglect under pressure becomes the hinge on which his future turns.

Here is a Driver Seat moment. The door that eventually opens for Joseph does not swing on ambition. It swings on empathy.

Genesis 40:8 "And they said unto him, We have dreamed a dream, and there is no interpreter of it. And Joseph said unto them, Do not interpretations belong to God? Tell me them, I pray you."

Notice the order, glory to God first, then the offering of skill. Joseph does not begin with ability. He begins with acknowledgment. He locates the source before he presents the service. That order matters. Humility secures the gift from manipulation. When leaders forget the source of their gifting, they begin to use the gift to secure themselves instead of serving others. When they remember the source, they steward it.

Joseph is still Joseph. In prison. In delay. In obscurity. And he says, "Interpretations belong to God." No self-pity. No bitterness. No insecurity. He does not say, "I used to interpret dreams." He does not say, "That was my old life." He does not say, "God abandoned me." He gives God credit. And he steps forward. The gift is still functioning.

This is consistent with a biblical pattern. Proverbs 3:6 instructs us, "In all thy ways acknowledge him, and he shall direct thy paths." Psalm 75:6–7 reminds us, "Promotion does not come from the east or the west, but God is the judge; He puts down one and sets up another." James 1:17 declares that "every good and perfect gift is from above." Joseph embodies that theology in real time. He refuses to detach his ability from its Author.

This is where many leaders stall. When life stops moving, they stop using what is in them. When they are not celebrated, they go silent. When they are not promoted, they withdraw. When recognition pauses, their confidence fades. But Joseph proves something essential. Your gift is portable.

You can be gifted while unemployed. Gifted while divorced. Gifted while grieving. Gifted while misunderstood. Gifted while restricted. Gifted while waiting. Location does not cancel calling.

Portability means your contribution is not geographically dependent nor title dependent; it is identity dependent. Your gift travels because its source is not your platform. It is God. When leaders acknowledge God first, they free themselves from the pressure of self-sustainment. They no longer have to manufacture outcomes. They simply steward what has been entrusted.

Joseph's acknowledgment also protects his heart. By giving God credit first, he guards himself from pride if the interpretation succeeds and from despair if it is ignored. His identity is anchored beyond the result. That is leadership stability. When glory is settled upward, confidence remains steady inward.

Genesis 40 shows us that the chains did not silence his calling. They clarified it. And because Joseph honored God before he exercised the gift, the gift remained clean. It remained aligned. It remained powerful.

Integrity in the Middle: When Your Gift Works but Your Life Does Not

Joseph interprets both dreams accurately. Genesis 40:9–13 records that the cupbearer will be restored in three days. Genesis 40:16–19 records that the baker will be executed in three days. Notice the integrity. He does not soften the difficult interpretation. He does not distort the truth to gain favor. He is accurate in both encouragement and warning. Three days later, Genesis 40:20–22, everything happens exactly as Joseph said. His gift works. Even when his life does not.

That is the paradox. Your internal capacity can be fully functioning while your external world feels stalled. You can be clear, precise, and anointed, and still confined. You can speak the truth that comes to pass for others while nothing changes for you. That internal strain is uncomfortable. But it is formative. Formation happens where feelings and faith collide. Accuracy without advancement tutors the soul in purer motives.

There is a deeper layer here that many readers will recognize. Joseph proves that your effectiveness for others is not evidence of your immediate deliverance. He accurately interprets the cupbearer's restoration, yet he remains imprisoned. He speaks freedom over someone else while staying bound himself. That is a difficult space. Many leaders quietly wrestle there. You counsel others through breakthroughs you are still waiting on. You advise marriages while navigating tension in your own home. You help build organizations while your personal visibility remains delayed. You pray for others and watch their prayers answered first.

That reality can expose motive. Do you serve because it works for you, or because it is who you are? Do you tell the truth only when it benefits you, or because you are anchored in truth? Joseph's refusal to distort the baker's outcome is critical. He does not manipulate the message to secure influence. He does not trade honesty for advantage. He speaks what is revealed, not what is strategic. That is leadership purity.

Here's another Driver Seat moment for you, maturity is revealed in how you handle accuracy without immediate reward. Many people can operate in gifting when there is a visible return. Fewer can operate in gifting when the return is delayed. Joseph's integrity in interpretation proves that his gift is not transactional. He is not leveraging revelation to negotiate release. He is stewarding revelation because it belongs to God.

There is also a sobering truth in this moment. Both interpretations were correct. One man lives. One man dies. Leadership requires the courage to carry both outcomes. Encouragement and warning. Restoration and consequence. Comfort and clarity. Joseph models balanced fidelity. He does not exaggerate mercy. He does not dramatize judgment. He remains aligned.

Perhaps this will become deeply practical for you. There will be seasons where your insight is sharp, your skill is intact, your discernment is precise, and yet your personal circumstances appear unchanged. Do not misinterpret delay as dysfunction. Your gift working in confinement is evidence of internal health. God is proving that your contribution is not circumstantial. It is covenantal.

When you continue to operate faithfully without visible promotion, your heart is refined. Applause loses its grip. Validation loses its necessity. Identity becomes anchored in obedience rather than outcome. And that is how Driver Seat leaders are formed who cannot be bought, rushed, or easily shaken.

Joseph's gift worked. Even when his life did not appear to. That is not a contradiction. That is construction.

Advocacy Without Anxiety

After interpreting the cupbearer's dream, Joseph does something important. Genesis 40:14–15 records his words: "But think on me when it shall be well with thee... and make mention of me unto Pharaoh... For indeed I was stolen away... and here also have I done nothing that they should put me into the dungeon." Advocacy is not unbelief; it is stewardship of voice. Joseph names truth without threatening timing.

Joseph advocates for himself. He names injustice. He asks for help. He does not spiritualize passivity. He does not pretend prison is fine. He does not pretend he does not want release. He does not pretend injustice is comfortable. This dismantles a dangerous religious myth that says if you have faith, you never ask. Joseph has faith and enough hope to ask, and he speaks. He does not demand. He does not manipulate. He does not panic. He simply asks.

But let us go deeper, because this is where many strong leaders quietly bleed. Joseph helps the cupbearer. Joseph serves him. Joseph accurately interprets his restoration. And then Joseph says, remember me. That request is not merely strategy. It is vulnerability. It reveals something profoundly human. When you are the one who shows up for others, you naturally believe that when their elevation comes, they will reach back. When you open doors, you assume someone will hold one for you. When you advocate, you expect advocacy. When you are loyal, you assume loyalty.

And here is the pain point. People are not always built like you.

Many leaders carry unspoken disappointment because they projected their own character onto others. You help because that is who you are. You show up because that is how you are wired. You keep your word because integrity is your default. Then you expect reciprocity as a moral reflex. But reciprocity is not automatic. Gratitude is not guaranteed. Character is not contagious.

Joseph's request is honest. His disappointment will be real. Genesis 40:23 says the chief butler did not remember Joseph, but forgot him. That verse is brief, but it is heavy. It captures the ache of being forgotten by someone you helped. It captures the silence after you thought the call would come. It captures the moment you realize that your expectation was not met.

This is where advocacy without anxiety becomes critical. Joseph asks, but he does not attach his identity to the answer. He speaks, but he does not spiral when silence follows. He plants the seed, but he does not attempt to control the harvest. That is maturity. Advocacy is your responsibility. The outcome is not.

Faith is not silence. Faith is steadiness. Joseph understands something critical. God can open doors, but humans must walk through conversations. He does not try to force Pharaoh. He speaks to the cupbearer. He plants the seed. He trusts the timing. And when the cupbearer forgets him, Joseph remains who he is.

Here is the deeper lesson for you. Do not build expectations on the assumption that others share your wiring. Do not mistake your generosity for a guaranteed return. Serve because it is your nature. Ask because it is wisdom. But anchor your hope in God, not in gratitude. Psalm 75 reminds us that promotion comes from God. Not from memory. Not from loyalty. Not from human fairness.

That is advocacy without anxiety. It is the courage to ask without collapsing when forgotten. It is the discipline to serve without making people your source. It is remaining in the Driver Seat of your character even when someone else drops the wheel of theirs.

The Trauma of Being Forgotten

The trauma of being forgotten sits at the intersection of psychology and Scripture, and Joseph's story captures it with painful clarity. When Joseph asked the cupbearer to remember him, he was not asking for a shortcut or a favor. He was asking for dignity. He was asking to matter. He had used his gift to bring clarity and hope to another man's life, and in return he asked for the most basic form of relational reciprocity: acknowledgment. Yet Genesis hits us with a devastating line: the cupbearer forgot him. Could you imagine being forgotten by someone you served, helped, and trusted?

Being forgotten wounds the human psyche because it disrupts the core need to be seen. People are created for connection, and connection depends on recognition. When someone you supported does not support you, the mind begins to question its own worth. You replay the moment. You wonder if you misread the relationship. You ask whether your contribution mattered at all. This is not the pain of waiting; it is the pain of feeling erased. Psychologically, this kind of wound can create emotional isolation, not because you are alone, but because you were left alone by someone who promised not to leave you there. It is the loneliness that follows broken expectation, and it cuts deeper than circumstantial delay.

Scripture does not hide this experience. David cries out in Psalm 13, asking God if he has been forgotten forever. Zion laments in Isaiah 49 that the Lord has abandoned her, and God responds not with speed but with remembrance, saying she is engraved on His hands. Even the thief on the cross understood that remembrance is a form of redemption when he said, "Remember me." These passages reveal that the fear of being forgotten is one of the most ancient human anxieties. It is not weakness; it is part of the human condition.

Joseph's trauma is intensified by the fact that he did everything right. He served faithfully. He interpreted accurately. He showed compassion. Yet the person he helped moved on with his life while Joseph remained in confinement. Leaders often experience this same emotional fracture. They pour into others, support others, advocate for others, and then discover that the people they invested in do not always invest back. This is not because people are cruel but because people are limited. They forget. They get distracted. They prioritize their own survival. The trauma of being forgotten becomes part of the leadership journey because it forces leaders to confront the truth that their destiny cannot rest in human memory.

This is where Joseph's story becomes spiritually transformative. The cupbearer's forgetfulness did not derail Joseph's future. It simply removed the illusion that his future depended on the cupbearer. Joseph's rise to power did not begin when the cupbearer remembered him; it began when God decided the time was right. What looked like abandonment was actually alignment. What felt like erasure was actually cultivation. God allowed Joseph to experience the trauma of being forgotten so that when he was finally remembered, he would know the difference between human recognition and divine appointment.

The trauma of being forgotten is real, but it is not final. People may forget you, but God does not. People may overlook you, but God sees every hidden act of faithfulness. People may fail to speak your name in rooms of influence, but God can create a moment where your name is the only one that matters. Joseph's story teaches that the pain of being forgotten is often the soil where God grows the kind of character that can carry destiny without unraveling under it.

The Theology of Delay

The story of Joseph's delay reveals how God shapes the inner life long before He elevates the outer life. Genesis holds the tension deliberately. It does not rush to resolution but allows the weight of waiting to settle on the reader. When Genesis 41 opens with the quiet line "at the end of two full years," it exposes the psychological reality of prolonged uncertainty. Two years is long enough for hope to fade, long enough for memory to blur, long enough for a person to question whether the promise they believed was ever real. Waiting becomes a crucible where the mind replays conversations, revisits expectations, and wrestles with the fear of being forgotten. In psychological terms, delay destabilizes the illusion of control. It forces a person to confront the gap between desire and reality, between what they believe should happen and what is actually unfolding.

In Scripture, delay is not framed as divine neglect but as divine formation. The human impulse is to equate speed with blessing and slowness with abandonment, yet the biblical narrative consistently reverses this assumption. Delay stretches internal capacity in ways that immediate fulfillment never could. It strengthens emotional resilience, deepens spiritual roots, and exposes the motivations that drive a person's identity. Leaders rarely break under betrayal or accusation alone; they break under the slow erosion of waiting. Delay forces the question: Who am I when nothing is happening? If identity is anchored in outcomes, delay becomes unbearable. If identity is anchored in recognition, delay becomes distorting. But if identity is anchored in God's presence, delay becomes formative rather than destructive.

Joseph's response to delay is psychologically remarkable. The text does not portray bitterness, collapse, or emotional regression. Instead, it shows consistency. He keeps serving. He keeps interpreting. He keeps showing up with the same integrity he had when he first entered the prison. His gift is not erased by delay; it is refined by it. The hidden years become the training ground where endurance is strengthened, humility is deepened, and character is shaped to match the weight of future responsibility. In biblical theology, this is the pattern of God's preparation: obscurity before influence, silence before speech, confinement before calling.

This is the essence of what might be called Driver Seat theology. God is not late; He is layering capacity. What looks like pause is often preparation. What feels like stagnation is often strengthening. The years that seem wasted become the very years that make a person ready for the moment that will define their story. Joseph's rise to power in a single day was only possible because of the slow work God did in him over many days. Delay was not the denial of his destiny; it was the development of his soul.

The Psychological Weight of Unmet Expectations

When someone you have supported fails to support you, the mind enters a cycle of questioning. You replay the conversation. You wonder if you misread the moment. You ask yourself whether you were foolish to hope. Psychologically, this is where disappointment becomes disorientation. Humans are wired for reciprocity. We expect relational symmetry. When that symmetry breaks, it can feel like a fracture in identity. You begin to wonder if your value was misjudged or if your contribution was invisible. Joseph lived in that tension for two full years. Not two days. Not two weeks. Two years of silence from someone who promised to speak on his behalf.

The Biblical Pattern of Delayed Recognition

Scripture repeatedly shows that God allows delay not to diminish a person but to deepen them. David was anointed long before he was enthroned. Moses waited forty years before he was commissioned. Hannah endured years of barrenness before Samuel was born. Even Jesus lived thirty hidden years before three public ones. Delay is not a biblical anomaly; it is a biblical pattern. This means that even when people forget you, overlook you, or fail to advocate for you, your destiny is not in their hands. Joseph's story reinforces this truth. The cupbearer's silence did not sabotage Joseph's future. It simply removed the illusion that his future depended on human memory.

The Pain of Human Disappointment and The Faithfulness of God

There is a unique pain in realizing that people cannot carry the weight of your expectations. Even good people, like the cupbearer, forget. God uses these moments to gently detach your hope from human hands and anchor it in His. Joseph's promotion came in a single day, but it was not triggered by the cupbearer's loyalty. It was triggered by God's timing. When Pharaoh dreamed, Joseph was remembered. Not because the cupbearer suddenly became faithful but because God made the moment ripe.

The Leadership Truth Joseph Teaches

Joseph's story teaches a leadership truth that is both sobering and liberating: people may contribute to your journey, but they do not control your destiny. God alone does. Human disappointment becomes the soil where divine appointment grows. The very people who forget you cannot stop what God has ordained for you. Joseph's rise to power was not delayed by the cupbearer's forgetfulness; it was aligned with God's preparation. When the moment came, Joseph was not just gifted. He was ready.

Being Used Before Being Rewarded

Being used before being rewarded is one of the most difficult realities in leadership and spiritual formation because it confronts the human desire for fairness, reciprocity, and recognition. Joseph embodies this tension. He was needed but not honored. He was valuable but not remembered. His gift served others long before it ever served him. This is not redundancy; it is a distinct emotional and spiritual experience that shapes leaders in ways applause never could. Joseph's accuracy did not earn him advancement. His faithfulness did not secure acknowledgment. His brilliance did not produce immediate elevation. He was used, but he was not yet rewarded, at least not yet.

This dynamic is psychologically disorienting because people naturally assume that contribution leads to compensation. When you help someone, you expect gratitude. When you solve a problem, you expect recognition. When you serve faithfully, you expect doors to open. Joseph's story disrupts that expectation. His interpretation of the cupbearer's dream directly benefited Pharaoh's court before Joseph ever met Pharaoh. His gift was already influencing the palace while he remained confined in a prison. This is the emotional paradox of leadership: you can be essential to a system that does not yet acknowledge your existence.

Why This Experience Forms Leaders

Being used before being rewarded exposes the motives beneath your service. It reveals whether you serve for validation or from identity. It tests whether your gift is a performance for people or an offering to God. Joseph continued to interpret dreams in prison not because it advanced him but because it was who he was. He did not stop being gifted simply because he was not being celebrated. He did not stop serving simply because he was not being promoted. His consistency in obscurity became the foundation of his credibility in influence.

The Biblical Pattern of Unseen Preparation

Scripture repeatedly shows that God trains leaders in hidden places before He trusts them with visible ones. David killed lions and bears before he killed Goliath. Moses shepherded sheep before he shepherded Israel. Joseph interpreted dreams in a prison before interpreting dreams in a palace. The pattern is unmistakable: God develops competence in obscurity so that character can sustain influence in visibility.

Why Being Used Without Reward is Not Exploitation

It is tempting to interpret this season as unfairness or exploitation, but Joseph's story reframes it. What looks like being used is often God using the moment to sharpen your gift. What feels like being overlooked is often God strengthening your endurance. What seems like stagnation is often God building the internal structure required for future responsibility. Joseph was not being exploited; he was being prepared. When Pharaoh finally called for him in Genesis 41, Joseph was not scrambling to remember how to interpret dreams. He had been practicing. In prison. In obscurity. In silence. His readiness was not accidental. It was the residue of repetition. Practice under pressure became poise under promotion.

The Blindside of Leadership: A Gift You Cannot Use on Yourself

There is a blindside to leadership that Joseph's story exposes with unsettling clarity. God gave Joseph dreams, but Joseph could not interpret his own dreams. He could explain the mysteries of others, but he could not decode the mysteries of his own life. The very gift that would one day elevate him was the same gift that initially isolated him. His dreams were the tool God used to call him, but they were also the tool that provoked his brothers to bind him. This is the paradox leaders rarely see coming: the gift that marks you is often the gift that wounds you first.

Joseph could interpret the cupbearer's dream. He could interpret the baker's dream. He could interpret Pharaoh's dream. But he could not interpret the meaning of his own journey.

This is the blindside of leadership, you can be gifted and still confused about your own life. You can bring clarity to others while walking through seasons that feel unclear to you. You can help others move forward while having no idea when your own breakthrough will come. Joseph's gift worked everywhere except on himself, and that was not a flaw. It was refinement.

Because if Joseph could interpret his own dreams, he would have tried to manage his own destiny. If Joseph could decode his own future, he would have tried to accelerate it. If Joseph could see the meaning of his own suffering, he would have tried to escape it. God blindsides leaders not to punish them but to protect them. He withholds interpretation so He can preserve dependence. He hides clarity so He can cultivate trust.

Joseph's inability to interpret his own dreams forced him to rely on God rather than on his gift. It kept him humble. It kept him surrendered. It kept him from manipulating outcomes. Leaders often assume that gifting guarantees understanding, but Joseph proves that gifting guarantees responsibility, not clarity. And here is the deeper truth:

The gift that first bound Joseph would one day free him.

The dreams that caused his brothers to hate him would one day save them. The visions that made him a target would one day make him a leader. This is the blindside of calling, your gift may hurt you before it helps you. It may confuse you before it clarifies you. It may isolate you before it elevates you. But none of that means the gift is broken. It means the gift is bigger than you.

Joseph's story teaches that leaders are often the last to understand what God is doing in their own lives. And that is not a deficiency, it is divine design. Because if you could interpret your own dreams, you would not need God to fulfill them.

The Driver Seat Principle

The Driver Seat Principle emerges in the tension that closes Genesis 40. Joseph is accurate, faithful, gifted, advocating, and forgotten, yet he remains internally stable. His circumstances are chaotic, but his character is not. He does not allow being forgotten to make him shrink. He does not allow delay to rewrite his personality. He does not allow silence to convince him he is unseen. This is the rare leadership muscle most people never build: the ability to remain in the driver seat of your identity when life places you in the back seat of your circumstances.

Joseph's stability is not denial; it is discipline. It is the refusal to let external inconsistency create internal instability. Many leaders fail not because they lack gifting but because they lack grounding. They allow disappointment to define them. They allow delay to drain them. They allow the absence of recognition to distort their sense of worth. Joseph shows a different way. He demonstrates that your gift must outlive your disappointment, your discipline must outlive your delay, and your identity must outlive your recognition. This is not motivational language; it is spiritual formation. It is the shaping of a leader who can carry influence without being crushed by it.

The Psychology of Staying in The Driver Seat

Remaining stable in seasons of uncertainty requires more than patience. It requires structure within the soul. Joseph does not drift emotionally when forgotten. He demonstrates three traits that every Driver Seat leader must possess if they are going to remain steady when life feels stalled.

1. Identity Anchored Internally, Not Publicly

Joseph's sense of self is not tied to who remembers him. He knows who he is even when no one else does. Great leaders do not outsource identity to recognition. Titles shift. Visibility fluctuates. Applause fades. If affirmation is the fuel, instability will follow. Driver Seat leaders build identity on conviction, not attention. They understand that obscurity does not erase calling. When your identity is internal, silence does not dismantle you. You are not defined by who mentions your name in the room. You are defined by who you are when no one does.

In everyday leadership, this shows up when you are overlooked for promotion but continue producing excellence. It shows up when your contribution is not acknowledged, yet your standards remain intact. It shows up when no one validates your effort, but you do not lower your integrity to be seen. Identity anchored internally is emotional independence from applause.

2. Purpose Driven, Not Platform Dependent

Joseph continues interpreting dreams because it is his calling, not because it is his platform. His gift is not contingent upon environment. Great leaders operate from purpose, not position. They do not wait for optimal conditions to contribute. They do not suspend their discipline because circumstances are unfavorable. They understand that calling precedes visibility.

This is the leader who mentors even when their own career feels paused. This is the entrepreneur who keeps building even after setbacks. This is the pastor who keeps serving even when attendance fluctuates. Platform dependent leaders shrink when spotlight dims. Purpose driven leaders remain consistent because their why is larger than their where.

3. Consistency Governed by Character, Not Reaction

We touched on Joseph not becoming bitter, passive, or cynical. He stays aligned with his character even when his environment is misaligned with his destiny. Great leaders do not allow disappointment to rewrite their disposition. They do not let silence produce sarcasm. They do not let delay produce disengagement. Reaction is easy. Regulation is discipline.

This trait is visible when others change and you remain steady. When someone forgets you and you do not harden. When progress is delayed and you do not compromise. Emotional maturity is not the absence of feeling. It is the governance of feeling. Driver Seat leaders feel the weight but refuse to be ruled by it.

These three traits keep Joseph behind the wheel of his own soul. He cannot control the timing, but he can control his posture. He cannot control the cupbearer's memory, but he can control his own maturity. He cannot control when Pharaoh calls, but he can control who he is when the call comes. And that is the essence of staying in the Driver Seat.

Stability is Not Stagnation

Joseph's steadiness is not passivity. It is strength restrained. It is the quiet confidence of someone who knows that God's timing cannot be manipulated and God's purpose cannot be rushed. Stability is not the absence of movement; it is the presence of mastery. It is the ability to remain aligned with your calling even when your conditions are misaligned with your expectations. Joseph is not stuck; he is being fortified. He is not sidelined; he is being shaped. He is not forgotten by God; he is being established for God's moment.

The Leadership Truth Beneath The Principle

The Driver Seat Principle teaches that leadership is not proven when doors open but when they stay closed. It is not proven when people applaud but when people forget. It is not proven when you are promoted but when you are overlooked. Joseph's greatness is not revealed when he stands before Pharaoh; it is revealed when he sits in prison and remains himself. His readiness in Genesis 41 is the residue of repetition in Genesis 40. Practice under pressure becomes poise under promotion. He is ready because he never stopped being who he was.

Chapter 7 ends with Joseph confined but emotionally regulated, and that detail mattered more than the confinement itself. The walls around him are still present, but the chaos inside him is no longer in charge. This is the quiet victory most readers rush past. We are conditioned to celebrate open doors and visible breakthroughs, but Scripture lingers here on something far rarer: a man who has lost freedom without losing himself. Joseph is restricted, but he is not reactive. He is limited, but he is not unstable. The storm that once lived inside him has learned how to be still, and that is no small miracle.

Emotional regulation is not the absence of feeling; it is the refusal to let feelings dictate directions. Joseph is no longer ruled by the moment. He has moved from being driven by circumstances to sitting firmly in the driver's seat of his inner life. There is a profound difference between confinement and captivity, and Joseph teaches us that captivity is internal long before it is external. Many people walk free while remaining imprisoned by resentment, fear, and unfinished grief. Joseph, however, sits confined while emotionally grounded, and this reversal is intentional. Before God entrusts him with movement, He ensures that stillness no longer threatens him. Before Joseph is allowed to steer outcome, he must prove that he can govern himself once again.

This is the hidden curriculum of leadership. If you cannot regulate your inner world, you will inevitably abuse the outer world once power is placed in your hands. That's why we move into chapter 8 quietly, almost unremarkably, with Joseph contributing while still restricted. No announcements, no ceremonies, just usefulness emerging from limitations. This is the shift from internal formation to external usefulness, and it is one of the most misunderstood transitions in the entire narrative. Joseph does not wait for freedom to be valuable. He does not postpone contribution until conditions improve. He begins to serve, he begins to interpret, he begins to assist, to bring clarity while still being confined.

The most uncomfortable truth in life is how you deal with what you do not see coming. And this is where many people miss their moment because they have been taught that usefulness requires permission. Joseph demonstrates that usefulness flows from maturity, not mobility. This is where driver seat language becomes essential. Joseph is not in control of his environment, but he is in command of his responses. He is not steering a vehicle of circumstances, but he is firmly seated behind the wheel of self-awareness, restraint, and discernment. Too many people confuse the passenger seat with powerlessness and the driver's seat with authority, but the driver's seat is not about position; it's about posture. It's about who is making decisions when pressure rises. It's about what voice you listen to when fear offers directions. Joseph is confined, but he is not being dragged by his emotions. He is not hijacked by bitterness. He is not negotiating with despair. He is driving himself even while the road remains closed.

There is philosophical weight to the moment that deserves attention. The ancient thinkers understood something we often forget. Freedom is not primary; it's partial. It is existential. You can be limited in movement and expansive in meaning. You can be restricted in access and rich in agency. Joseph embodies this truth. His body is confined, but his mind is disciplined. His options are limited, but his integrity is expansive. He is no longer asking, "Why is this happening to me?" He is asking, "Who am I becoming while this is happening?" This is the question of a man who has moved from reaction to reflection.

Here is the unsettling thought many would rather avoid: God often allows restrictions to remain long after regulation has been achieved. Why? Because regulation proves maturity, but contribution proves readiness. Emotional stability alone is not the goal; it is the foundation. God is not simply shaping who Joseph is; He is preparing how Joseph will serve. And service is the real test of formation. Can you add value without visibility? Can you bring clarity without credit? Can you help others move forward while you yourself remain stationary? These are not rhetorical questions meant to inspire; they are diagnostic questions meant to reveal.

Joseph began interpreting dreams not as a strategy for escape but as an expression of stewardship. This distinction matters. When contributions become transactional, they poison the soul. When usefulness is offered merely as a means to an end, it corrupts integrity. Remember, Joseph does not interpret to manipulate his release. He interprets because clarity is now a part of who he is. He has become the kind of man who brings order where confusion reigns. He has become the kind of man who listens deeply enough to name meaning. Stop using your gifts as leverage and start offering them as service. There's a quote I want to leave with you: maturity is when your gift no longer needs to be used as a bargaining chip.

Joseph is no longer hustling for freedom. He is anchored in faithfulness, and faithfulness, contrary to popular belief, is not passive. It is active alignment with purpose even when outcomes are delayed. Joseph has not resigned. He is resolved. He has accepted that his worth is not suspended until circumstances change, and that acceptance frees him to be useful without being desperate. This chapter forces an uncomfortable realization upon us as readers. Many of us want external usefulness without internal formation. We want influence before introspection, platforms before patience, and visibility before vulnerability. But Joseph's story dismantles that sequence entirely. He shows us that usefulness divorced from formation produces damage, not deliverance. Influence without emotional regulation becomes tyranny. Insight without humility becomes manipulation. Authority without restraint becomes destructive.

God is not delaying Joseph's rise. He is safeguarding the world Joseph will one day touch. Consider this question carefully. What would happen if God answered your prayers for expansion before your inner life could handle the pressure of being seen? What if the delay you resent is actually the protection you need? Joseph's confinement is not evidence of divine indifference. It is evidence of divine precision. God is not merely preparing Joseph for a role. He is preparing Joseph for the weight of consequences that role will carry. Leadership is not about control. It is about consequence management. Every decision Joseph will one day make will ripple across nations. That kind of responsibility demands a man who is no longer governed by impulse.

The prison did not change Joseph's future; it changed Joseph's reflexes. He no longer reacts from fear. He no longer interprets reality through the lens of betrayal. He no longer needs affirmation to function. He contributes from wholeness, not hunger, and this is the true mark of someone who belongs in the driver's seat. They do not need the road to cooperate in order to remain composed.

There is a contrast worth noticing here, one that Scripture quietly invites us to see. Joseph's stability in confinement stands in sharp opposition to Saul's instability in kingship. Saul had position, visibility, and authority, yet he was governed by insecurity and impulse. Joseph had none of those things, yet he was governed by clarity and restraint. Saul threw spears when he felt threatened. Joseph interpreted dreams when he felt forgotten. Saul's inner world corrupted his leadership; Joseph's inner world prepared him for leadership. This contrast reveals a sobering truth: God is far more concerned with the condition of a leader's interior life than the size of their platform. Influence without regulation becomes dangerous, but confinement with regulation becomes preparation.

Joseph's posture in prison also foreshadows the way Jesus carries Himself in His own unjust confinement. Jesus stands before Pilate silent, centered, and unshaken, not because the moment is fair but because His identity is not dictated by external injustice. He does not retaliate. He does not panic. He does not negotiate with fear. He remains aligned with His mission even when misunderstood and mistreated. Joseph's prison and Jesus' trial reveal the same spiritual pattern: God entrusts the greatest assignments to those who can remain grounded when falsely confined. Emotional regulation is not a modern concept imposed on an ancient text; it is a thread woven through the entire biblical story.

What Joseph displays is not a single moment of heroic self-control. It is the cumulative effect of repeated choices. Every time he refuses bitterness, he is rewiring his reflexes. Every time he chooses service over self-pity, he is training his nervous system to respond differently to pressure. By the time Pharaoh calls, Joseph is not improvising calm; he is expressing what has been rehearsed in hiddenness. Formation is not only spiritual; it is neurological. Your nervous system learns what your soul repeats. Joseph's steadiness is not accidental. It is the fruit of disciplined repetition in obscurity.

And Joseph's inner work does not benefit only Joseph. Emotional regulation is never a private luxury; it is a communal safeguard. The stability he cultivates in prison becomes the stability he offers to a starving world. When famine arrives, Egypt does not need a reactive leader. It needs a regulated one. Your inner life is not just about your peace; it is about the safety of everyone who will one day live under the influence of your decisions. This is why God takes His time with some of us. He is not only protecting our future. He is protecting the people our future will touch. Joseph's formation is not merely personal—it is generational.

This leads to a question Joseph's story presses upon us with uncomfortable clarity: Where do you still require external change before you will allow internal change? If your peace depends on promotion, your peace is fragile. If your usefulness depends on visibility, your usefulness is conditional. Joseph's story invites you to locate the places where you are still bargaining with God for movement before you will offer maturity. Those are the very places God is most committed to transforming. Joseph's confinement exposes the truth many avoid: God is not waiting for your environment to shift. He is waiting for your interior world to stabilize.

Prayer

Father, shape my inner world before You expand my outer one. Teach me to be steady when life is unstable, faithful when I feel unseen, and useful even when I am confined. Regulate my emotions, purify my motives, and strengthen my reflexes. Make me the kind of person who can carry responsibility without being crushed by it. Prepare me in hidden places so I can serve well in visible ones. And when the moment comes, let me be ready not because I forced my way forward, but because You formed me in the dark. Amen.

Driver Seat Key Takeaways

- Emotional regulation is the first victory, not external freedom. Joseph's breakthrough begins inside him long before anything changes around him. Stability precedes mobility.

- Confinement and captivity are not the same. Joseph is confined physically but free internally. Many people live the opposite—externally free but internally imprisoned.

- God tests stillness before He trusts movement. Before Joseph can steer outcomes, he must prove he can govern himself.

- Usefulness does not require visibility. Joseph serves, interprets, and contributes while unseen. Maturity expresses itself even in obscurity.

- Gifts become dangerous when used as leverage. Joseph interprets dreams as stewardship, not manipulation. His gift is no longer a bargaining chip.

- Formation is proven through contribution, not comfort. God leaves Joseph in restriction long enough to reveal whether he can add value without applause.

- Leadership requires mastery of reflex, not just mastery of skill. Joseph's prison years reshape his instincts—he no longer reacts from fear, insecurity, or hunger.

- Inner work is never private; it protects the people you will one day lead. Joseph's emotional stability becomes Egypt's salvation. Regulated leaders create safe environments.

- The gift that marks you may wound you before it elevates you. Joseph could interpret everyone else's dreams except his own. His gift confused him before it clarified him.

- God delays elevation not to punish you but to protect what your influence will touch. Joseph's confinement is divine precision. God is shaping a man who can carry national consequence without collapsing.

***

Joseph has now reached the point where his inner world is steady, his gift is purified, and his reflexes are aligned with purpose. He is no longer driven by desperation or shaped by the need to be seen. He is ready, even though he does not know it. And this is where the story turns.

Because while Joseph is practicing faithfulness in a forgotten place, God is stirring a crisis in a palace. While Joseph is interpreting dreams in confinement, Pharaoh is about to dream a dream that no one in Egypt can interpret. The moment Joseph has been prepared for is forming outside his awareness.

Chapter 9 opens with a truth every leader must eventually face:

When God decides the time is right, your name will be called in rooms you've never entered.

Joseph's preparation is about to collide with Pharaoh's need. The years of obscurity are about to meet a moment of opportunity. And the man who once begged to be remembered is about to be summoned because God remembered him.

Now we step into the day Joseph's preparation pays off, the day Pharaoh calls.

SECTION THREE

THE RISE OF A DRIVER

CHAPTER NINE

Pharaoh's Call: The Day Your Preparation Pays Off

Every life contains moments that arrive so quietly they almost escape notice, yet they hold enough weight to bend the story in a new direction. We often imagine destiny announcing itself with sound and sign, but Scripture reveals something far more subtle: turning points rarely knock; they simply appear. Genesis 41 opens with one of those understated disruptions. There is no trumpet, no warning, no emotional preparation, just a line that shifts the atmosphere of Joseph's life without asking permission. **"And it came to pass at the end of two full years, that Pharaoh dreamed..." (Genesis 41:1).** It is an introduction without drama, but it signals that heaven is moving again.

The text does not linger to rehearse Joseph's pain or repeat the emotional toll of the previous chapters. It simply marks time, two years, and moves forward. What makes this significant is not the length of the wait but the silence surrounding it. Nothing in Joseph's environment suggested that anything was changing. Nothing around him hinted that a door was forming. The prison looked the same, the routines felt the same, the responsibilities remained the same. The two years represent the mystery of God's timing rather than the burden of Joseph's waiting. They show us that God often finishes what He is building long before He reveals what He has planned. Timing is not measured in emotion; it is measured in divine readiness.

This is the subtle power of the opening: the chapter does not focus on how long Joseph waited, it focuses on how quickly God moved once the moment arrived. One sentence collapses years of stillness, making it clear that God's pace does not follow human logic. Joseph moves from confinement to summons without transition, without buildup, and without explanation. The shift is abrupt, almost jarring. It reminds us that God's movements are often imperceptible until the very moment they break through. When the text says, "Then Pharaoh sent and called Joseph," it is describing more than a royal request, it is describing the collision of preparation and divine timing.

What makes the moment remarkable is not simply that God acted, but that He acted suddenly. We assume that suddenness means emergency, but Scripture often uses suddenness to signal confidence. God does not hurry because He is late or pressured; He moves quickly because the vessel is ready. Sudden acceleration is not divine panic, it is divine assurance. Heaven does not rush Joseph; heaven reveals Joseph. What looks abrupt to the human eye is simply the unveiling of what God has been forming in secrecy.

The stability Joseph carries into this moment is not accidental. God does not move suddenly until He knows the person He is promoting will not be destabilized by the speed. Sudden opportunity is not a sign of crisis but a sign of completion. This is why the moment feels both shocking and intentional. Joseph does not ease his way into influence; he is interrupted into it. One moment he is navigating the rhythms of obscurity, and the next he is standing before the throne of the most powerful man in the world. The text gives no indication that Joseph had time to prepare emotionally, reenvision his life, process the implications, or rehearse what he might say. It is a reminder that divine timing does not consult human readiness; it reveals it.

Then the narrative shifts to Pharaoh himself, a man disturbed by dreams no one can interpret. His spirit is troubled, his advisors are ineffective, and his intellect cannot give him rest. The palace is confused, the experts are silent, and the nation's leader is unsettled. And while the kingdom freezes under uncertainty, a memory awakens in the mind of the cupbearer. What Joseph could not make happen for himself, God brought to the surface through someone who had forgotten him completely. The timing is not manipulated, influenced, or orchestrated by Joseph's effort; it is summoned by the weight of what Joseph carries. That is the Driver Seat truth revealed in this moment: preparation always meets opportunity at the intersection of divine timing, not human striving.

From Forgotten to Summoned

Genesis 41:14 records the moment everything shifts: "Then Pharaoh sent and called Joseph, and they brought him hastily out of the dungeon…" The summons comes with startling speed. One moment Joseph is living the quiet, repetitive rhythm of confinement, and the next he is being pulled into a moment he did not request and did not expect. The swiftness of the shift is almost disorienting. Divine timing rarely gives a countdown. Heaven moves when heaven decides, and Joseph's entire environment changes before he has time to process what is happening around him.

Yet Scripture immediately pauses to highlight a detail so understated it is often overlooked, yet so revealing it reframes the entire moment: Joseph shaves, changes his clothes, and presents himself. Before he interprets a dream. Before he stands before power. Before the outcome is known. He attends to himself. This is not cosmetic. It is psychological. It is theological. It is the quiet declaration of someone who has learned how to sit in the Driver Seat of his own life. The Driver Seat is not about controlling circumstances; it is about governing self. Too many people confuse power with position and authority with arrival, but Joseph shows us something deeper. Long before he governs a nation, he governs his responses. Long before he commands resources, he commands himself. Joseph does not rush from captivity into presence as a desperate man hoping to be rescued. He moves deliberately as a composed man prepared to be revealed. Destiny does not excuse disorder. Joseph understands that how he enters Pharaoh's court will speak as loudly as anything he says once he is standing there.

The single act of shaving is loaded with meaning. It speaks of self-regulation, the discipline to pause rather than panic. It reveals readiness, not as ambition, but as preparedness. Joseph does not know if this meeting will elevate him or end him, yet he refuses to show up fragmented. He refuses to let urgency dictate his presentation. In Driver Seat language, this is mastery over impulse. This is the refusal to let circumstance grab the wheel. If urgency can rush you, it can rule you. Joseph will not be ruled by the moment. He will not be dragged into opportunity unprepared or undone.

And the act of changing clothes is not merely cultural; it is symbolic. Joseph has worn many garments in his life, the robe of favor, the stripped fabric of betrayal, the plain clothes of servitude, the anonymity of confinement. Now he chooses what he will wear. For the first time in the narrative, Joseph is not dressed by someone else's decision. He steps into self-authored readiness. This is Driver Seat maturity, when identity is no longer assigned by trauma, injustice, or environment, but consciously assumed with intention. Many people reach opportunity still dressed in the garments of their last wound. They carry bitterness into boardrooms, insecurity into pulpits, and fear into influence. Joseph refuses this. He does not drag yesterday's humiliation into today's possibility. He does not allow the prison to speak louder than the moment. This is not denial; it is discernment. He knows unresolved pain cannot be allowed to drive. Healing begins when you stop letting yesterday dress you for today.

Joseph's emergence from confinement is not simply a rescue; it is a revealing. Pharaoh's call is not just Joseph's breakthrough; it is his audit. Everything he learned in confinement will now be measured under exposure. And because Joseph learned how to listen before he learned how to lead, he does not rush to impress. He interprets. He explains. He points upward. He refuses to confuse insight with ownership. He is steady because his formation was slow. He is calm because his preparation was deep. He is ready because his reflexes were reshaped in obscurity. This is why preparation matters. Preparation is not about rehearsing the role; it is about reshaping the reflexes. Who you become in slow seasons determines how you respond in sudden ones. When pressure hits, you do not rise to the level of opportunity; you default to the level of formation. Joseph is not overwhelmed by the acceleration because the acceleration is not creating who he is, it is revealing who he has become.

The Psychology of Sudden Elevation

Genesis 41:15 captures the moment Joseph stands in a room his suffering once made unthinkable: "I have dreamed a dream, and there is none that can interpret it: and I have heard say of thee, that thou canst understand a dream to interpret it." Now the spotlight is on Joseph. Imagine the pressure: thirteen years of betrayal, servitude, confinement—and now one conversation determines trajectory. The weight of sudden visibility can overwhelm even strong leaders. Promotion shock is real. Psychologically, sudden elevation can destabilize identity if preparation was shallow. Many rise into opportunity but collapse under the emotional speed of it. But Joseph's response reveals internal stability. His spirit is not trembling in the presence of power, because he has already learned how to carry weight in the absence of witnesses.

Genesis 41:16 records Joseph's answer, and it arrests the moment with humility and clarity: "And Joseph answered Pharaoh, saying, It is not in me: God shall give Pharaoh an answer of peace." And yet again, he does not grab credit. He does not shrink in insecurity. He does not overperform to impress. He redirects glory and remains calm. This is integrated leadership: confidence without ego, humility without timidity. Joseph is not the 17-year-old dreamer anymore. He is refined. The trials did not break him; they balanced him. The years did not silence him; they sobered him. He stands before Pharaoh with a posture that announces formation, not performance.

Driver Seat principle: You do not rise to the level of opportunity, you default to the level of formation. When pressure hits, you don't think your way forward; you reveal your training. Pharaoh does not just summon Joseph's gift; he summons Joseph's composure, a man who can stand under power without craving it, who can speak clearly without needing validation, who can influence a king without being intoxicated by proximity. That kind of presence is not learned in public; it is forged in restriction. The paradox of readiness is that the ones most prepared often feel the least entitled. When you've already been stripped, elevated moments don't intoxicate you. When you've already been humbled, power doesn't confuse you. Preparation produces calm. Those who have nothing to prove cannot be provoked. Those who have learned contentment cannot be manipulated. Joseph does not perform; he simply stands as who he already is.

Sudden elevation is only dangerous to those who were inflated privately. Joseph's stability in this moment is evidence that his identity was no longer attached to circumstance. He could serve in prison without collapsing, and now he can stand in Pharaoh's court without craving. This emotional equilibrium, this groundedness, is what makes him trustworthy. God does not promote giftedness; He promotes wholeness. And Joseph stands whole.

Interpretation and Strategy

Pharaoh recounts the dreams: seven fat cows, seven lean cows; seven full ears of corn, seven thin ears. Joseph interprets without hesitation. Genesis 41:25–27 records his words: "God hath shewed Pharaoh what he is about to do..." Seven years of abundance. Seven years of famine. Joseph moves through divine revelation with a steadiness that reflects both clarity and confidence. But Joseph does something remarkable. He does not stop at interpretation. He moves into strategy.

Genesis 41:33 captures this transition: "Now therefore let Pharaoh look out a man discreet and wise, and set him over the land of Egypt." Joseph shifts from prophetic insight to executive planning. This is leadership evolution. In prison, he interpreted dreams. In the palace, he builds policy. He proposes storage systems, administrative structure, resource management, and long-term planning. This is systems thinking under pressure. Joseph is not simply spiritual; he is strategic. Not simply insightful; he is infrastructural. Not simply gifted; he is governmental. He has learned that revelation without structure cannot sustain itself.

Driver Seat principle: Vision without structure collapses. Interpretation without implementation is incomplete. Joseph is not just spiritually insightful; he is administratively competent, built in Potiphar's house, refined in prison, stabilized in delay. The environments that frustrated him the most forged him the deepest. The systems he served under now empower him to build systems of his own. This is why the palace recognizes him: not for his hope but for his handling, not for his dreams but for his design.

This leads naturally into one of the most foundational theological and psychological frameworks of Joseph's leadership: why destiny never rides shotgun.

There is a theology many people inherit without ever questioning it, a belief that sounds humble but quietly erodes responsibility. It shows up in songs, in prayers, and in Christian slogans: "God, take the wheel." It sounds spiritual. It feels surrendered. But it is dangerously incomplete. Scripture does not present God as a chauffeur driving passive passengers toward purpose. Scripture presents God as an architect who hands us keys, gives directions, and expects participation. Destiny is not automatic. It is collaborative. And the moment we confuse surrender with inactivity, we step out of alignment with how God actually works in the world.

Joseph's story dismantles this theology without ever announcing its intent. At no point does Joseph sit back and wait for destiny to arrive. He interprets dreams. He offers strategy. He explains outcomes. He manages systems. He reads seasons. He prepares for famine before famine ever arrives. Faith in Joseph's life is not spiritual idleness; it is engaged obedience. He prays, but he also plans. He trusts God, but he also thinks. He honors heaven without abandoning responsibility on earth.

This is where the Driver Seat metaphor becomes unavoidable. Destiny does not unfold for those waiting in the passenger seat. Destiny responds to those who are willing to sit upright, hands on the wheel, eyes forward, aware that God governs direction while expecting participation. God determines the destination, but He never removes human agency from the journey. The wheel was never meant to be surrendered; it was meant to be stewarded.

Driver Seat Quote: "Faith is not letting go of the wheel. Faith is learning how to drive without panicking when the road bends."

The illusion that God will do everything while we do nothing is not biblical; it is convenient. It absolves us from thinking deeply, choosing wisely, and acting courageously. But Joseph's life exposes a deeper truth: God does not override human involvement, He dignifies it. Destiny does not replace decision-making; it demands it.

Joseph does not rise because he waits correctly. He rises because he engages correctly. Notice the progression. When Joseph is asked to interpret dreams, he does not say, "God will handle it." He listens. He discerns. He speaks. When he recognizes what the dreams mean, he does not stop at revelation. He moves into strategy. He designs storage systems. He calculates years of abundance and scarcity. He proposes logistics. He assigns roles. This is not mystical passivity. This is disciplined participation.

> **Driver Seat Quote:** "Revelation without responsibility creates spectators, not stewards."

This is the core failure of "God take the wheel" theology. It treats destiny as something that happens around us rather than something that flows through us. It assumes God prefers silence over thought, waiting over wisdom, and stillness over stewardship. But Scripture reveals something far more demanding: God entrusts destiny to those willing to engage their mind, discipline their will, and align their actions with divine intention.

Joseph's faith is not proven in worship alone; it is proven in systems. Not just in prayer but in preparation. Not just in vision but in execution. Destiny does not reward intention alone; it responds to alignment.

This is where the Driver Seat framework clarifies everything. To sit in the Driver Seat means you acknowledge three truths simultaneously. First, God determines purpose. Second, you are responsible for posture. Third, movement requires cooperation. God is sovereign, but sovereignty does not cancel stewardship. Grace does not eliminate effort; it directs it. Calling does not excuse immaturity; it demands development.

> **Driver Seat Quote:** "God writes purpose in ink. We trace it in action."

Joseph never confuses divine favor with divine micromanagement. He understands that God reveals direction, but humans must navigate terrain. He reads the signs of the times and responds accordingly. He does not wait for famine to arrive before preparing. He does not pray away responsibility. He does not spiritualize avoidance. He engages.

This is why Joseph survives power without being corrupted by it. Because he learned early that destiny does not drive itself. Many people want prophetic insight without strategic thinking. They want promises without process. They want arrival without accountability. But destiny resists entitlement. It yields only to participation.

> **Driver Seat Quote:** "Destiny is not drawn to those who believe loudly; it is drawn to those who live deliberately."

There is a subtle but critical distinction between surrender and abdication. Surrender submits your will to God's direction. Abdication refuses responsibility under the guise of spirituality. Joseph surrenders; he never abdicates. He bows his heart without disengaging his mind. He honors God without abandoning agency.

This reframes faith entirely. Faith is not waiting for clarity before moving; it is moving responsibly with the clarity you have. Faith is not the absence of planning; it is planning in alignment with revelation. Faith is not passive trust; it is active obedience.

Joseph's ability to interpret dreams would have meant nothing if he refused to act on them. Revelation without response is spiritual negligence. God did not give Joseph insight so he could feel special; He gave him insight so he could save lives.

> **Driver Seat Quote:** "God reveals the future to those willing to take responsibility for the present."

This is where human inactivity becomes the greatest threat to destiny.

Not sin. Not failure. Not opposition. But passivity. The refusal to engage. The tendency to spiritualize delay. The habit of waiting for conditions to be perfect before committing to action.

Joseph does not wait for certainty to become complete before acting. He acts decisively within uncertainty. He prepares for what he believes is coming, trusting that obedience will meet provision along the way.

The Driver Seat requires courage. It requires thought. It requires risk. You cannot sit in it and pretend ignorance. You cannot blame circumstances. You cannot outsource responsibility to God and call it faith.

Driver Seat Quote: "The Driver Seat is where prayer meets planning and belief meets behavior."

Joseph's leadership reveals a God who partners, not puppeteers. A God who entrusts responsibility rather than removes it. A God who expects maturity, not magical thinking. Destiny unfolds not because Joseph waits correctly, but because he responds wisely.

This chapter is not about control. It is about cooperation. Not about independence from God, but alignment with Him. Sitting in the Driver Seat does not mean you know every turn ahead. It means you are willing to stay alert, responsive, and obedient as the road unfolds.

Driver Seat Quote: "God governs direction. We govern response. Destiny happens where the two meet."

When faith becomes disengaged, destiny stalls. When obedience becomes embodied, destiny accelerates. Joseph understood this, and that understanding made him trustworthy with influence. He did not wait for destiny to rescue him; he prepared himself to steward it.

The Driver Seat is not a place of arrogance; it is a place of responsibility. It is where humility meets intentionality. It is where prayer informs action. It is where destiny stops being abstract and becomes embodied. And the quiet truth is this: God has never been looking for passengers. He has always been forming drivers.

Driver Seat Quote: "Destiny does not need spectators. It needs participants willing to stay awake on the road."

The Day Capacity Is Recognized

Pharaoh responds with words that reveal both discernment and divine orchestration. Genesis 41:38–39 records the moment: "Can we find such a one as this is, a man in whom the Spirit of God is?... Forasmuch as God hath shewed thee all this, there is none so discreet and wise as thou art." Recognition arrives, but notice something important: Joseph did not announce himself. He did not campaign. He did not defend his résumé. He did not try to open the door. He simply showed up ready. That is the mystery of capacity in God's economy, when the moment requires what you carry, you do not need to force visibility; visibility finds you.

Genesis 41:41 continues the revelation: "And Pharaoh said unto Joseph, See, I have set thee over all the land of Egypt." From prisoner to Prime Minister. In a day. But not in a moment. It took thirteen years to build what was revealed in a conversation. Elevation is not sudden; it is revealed suddenly. Capacity was layered slowly. Joseph's authority is not manufactured in the throne room; it is recognized there. Pharaoh does not just see Joseph's theology; he sees Joseph's functionality. He sees a man who can think beyond crisis, who can forecast seasons, who can build structures, who can bear weight. He does not see a man who was human trafficked, betrayed, lied on, or falsely accused; he does not see the residue of Joseph's past because a Driver Seat leader carries their history without wearing it. Like a skilled driver who knows every scar on the road they traveled, Joseph arrives without looking like the miles he survived. Pharaoh sees not the trauma that tried to break him, but the stewardship that shaped him. He sees Joseph the way God sees Joseph, not through the lens of what wounded him, but through the lens of what he became. Pharaoh responds to capacity, foresight, design, restraint, and competence. True authority does not announce itself; it explains what others cannot see. It is not noisy; it is necessary. When Joseph speaks, Pharaoh hears not talent but trustworthiness.

Recognition is never about charisma; it is always about capacity. Charisma can open a door, but only capacity can keep you in the room. Joseph is elevated not because he is impressive, but because he is integral. Not just because he is gifted, but because he is favored by God. Favor does not excuse the need for formation; it empowers the formation God has already done. Favor gives access, but integrity sustains it. Joseph stands before Pharaoh as a man whose life carries the weight of divine endorsement, not the polish of human performance. This is the kind of leader heaven backs, a leader who can be trusted privately long before being promoted publicly. Joseph's story proves that when your formation is real, your fruit will speak for itself. Favor does not shout; it shows. Capacity does not boast; it is revealed. And when both converge in a single life, elevation becomes recognition rather than rescue.

Promotion Without Collapse

Joseph is given Pharaoh's ring, fine linen, a gold chain, a new name, a wife, and authority. Genesis 41:43 adds the public spectacle: "And he made him to ride in the second chariot which he had..." Public validation. Visible honor. Power. Psychologically, this is dangerous. Many leaders collapse under sudden authority because their identity is still fragile. Recognition can become intoxication. Access can become an addiction. Influence can become instability. But Joseph has survived rejection, injustice, isolation, and being forgotten. He is not intoxicated by applause. He is not reactive to power. He has already learned restraint. Before he ever carries Egypt, he learned how to carry himself.

What is striking about this moment is not only the elevation but the redemption embedded within it. Joseph receives in one chapter what most hope to gather over decades. He receives position, honor, marriage, responsibility, provision, and legacy in a single sweep of divine acceleration. This is not coincidence; it is Scripture's witness that God restores lost years. Joel 2:25 declares, "I will restore to you the years that the locust has eaten," and Joseph's story becomes a living illustration of that promise. Thirteen years that looked wasted, stolen, and shattered are suddenly recovered in one decisive moment of divine favor. God is not simply elevating Joseph; He is compressing time on Joseph's behalf. He is proving that no season of loss can restrict a God who redeems time and rewrites outcomes.

At thirty years old, Joseph steps into the fullness of what most would expect much earlier. Age thirty is biblically symbolic; it is the age priests begin service, the age David becomes king, and the age Jesus begins His public ministry. It marks maturity, readiness, and spiritual completeness. At thirty, many dream of being established, settled, and secure, yet Joseph's twenties were consumed not by stability but by survival. Still, when the moment comes, God ensures Joseph stands not lacking but laden, given a family, given authority, given honor, given influence. God provides in one season what pain tried to delay in the previous ones. Restoration is not always God returning what you lost; sometimes it is God giving you what you never had the chance to receive.

Driver Seat principle: If you were not trained in the pit, promotion would crush you. Power does not test your ambition; it tests your integration. Can your inner life support your outer influence? Can your values survive proximity to control? Can your discernment function when applause enters the room? Opportunities do not expose your gifting; they expose your wiring. Joseph does not bring the prison into the palace. He brings discipline. He does not bring resentment; he brings discernment. He does not bring self-pity; he brings structural integrity. Preparation is not rehearsing the role; it is reshaping the conditioned responses. Joseph can sit in the second chariot because he first learned to sit with himself.

Elevation reveals what obscurity formed. Some leaders rise and immediately implode because the stage magnifies what still lives in their soul. But Joseph rises and remains steady. He walks into authority carrying not entitlement but endurance. He carries not ego but empathy. He carries not hunger for power but hunger for purpose. This is why his promotion does not collapse him. He was not shaped by applause; he was shaped by adversity. He was not validated by people; he was validated by God. Promotion simply reveals what preparation poured into him.

And in Joseph's elevation, we witness a final Driver Seat truth: God does not simply restore Joseph's years, He restores Joseph's trajectory. He restores Joseph's dignity. He restores Joseph's relational future. He restores Joseph's influence. God redeems the time Joseph lost by accelerating the fulfillment Joseph was destined for. What looked stolen becomes seed. What looked wasted becomes weave. What looked delayed becomes delivered. Joseph does not simply rise; he recovers. And every mile of his past becomes material for the leader he is now entrusted to be.

And here's a Driver Seat moment: If God did it for Joseph, He can do it for you too.

The Age Detail Matters

Genesis 41:46 gives us a detail so subtle it is often skimmed, yet so significant it reframes Joseph's journey: "And Joseph was thirty years old when he stood before Pharaoh king of Egypt." Seventeen when he was betrayed. Thirty when he was elevated. These numbers are not just markers of age; they are markers of formation. Thirteen years of shaping, stripping, stretching, and strengthening. Thirteen years of development, unwanted transitions, and stamina building. Years of misunderstanding, years of silence, years of discipline, years of being unseen. Thirteen years of responsibility without recognition that trained his character for authority without corruption. The palace did not make him a leader. The process did. The pit did. Potiphar's house did. The prison did. Leadership is not proven in visibility. It takes shape in the shadows. The call is fast; the making was slow.

The age detail tells us something profound about the making of a leader: God does not rush development. He does not elevate what has not been established. He does not graduate those who have not endured the curriculum. Many leaders never step into the fullness of what God intended, not because they were never called, but because they quit during the making. The pressure felt pointless. The waiting felt wasted. The process felt too long. Joseph's age proves that the process was not a penalty; it was positioning. The seasons that felt like detours were actually deposits. What looked like a delay was actually construction. Nothing was wasted, not the pain, not the silence, not the restraint, not the lessons. And like Joseph, nothing in your life will be wasted either. Not the pain that broke you, not the betrayal that stunned you, not the seasons that bruised you, not the silence that stretched you. God does not discard your story; He develops it. Every bruise becomes building material. Every setback becomes training. Every unanswered question becomes shaping. The very chapters you thought disqualified you are often the ones God uses to define you.

The making is what preserves the mandate. The process is what protects the purpose. And when the making is complete, elevation no longer feels like escape, it feels like assignment. Joseph's age is not a reminder of how long it took; it is a reminder that what God builds slowly, He trusts deeply. Joseph's age reminds us of something we resist in a culture obsessed with speed. We live in a microwave society that wants maturity without time, authority without process, influence without integration. We want it fast, visible, and now. But Joseph's story challenges us to pause. The age detail reminds us that maturity is never microwaved. It is formed through time, tension, and trust. It is built slowly, strengthened quietly, and proven under pressure before it is ever displayed in public.

Driver Seat Principle

Pharaoh's call is not random. It is timed. Joseph was ready, stable, humble, strategic, integrated. This chapter teaches: preparation pays off, but not always on your timeline. When timing meets preparation, doors open fast. But if preparation is missing, doors become pressure. Elevation does not create leaders. It reveals them. Destiny is not activated by desire; it is sustained by discipline. Joseph's emergence in this moment confirms that God does not simply schedule opportunity, He safeguards it by ensuring the one called will not erode under its weight.

You may feel forgotten. You may feel stalled. You may feel invisible. But if you stay behind the wheel, if you steward your gift in confinement, regulate your emotions in delay, and refuse to let bitterness rewrite your personality, the day will come when your preparation is required. And when it does, you will not scramble. You will respond. Prepared people do not fear, they step into alignment. Joseph does not perform for the moment, he matches it. His story is a reminder that God does not forget what you have built with integrity, what you have carried in your unseen season, or what you have maintained in silence. Heaven remembers formation even when earth ignores it.

Driver Seat Quote: "God moves suddenly only when He knows you won't lose yourself in the speed."

Prayer

Father, anchor me while You prepare me. Form my reflexes in hidden places so I can carry weight in public places. Give me the wisdom to shave what no longer belongs to this season, the courage to change what must be changed, and the humility to say, "It is not in me, God will give the answer of peace." Teach me to steward insight with strategy, power with purity, and opportunity with obedience. When the call comes, let me be calm, clear, and whole. Amen.

Driver Seat Key Takeaways

- **God prepares slowly; He moves quickly.** Delay is not divine disinterest; it is divine development. When God appears to move suddenly, it is only because He has been forming quietly.

- **Formation beats performance.**
  Under pressure, you default to training, not talent. Gifting may open a door, but formation determines whether you can survive what waits on the other side.

- **Presentation is participation.**
  Joseph shaved; he changed. Readiness is spiritual and practical. Stewardship includes showing up with intention, excellence, and dignity, because preparation is worship.

- **Strategy is spiritual.**
  Interpretation without implementation is incomplete; systems are sacred. God reveals direction, but humans must design structure. Heaven gives insight; earth demands execution.

- **Authority tests integration.**
  Power reveals whether your inner life can support your outer role. When doors open, whatever is unresolved will rise with you. Influence magnifies identity.

- **Destiny requires partnership.**
  God governs direction; you govern response. Favor is not a substitute for responsibility. Spiritual maturity is cooperation, not passiveness.

- **Process builds permanence.**
  Elevation reveals what obscurity formed. Sudden promotion is safe only when slow formation has done its work. The moments you thought were wasted were actually welding your foundation.

- **Readiness is identity in alignment.**
  Joseph's shaving, changing, and presenting himself show that leadership begins with governing self. Before God trusts you with people, He watches how you manage your posture.

- **Urgency is not leadership.**
  If urgency can rush you, it can rule you. Leaders who cannot regulate impulses will always interpret opportunity through fear rather than faith.

- **Wholeness precedes weight.**
  Joseph did not collapse under elevation because adversity had already sculpted his resilience. God promotes wholeness, not hype.

***

Joseph is now in position, authority in his hands, systems under his command, a nation depending on his decisions. But elevation is not the end of leadership development; it is the beginning of new pressure. Authority does not cancel family history. It exposes what formation has healed and what remains. The final tension arrives: you cannot lead your future if you are still negotiating with your past. Chapter 10 will ask: What happens when destiny finally hands you the wheel? Because getting the seat is one thing. Staying steady in it is another. Joseph is about to prove that leadership is not about arrival; it is about stewardship at every altitude.

CHAPTER TEN

THE REUNION: Confronting Trauma Without Losing Yourself

Genesis 42–44

There are some rooms you hope you never walk back into. Some faces you pray you never have to look at again. Some chapters you close with force, not peace. Joseph had built an entire life in Egypt with a new name, new language, new wardrobe, new wife, new title, and new authority. But trauma does not dissolve because you become successful.

The Famine Reaches Jacob's House

Genesis 42:1–5

The famine drives the story forward. While Joseph flourished in Egypt, famine pressed against Canaan. Scarcity forced Jacob to send Joseph's brothers to Egypt for grain, never imagining the son he mourned was the man controlling the distribution. Pain eventually comes back into the room, but when it does, you come back different. What resurfaces is not punishment—it is timing. Divine timing.

The famine forces a return to the unresolved. God will sometimes use external crisis to initiate internal confrontation. Joseph's brothers are heading toward Egypt believing they are chasing survival, unaware they are walking into a destiny fulfilled.

Joseph Recognizes His Brothers, But They Do Not Recognize Him

Genesis 42:6–8

"And Joseph was the governor over the land... and Joseph's brethren came, and bowed down themselves before him..." (Genesis 42:6). The dream had come true. The same brothers who stripped, threw, and sold him now bowed. "And Joseph remembered the dreams..." (Genesis 42:9). Not just the dreams, the moment, the pit, the betrayal, the sound of their voices. Trauma has memory. Trauma has memory. It resurfaces not to weaken you, but to show you what still needs integrating. Because trauma doesn't travel by logic, it travels by association. A voice that sounds like someone who hurt you. A room arranged like a place where you were dismissed. A conversation that echoes an old betrayal. A moment where your body suddenly doesn't feel safe, even though nothing "dangerous" is happening. This is how the nervous system works: it stores pattern, tone, sensation, and threat long after the event ends. Joseph remembered the dreams, yes, but he also remembered the tone of their mockery, the coldness in their faces, the echo of the pit walls, the tightening grip of the hands that threw him, the dust rising as the caravan of men enslaved him and sealed his fate. Trauma carries the full sensory file, not just the highlight reel. And here's the hard truth: healing doesn't erase memory; it transforms the meaning of it.

Leadership does not exempt you from emotional collision. In fact, leadership will place you in rooms you prayed never to see again, with people you thought were permanently behind you, and in scenarios that resurrect emotions you thought were long buried. Leadership doesn't shield you from triggers; it trains you to respond to them differently. Joseph was second in command of the most powerful empire in the world, and still, the sight of his brothers triggered tears he had to hide. Authority does not silence your humanity. Titles do not delete your triggers. Success does not sterilize your story.

Because leadership will always demand collisions:

Collisions between your past and your present

Collisions between your healed self and your old memories

Collisions between your wisdom and your wounds

Collisions between your assignment and your emotions

And if we're honest, Joseph's collision was profound. I couldn't imagine hearing the voices of the very brothers who trafficked me, sold me, abandoned me to strangers, and then went home and lived their lives as if mine did not matter. Psychologically, this is what is called trauma reactivation, when your brain encounters a familiar stimulus and instantly pulls the old file. The body reacts before the mind can reason. Your heart races. Your breathing shifts. Your internal alarms activate. Not because you are weak, but because your body remembers danger even when you are no longer in it.

Joseph didn't fall apart because he was fragile, he stepped away to weep because he was wise. He honored the collision without surrendering to it. That is the difference between a wounded leader and a healed one: a wounded leader reacts; a healed leader regulates. Collisions are inevitable; collapse is optional. The collision is not a sign that you're failing, it's a sign that you're feeling. And feeling is how God reveals what still needs refining.

For the reader who is here right now, standing in front of something or someone who mirrors an old wound, this is how you navigate it:

Honor your humanity. If Joseph needed a moment, so can you. Stepping away is not weakness; it's stewardship.

Recognize what your body is saying. Your nervous system reacts to patterns, not permission. Pay attention. Regulate before you respond.

Face the moment from your healed identity, not your old injury. Joseph didn't face his brothers as the boy who was thrown in the pit, he faced them as the man God had raised in the palace.

Seek clarity, not closure. Joseph assessed their behavior before offering reconciliation. Collisions are for discernment, not rush decisions.

Allow God to reframe what memory can't erase. Healing doesn't delete the story, God simply gives you power over the chapters that once held you hostage.

This is what leadership looks like: not the absence of triggers, but the presence of tools; not perfection, but regulation; not denial, but discernment; not collapse, but clarity. Driver Principle: Elevation can put you back in front of what once broke you, not to break you again, but to prove what healing has built.

Joseph Tests Them to See If They Have Changed

Genesis 42:9–20

Let's unpack this a little more and address what happens when you face the same people who wounded you. Joseph recognizes them immediately. They do not recognize him. When you heal, you evolve; if they haven't, they often don't recognize who you've become. Joseph could have exposed them, humiliated them publicly, or withheld food entirely. He had leverage. He had power. But power does not remove trauma; it reveals whether you've processed it. His authority didn't erase the pit. His position didn't delete the betrayal. His success didn't sterilize the story. Standing in front of the very men who trafficked him was not just a moment; it was a collision we discussed earlier that leaders often face. This time it was a collision between past wounds and present wisdom. And yet Joseph does not react; he responds. He observes, questions, and tests (Genesis 42–44). He watches how they treat Benjamin. He listens to Judah plead and offer himself (Genesis 44:18–34). He studies their behavior, their tone, their unity, their remorse. Joseph is not playing games; he is assessing transformation. He needs to know: Are you the same men who threw me away, or have the years carved something new into you?

Driver Seat principle: Trauma tries to pull you backward. Destiny demands you stand where you are.

Before reconciliation, you must discern. Because reconciliation without discernment is not grace, it is self-sabotage. Joseph did not run into his brothers' arms the moment he saw them. He did not announce, "It's me!" out of sentiment or shock. He observed. He questioned. He tested. He watched their interactions with one another. He studied their treatment of Benjamin. He listened to how they talked when they didn't know he could hear. Discernment is the distance you create long enough to see who people actually are, not who they say they are.

Joseph shows us that reconciliation is not a reflex; it is a responsibility. Just because your heart forgives does not mean your life must immediately reconcile. Forgiveness is internal, but reconciliation is relational. Forgiveness takes place in your spirit, but reconciliation requires evidence in someone else's character. Joseph is showing leaders and believers something many never learn: reconciliation is holy, but premature reconciliation is harmful. It reopens wounds God intended to heal. It gives access to people who have not yet proven they can be trusted. It places your healed places back into the hands of people who helped break them.

Joseph's restraint in this moment is not bitterness; it is wisdom. Many people confuse discernment with distrust, but they are not the same. Distrust assumes the worst. Discernment watches for the truth. Distrust reacts out of fear. Discernment responds out of clarity. Distrust closes every door. Discernment decides which doors should open. Joseph is not withholding reconciliation out of resentment. He is protecting the work God did in him. He is ensuring that the next chapter of his story will not repeat the pain of the last one.

Discernment is leadership's emotional intelligence at work. It is your spirit, your experience, your healing, and the Holy Spirit's wisdom all partnering together to help you see reality clearly. Discernment is the ability to pause long enough to separate apology from transformation, sorrow from change, emotion from accountability. Joseph proves that discerning leaders do not rush to restore what broke them. They wait, they watch, and they weigh behavior. They pay attention to fruit, not feelings. They listen for consistency, not convenience. They do not confuse remorse with repentance, and they do not confuse nostalgia with newness.

Joseph's testing of his brothers is not spite; it is stewardship. He is not being dramatic; he is being responsible. He is not punishing them; he is protecting what God entrusted to him. For years, Joseph has been faithful with assignments, faithful with emotions, faithful with power, faithful with pain. This is not the moment to abandon that stewardship just because familiar faces walked into the room. Joseph teaches us that healed people do not rush back into relationship simply because the opportunity appears. They discern the moment. They guard their healing. They evaluate character. They value safety. They move slowly. They allow wisdom to lead the conversation, not sentiment.

This is the lesson leaders and everyday people must learn: reconciliation requires discernment. Before you let someone close again, you must ask, "Are you safe for the healed version of me?" Before you rebuild trust, you must ask, "Have you grown enough to hold this relationship without breaking it again?" Before you reenter what once wounded you, you must ask, "Has God given me peace, or am I walking in pressure?" Joseph asked these questions through tests, through observation, through silence, through boundaries, and through wisdom. He teaches us that the heart can be open, but access must be earned. Forgiveness is something you give freely; reconciliation is something others must qualify for.

This is the wisdom of Joseph. This is the maturity of a healed leader. This is the way of a Driver Seat leader. And this is your permission to live by this leadership principle: before reconciliation, discernment.

This is why discernment must always come before reconciliation, because discernment protects the very healing God has built in you. Joseph shows us that wisdom is not cold and boundaries are not cruel; they are the way you honor what God has restored. Discernment allows your heart to forgive without your life becoming vulnerable to repeated injury. It allows you to love people without losing yourself. And once discernment has done its work, another truth becomes clear: forgiveness without wisdom is immaturity. It is giving full access to people who have only given partial repentance. It is allowing the most broken parts of others to repeatedly collide with the most healed parts of you. Forgiveness is holy, but reconciliation is strategic. Joseph forgave them long before they arrived in Egypt, but he did not reconcile with them until he saw proof that they had changed. Forgiveness is a heart posture; reconciliation is a behavioral decision.

And this is where many people fail, because without discernment, forgiveness can drift into bitterness when boundaries are absent.

Bitterness without boundaries is destruction. Bitterness punishes you; boundaries protect you. Bitterness hardens your heart; boundaries guard it.

Bitterness keeps the wound open; boundaries give it space to close. Some people do not need revenge, they need regulation. Some situations do not require retaliation, they require distance, clarity, and conditions. Joseph did not retaliate, but he did not rush either. His boundaries were not punishment, they were wisdom in motion. And it is this wisdom that leads us into one of the most essential principles of relational restoration, a principle most people never learn until they have been deeply wounded: reunion is not the same as restoration; restoration requires evidence.

Reunion is a moment; restoration is a measurable process. Reunion says, "We are in the same room again." Restoration says, "Your fruit matches your apology." Reunion is proximity; restoration is proof. Reunion is emotional; restoration is spiritual, behavioral, and observable. Joseph models this perfectly. This was not cruelty; it was assessment. Reconciliation cannot be based on nostalgia or need. It must be based on demonstrated change.

How Joseph assessed transformation is clear and scriptural. He tests their honesty. He evaluates their loyalty. He listens for remorse, not in their tears but in their choices. He looks for transformation in Judah's willingness to sacrifice himself. Evidence mattered then, and evidence matters now. It matters in the workplace when the colleague who undermined you now wants back on your project. Evidence looks like honest ownership, changed patterns, clear timelines, and accountability, not flattery and urgency. It matters in family dynamics when a relative returns after chaos. Evidence looks like consistent stability or sobriety, counseling follow-through, and boundaries honored, not tearful apologies without change. It matters in ministry teams when a leader who harmed trust seeks stage time. Evidence looks like a submitted process, quiet serving, restitution, and a willingness to be pastored, not entitlement to the platform.

Joseph's story shows us that discernment is love with eyes open. It refuses to confuse sentiment with safety. It does not romanticize the past or rush the future. It sits in the tension long enough to see whether fruit has replaced familiarity. Discernment protects your healed places from being re-injured. Discernment makes you slow, steady, prayerful, and observant. Reconciliation is not a sprint; it is a sequence, a series of revealed decisions, tested behaviors, and stable patterns that demonstrate someone is not who they used to be.

And Joseph models this sequence with holy precision. He does not weaponize his authority; he uses it to evaluate trust. He does not collapse under old emotions; he steps away to weep, then returns to lead. He does not seek revenge; he seeks revelation. He does not let the trauma of the boy override the wisdom of the man. Joseph shows us how healed people navigate old wounds: slowly, wisely, and with a clear eye on God's sovereignty. His discernment was not cold, it was careful. His boundaries were not judgment, they were protection. His testing was not manipulation, it was stewardship.

Psychologically speaking, trauma-informed wisdom distinguishes between emotional forgiveness and relational safety. Emotional forgiveness cleans the heart; relational safety protects the future. Joseph embodied both. His testing aligns with how trust is rebuilt; the nervous system needs new, consistent evidence before reopening old pathways. Joseph was not stalling; he was stabilizing. He was not being petty; he was protective. He was not withholding grace; he was stewarding it.

Joseph teaches every leader this: you do not owe instant reconciliation to anyone. You owe God your obedience, yourself your protection, and others the chance to show who they truly are now. And when evidence emerges, consistent, humble, transformed evidence, then, and only then, can restoration begin.

Simeon Is Bound — The First Test of Integrity

Genesis 42:21–24 says:

"And they said one to another, We are verily guilty concerning our brother, in that we saw the anguish of his soul, when he besought us, and we would not hear; therefore is this distress come upon us. And Reuben answered them, saying, Spake I not unto you, saying, Do not sin against the child; and ye would not hear? therefore, behold, also his blood is required. And they knew not that Joseph understood them; for he spake unto them by an interpreter. And he turned himself about from them, and wept; and returned to them again, and communed with them, and took from them Simeon, and bound him before their eyes."

This is where we are in the narrative. The brothers believe Joseph is dead or gone forever. They are standing before the brother they betrayed, confessing their guilt, unaware that he understands every word. Joseph hears them acknowledge his anguish. He hears them admit they ignored his cries. He hears them connect their current distress to their past sin.

And Joseph weeps.

Notice what happens. He does not interrupt them. He does not expose himself. He does not retaliate. He turns away and weeps privately. This is not regression. It is emotional honesty without emotional surrender. Old wounds are being revisited, but they are being revisited in a healed body.

Remember this: a wounded leader reacts. A healed leader regulates

Joseph's tears do not control him. They inform him. He allows himself to feel, but he does not allow himself to be ruled by what he feels. This is crucial. Many leaders think healing means the absence of emotion. Scripture shows something different. Healing means you can feel the collision without collapsing under it.

After weeping, Joseph returns and binds Simeon before their eyes.

Why Simeon? Simeon was one of the primary aggressors in the earlier violence against Joseph and later against Shechem in Genesis 34. Whether Joseph chose him for that reason or for strategic leverage, the act is intentional. It is structured. It is not wisdom. It is discernment. Joseph now holds power over the very men who once held power over him. This is the first true test of integrity. Integrity is not tested when you are powerless. It is tested when you are in control.

Joseph could have imprisoned all of them. He could have revealed himself and shamed them publicly. He could have retaliated. Instead, he chooses measured accountability. He keeps Simeon and sends the others back with grain, instructing them to return with Benjamin.

What is Joseph doing? He is testing transformation. He is creating a scenario that will reveal whether his brothers have changed. Will they abandon another brother as they abandoned him? Will they protect Benjamin? Will they take responsibility?

Here is "Before reconciliation, you must discernment," in motion.

Here are several learning principles from this moment.

First, emotional maturity does not mean emotional numbness. Joseph wept. Leaders who cannot weep are often leaders who have not processed. Feeling is not a weakness. Unregulated feeling is.

Second, power reveals character. Joseph's authority did not create integrity. It exposed whether integrity had been formed. The true test of leadership is not how you act when wounded, but how you act when you finally have the upper hand.

Third, reconciliation requires evidence. Forgiveness may be immediate in the heart, but trust is rebuilt through proof. Joseph does not rush restoration simply because guilt is confessed. He creates space for demonstrated change.

Fourth, discernment protects destiny. Joseph's role now affects nations, not just family. Emotional shortcuts could compromise everything. Mature leaders understand that personal healing must align with public responsibility.

Finally, integrity sometimes looks like restraint. Binding Simeon was not cruelty. It was clarity. Joseph refuses to let sentiment override wisdom. He does not deny the past, but he does not let it drive the present.

The Brothers Return to Jacob With Grain and Fear

Genesis 42:25–38

In this part of the story, Joseph's brothers have just completed their first encounter with him in Egypt. They still do not know who he is. Joseph fills their sacks with grain but secretly returns their silver. When they stop along the journey and discover the silver in their sacks, panic erupts among them. They assume judgment. They assume danger. They assume the worst. Their nervous system collapses into fear because fear is the language they were raised on. By the time they reach home and tell Jacob everything, Jacob spirals into deep despair and says, "Everything is against me." This is the generational pattern Joseph escaped. Trauma formed their responses; fear formed their worldview.

Jacob interprets life through loss because loss shaped him. The brothers interpret life through guilt because guilt shaped them. They are not reacting to the moment; they are reacting to the memories the moment awakens. What Joseph escaped through God's hand, they are still trapped in. Their emotional reflexes reveal what unhealed history does to a family: it turns every unknown into a threat and every crisis into catastrophe. This is why Joseph's story is so remarkable. Joseph was shaped by trauma, but he refused to be governed by it. His family allows fear to frame the future; Joseph allows God to frame it.

Driver Seat reminder: Your healing does not erase others' dysfunction, but it positions you to navigate it. You cannot control how they react, but you can control how you respond. You may grow, but the people you return to may still speak the language of fear, scarcity, blame, or panic. Leadership is learning to stay grounded in the presence of those who are still reacting from unhealed places. Joseph's brothers and father prove this. They interpret the silver as a curse. They interpret the famine as punishment. They interpret circumstances as loss upon loss. They are overwhelmed because they do not yet understand the sovereignty at work. But Joseph does. And that difference is the distinction between a leader who has been formed in God's process and a family still living in emotional survival.

Joseph's healing does not change their reactions, but it changes what their reactions produce. He is no longer shaped by the environment that once wounded him. He can see the panic but not absorb it. He can hear the fear but not inherit it. He can witness their despair but not sink into it. That is the evidence of healing. God did not heal Joseph so he could avoid dysfunction; He healed Joseph so he could lead within it. That is why the Driver Seat matters. Healing shifts you from reacting with your past to responding with your purpose.

The Second Journey — Judah Steps Up

Genesis 43

By the end of Genesis 42, the atmosphere in Jacob's household is thick with fear, guilt, and generational exhaustion. The silver in the sacks has shaken the brothers. Jacob's grief has resurfaced with force. The family is spiraling while the famine tightens its grip. Yet none of their panic changes the reality that more food will be needed. Crisis does not pause because emotions are overwhelmed. Life keeps moving, and eventually the family must move with it. Their grain runs out, and the pressure of survival pushes them back toward Egypt, back toward the brother they betrayed, and toward the next phase of God's unfolding plan. It is here, in Genesis 43, that a quiet but seismic shift happens in the family line. The narrative slows down long enough for us to see a different kind of leadership emerging. Benjamin must come. That is Joseph's condition. The brothers know it. Jacob resists it. The tension is real, and for a moment it appears that the family will fracture under the weight of fear. But then Judah steps forward. Judah takes responsibility, unlike Reuben. Judah offers his own life as assurance for Benjamin's. Judah speaks with clarity, courage, and accountability. This is character development in the family line. This is emotional maturity surfacing where immaturity once ruled. This is leadership being born in a place where betrayal once lived. And Joseph will see it. Joseph will notice it. Joseph will discern it as the first visible evidence that the brothers standing before him are not the same men who threw him into a pit. In Judah's willingness to carry responsibility, Joseph sees growth. In Judah's courage, Joseph sees integrity. In Judah's sacrifice, Joseph sees maturity. Finally, after years of chaos and dysfunction, Joseph witnesses the first signs of change in the men who once destroyed him.

And there is a lesson here for anyone reading who has ever failed, who has ever been the villain in someone else's story, who has ever been the source of hurt or the carrier of immaturity or the participant in wrongdoing. Judah proves that people can change. He proves that character can grow. He proves that history does not have to be your destiny. He proves that what you were is not the limit of who you can become. Judah once participated in Joseph's betrayal, but now he becomes the first brother willing to lay his life down for another. That is transformation. That is repentance with fruit. That is evidence of real growth. And this should comfort every leader, every parent, every spouse, every pastor, every entrepreneur, every sibling, and every person who fears their past disqualifies their future. Judah's evolution teaches us that God is not limited by who you were, because God is always forming who you can be. Responsibility can replace recklessness. Integrity can replace insecurity. Courage can replace cowardice. And sacrifice can replace selfishness. Judah shows us that people can grow, families can shift, leaders can mature, and those once trapped in dysfunction can rise to responsibility. His transformation is a reminder that no story is stuck and no person is beyond redemption.

The Emotional Breaking Point — Joseph Weeps Again

Genesis 43:26–34

Judah's transformation marks a turning point for the entire family, but it also prepares the emotional ground for what comes next. As the brothers make their way back to Egypt with Benjamin in tow, the narrative shifts its focus from the growth happening in Jacob's house to the weight that is about to hit Joseph's heart. Judah stepping up was evidence of change in the family line, but Benjamin stepping into the room will expose the deepest place in Joseph's story. Maturity in others often positions you to face the unfinished chapters inside yourself. Leadership will always require you to hold the tension between what you see in others and what you must still confront within your own heart. Judah has grown, the brothers have changed, and the evidence is beginning to show. But now the lens moves back to Joseph, because sometimes the greatest test is not whether others have been transformed, but whether you can stay grounded when the people connected to your most painful memories stand in front of you again. It is at this intersection of progress and pain that Scripture brings us to the next moment.

Joseph sees Benjamin, and the boy within him breaks again. He steps away to weep, collects himself, and returns. This is childhood memory meeting adult identity. This is past loss colliding with present love. This is family attachment confronting a life of calling. Joseph does not fall apart publicly; he processes privately. This is emotional regulation, not emotional denial.

Joseph weeps, again (Genesis 42:24; 43:30; 45:1–2). He steps away to cry. He regulates emotion privately so he can lead publicly. This is not regression; this is Joseph regulating himself again, the same way he did before, choosing composure over collapse. Once again, he is not pretending nothing happened; he is acknowledging everything that did. He is giving his heart the space it needs without handing his emotions the steering wheel. Joseph knows that if he collapses in front of them, the moment becomes about his pain; if he collapses within himself, the moment becomes about his past; but if he processes first, the moment can become about his purpose. That is the difference between reaction and response. Trauma unprocessed turns discernment into suspicion, boundaries into walls, and justice into revenge. Unprocessed pain hijacks leadership because it demands immediate relief rather than long-term wisdom. Joseph stabilizes first. He allows himself to feel so he does not allow himself to fracture. He releases the pressure so he can return with perspective. What he is doing in those private moments of weeping is sacred: he is metabolizing the emotion so the emotion will not master him.

Lesson: If you do not process your pain, you will project it. And projection is where many leaders unintentionally harm, turning past wounds into present policies, past betrayals into present accusations, and past abandonment into present control. Joseph refuses to let the pain of the boy dictate the decisions of the man. To the reader who feels emotionally flooded, triggered, or overwhelmed by people or situations that echo old wounds, Joseph provides a framework for emotional regulation that is both spiritual and psychologically sound.

Practical Tools for Regulation

- **Name it to tame it.** Put language to what is happening inside you. "I am feeling grief plus fear plus anger." Labeling emotion reduces its intensity and grounds the nervous system. When Joseph leaves the room to weep, he is identifying what his body already knows: this moment matters, and it hurts.

- **Step away rhythms.** Joseph exits to weep; you can pause a meeting, take a walk, breathe deeply, or pray in silence. Stepping away does not mean stepping back. It means giving your mind time to re-regulate before you return. Emotional leadership requires emotional pacing.

- **Truth anchors.** When old emotions threaten present peace, anchor yourself in truth: "I am safe. I have authority. God is with me. I do not need to retaliate to lead." These truths reset the internal narrative and remind you that you are not the person you were when the wound formed.

- **Wise mirrors.** Joseph had no mentor in that room, but you do. Seek a counselor, pastor, or coach who can reflect reality back to you without fueling revenge or minimizing your pain. Wise mirrors give perspective when emotion distorts clarity.

- **Re-enter with intention.** Joseph always returns to the room composed, collected, and clear. He models that you can feel deeply and still lead decisively if you take the time to regulate before re-engaging.

Identity Principle

Maturity is not the absence of triggers; it is the presence of tools. Healed leaders are not unfeeling; they are equipped. They know how to steward their inner world so their outer world does not become collateral damage. Joseph's tears were not a sign he had gone backward; they were evidence he was processing forward.

Maturity Under Power

By age 39, Joseph carries a restraint forged in years of obscuration. There is a weight that comes with leadership that only hidden seasons can build, and Joseph bore that weight well. So when Benjamin appears, his mother's son, his heart's memory, Joseph breaks again (Genesis 43:30). He loves, aches, and feels, yet he still refuses to let emotion dictate outcome. His tears do not weaken his judgment; they humanize it. His compassion does not cloud his discernment; it clarifies it. Joseph stands as proof that emotional depth and spiritual maturity can coexist inside the same leader.

Leadership requires more than gifting. It requires self-awareness, regulation, discernment, and timing. Self-awareness is knowing what is happening within you. Regulation is managing what you know so it does not spill in destructive ways. Timing is knowing when to speak, when to act, and when to wait. Joseph embodies all four. He does not rush to reveal himself when he sees Benjamin. He steps away, stabilizes, returns with composure, and continues the process God has given him. Healing integrates history; it does not erase it. Joseph did not forget what his brothers did, but neither did he lose what God formed in him.

Thermostat vs. Thermometer Leadership

A thermometer reports the temperature of the room; it mirrors the environment. It reacts. It absorbs. It reflects whatever is around it. A thermostat sets the temperature of the room; it regulates the environment. It leads. It stabilizes. It determines what atmosphere is allowed to exist. Restored leaders become thermostats. They refuse to let unhealed rooms set their responses. Joseph walks into a room filled with the men who tried to erase him, and instead of becoming what they were, he remains who God made him. His heart remembers the wound, but his character remembers the assignment. His emotions rise, but his maturity rules. He sets the tone. He decides the pace. He holds the room steady even when his internal world is shaking.

This is the power of maturity under power: you no longer respond from who hurt you; you respond from who healed you.

The Final Test — The Silver Cup in Benjamin's Bag

Genesis 44

By the time we reach Genesis 44, Joseph has observed enough to know that something has shifted in his brothers, but he needs to discern the depth of that change. Surface remorse is easy. Tears are easy. Apologies are easy. Transformation is not revealed in emotion; it is proven in behavior. Joseph understands that wounds this deep require clarity for sure. So he orchestrates one final test, a test designed not to hurt them but to reveal them. He places his silver cup in Benjamin's sack and sends his steward to confront them on the road. The moment is deliberate and decisive. The accusation falls, the cup is found, and tension fills the air. Suddenly, the brothers find themselves facing the same type of choice they faced twenty years earlier. Back then, they abandoned Joseph without hesitation. Now, in this moment, Joseph watches to see if they will abandon Benjamin too.

This is the climax of their transformation. This is the fullness of the test. This is the moment where character is proven by pressure. No speeches. No promises. No "we are different now" declarations. Just a choice. Raw and unfiltered. What will they do when self-preservation is the easy path?

Benjamin stands where Joseph once stood. Wrongly accused. Vulnerable. Powerless. Dependent on the courage and character of the same men who once threw his brother into a pit. And this is what Joseph needs to see. Not emotion. No apologies. Not sentiment. Evidence. Evidence that their hearts have changed. Evidence that their values have shifted. Evidence that their love has deepened. Evidence that their loyalty has matured. Evidence that they are no longer governed by jealousy, insecurity, and competition. This final test exposes whether their remorse has become repentance and whether their repentance has become responsibility.

This is where Judah steps forward. The same Judah who suggested selling Joseph now offers himself in Benjamin's place. The same Judah whose voice once fueled betrayal now becomes the voice of intercession. The same Judah who once abandoned a brother now refuses to abandon another. It is Judah, not Reuben, who stands in the gap. Judah pleads. Judah pushes. Judah protects. Judah sacrifices. Judah lays down his life so Benjamin can return home. Genesis 44:18–34 is one of the most powerful speeches in the Old Testament, not because of its eloquence but because of its evidence. Judah offers himself in Benjamin's place, and this is the proof Joseph has been waiting for. They are not who they used to be.

This moment teaches us another leadership lesson most people never grasp. The final test of transformation is consistency under pressure. Growth is not proven in comfort; it is proven in crisis. Joseph does not engineer this moment to be cruel. He engineers it to be clear. He knows the difference between guilt and growth, between grief and change, between regret and repentance. Leaders who steward wisely do not hand out reconciliation because someone cries. They discern the pattern. They evaluate the behavior. They watch the choices. Judah's willingness to sacrifice himself becomes the clearest sign that repentance has rewritten the family line.

There is also something profound happening in Joseph. He is not looking for a reason to punish them; he is looking for a reason to restore them. Joseph cannot safely give them access until he knows who they have become. The test reveals that what once broke him has now built them. Pain has shaped their character instead of hardening their hearts. Grief has softened them. Responsibility has matured them. Time has transformed them.

And here is where we find ourselves in the text. No matter who you are, this moment teaches you yet again that people can change. Family dynamics can shift. Brothers who betrayed can become brothers who protect. Leaders who once acted recklessly can become leaders who stand courageously. People who once failed you can become people who fight for you. Judah's transformation places hope in the hands of every person who fears their past. His sacrifice proves that God can rewrite a story from the inside out. Yet before we celebrate this moment, we must address the unavoidable truth beneath this moment. There is a familiar saying often echoed in leadership spaces, churches, and relationships: "When someone shows you who they are, believe them the first time." Dr. Maya Angelou's original wisdom was simply, "When someone shows you who they are, believe them."

In most cases, this is wise counsel. People often reveal their patterns long before they reveal their apologies. Past behavior can be a reliable predictor of future choices. Many have avoided heartbreak and catastrophe by taking this truth seriously. However, Joseph's story reminds us that this principle, while often true, is not absolute. Sometimes people do change. Sometimes character matures. Sometimes the heart softens. Sometimes the Holy Spirit breaks cycles that seemed permanent. And this is why discernment is essential for every leader. Discernment allows you to hold two truths at once: that what someone did matters and that who someone can become matters too. It is required, because this moment could have gone differently. This scene is proof that a brother who once hated Joseph enough to sell him could have hated Benjamin enough to abandon him too. One might even argue that perhaps Judah loved Benjamin more or disliked Joseph more, and we will never know. What we do know is that Joseph saw what mattered. He knew that his brother was no longer the monster he once was. He saw that Judah had a heart, and that was enough. Discernment allows leaders to see who a person is now without denying who they used to be. It allows room for transformation without being naive about history. It allows for restoration anchored not in sentiment but in evidence. Judah's actions offered that evidence, and Joseph's discernment recognized it.

Moments like this compel us to pause and consider the complexity of human change. Judah's transformation shows that people are not frozen in their failures and that time, conviction, and the hand of God can carve maturity where there was once immaturity. But Joseph cannot rely on sentiment alone. He cannot build restoration on emotion or nostalgia. He must build it on evidence. Discernment requires both compassion and clarity. Joseph's story teaches us that wisdom looks at a changed heart, but it also examines changed behavior. And as the narrative moves forward, Scripture brings us to the moment that would reveal everything Joseph needed to know. The next chapter of reconciliation will depend on what this final test has uncovered.

In your life, God may allow situations that feel similar to old wounds, not to retraumatize you but to reveal the transformation in others or in yourself. The final test is rarely about judgment. It is about clarity. It is about positioning. It is about ensuring the next chapter rests on proven character, not hopeful emotion. Joseph's restraint throughout this chapter reminds us that wisdom is slow, patient, and prayerful.

This is why Joseph could reveal himself in the next chapter without losing himself. Restoration is safest when evidence precedes emotion. And in Judah's offering, Joseph finally sees the evidence he needed. They are not who they used to be. And neither are you.

Prayer

Father, thank You for being present in every place my story has taken me, both the painful and the redemptive. As Joseph faced the very people who wounded him, give me the courage to face the chapters I once closed in fear. Strengthen my heart to recognize Your timing when old memories return, and help me discern what is healed, what is growing, and what still needs Your touch. Guard me from rushing into reconciliation without wisdom. Give me eyes to see evidence, ears to hear truth, and discernment to set boundaries that honor what You have restored in me.

When emotions rise, teach me to step away with grace rather than collapse in overwhelm. Regulate my heart, steady my mind, and anchor my identity in who You have called me to be, not in who hurt me. Do not let bitterness guide my decisions or fear shape my posture. Give me the maturity to respond from healing and not from history.

Like Joseph, help me recognize transformation in others without denying the truth of the past. Help me celebrate growth when it is real, and hold steady when it is not. And most of all, remind me that You are sovereign over every collision, every confrontation, and every test. What others meant for harm, You are always bending toward good. Lead me with clarity, protect my heart with wisdom, and guide me into restoration that is grounded in truth. In Jesus' name, Amen.

Driver Seat Key Takeaways

- **God will sometimes allow famine to push you into the very rooms where healing and destiny will collide.** The famine did not punish Joseph's family. It positioned them. Crisis forced old wounds into the open so God could complete what was left unresolved.

- **Trauma does not disappear with success. It resurfaces when destiny demands reintegration.** Joseph had risen in Egypt, but the moment he saw his brothers, the emotional file reopened. Healing does not erase memory. It transforms the meaning of it.

- **Leadership requires facing the rooms you hoped never to enter again.** Elevation will bring you back to the people, places, and patterns that once broke you, not to break you again but to reveal how deeply God has rebuilt you.

- **A healed leader regulates their emotions; a wounded leader reacts from them.** Joseph stepping away to weep was not weakness. It was stewardship. He felt fully and still led wisely.

- **Discernment must come before reconciliation.** Joseph tested before he trusted. Forgiveness is given freely, but reconciliation requires evidence. Love can be open, but access must be earned.

- **God will allow old relationships to reappear so you can evaluate change, not revive old cycles.** Joseph watched for loyalty, sacrifice, and honesty. He needed to see fruit, not feelings. Wisdom weighs behavior, not nostalgia.

- **Transformation is real, but it is revealed under pressure, not in apology.** Judah's willingness to offer himself for Benjamin proved change had taken root. Crisis exposes whether remorse has matured into responsibility.

- **Emotional regulation is a leadership skill, not a personality trait.** Joseph stepped away, processed privately, and returned with clarity. Regulation protects purpose. Unprocessed pain produces projection.

- **Healing prepares you to lead in environments that shaped your wounds.** Joseph could stand in the same atmosphere that once traumatized him and remain grounded. Healing does not remove dysfunction around you. It removes its power to shape you.

- **God uses final tests to confirm character before He releases restoration.** The silver cup incident revealed that the brothers were no longer who they used to be. God allows these moments so restoration can be built on truth, not sentiment.

***

Joseph did not collapse under the weight of reunion. He did not lose the man he had become. He faced the family that broke him with the stability God built in him. He discerned without becoming cynical. He loved without becoming foolish. He tested without becoming vengeful. He remembered without becoming imprisoned by memory.

This chapter shows what trauma-informed, spiritually grounded, psychologically integrated leadership looks like:

You can face what hurt you without becoming what hurt you.

SECTION FOUR
THE HEALING OF A DRIVER

CHAPTER ELEVEN

THE BLESSING: WHEN YOUR HARD SEASONS MAKE SENSE

There are moments in life that feel like completion. Moments where God pulls every scattered piece of your story into one room and shows you the pattern He was weaving all along. Joseph stands in such a moment. Not in the pit. Not in Potiphar's house. Not in the prison. But in a palace full of power, influence, and responsibility with the same brothers who broke him now standing before him trembling. This is not just reunion. This is reframing. This is redemption. This is revelation. This is when Joseph's entire arc, pit to house to prison to palace to purpose, finally makes sense.

To situate the scene, Scripture records that Joseph can no longer control himself in front of those who serve him. He orders everyone out, raises his voice in weeping that is heard in Pharaoh's house, and stands face to face with the history that once tried to end him. The geography is the palace, but the ground is holy. God is about to thread meaning through every chapter that preceded this one.

Before Joseph reframes the story in Genesis 45, he must first face it in Genesis 42. The brothers bow, and Scripture says Joseph remembered the dreams. Not only the dreams, but the pit, the betrayal, the silver, the silence. Trauma has memory. Leadership does not exempt you from emotional collision. Elevation does not erase what wounded you. It reveals whether you have integrated it.

When Identity Meets Interpretation (Genesis 45:1–4)

Joseph clears the room. For the first time in decades, he stands in front of the very people who tried to erase him and says the words he's carried through thirteen years of silence: "I am Joseph" (Genesis 45:3). Not the Egyptian name he was given. Not the title Pharaoh awarded him. Not the identity others projected onto him. Just Joseph. The boy they left. The leader he became. The man the process formed. His brothers cannot answer. Shame steals their tongues. Fear tightens their breath. Memory confronts them. Joseph calls them closer: "Come near to me, I pray you" (Genesis 45:4). This is not naïveté. This is not denial. This is not amnesia. This is integration.

Joseph does not immediately reconcile. He questions. He observes. He tests for transformation. Reunion is not restoration. Restoration requires evidence. Forgiveness without discernment is immaturity. Joseph proves that wisdom and compassion can coexist.

> **Driver Seat Quote:** "Healing is proven not by proximity to the past, but by mastery over its meaning."

Joseph's first move is identity. He reclaims name before he reframes narrative. "I am Joseph" is not a flourish. It is leadership. It says, I will not meet you as a costume or a title. I will meet you as a whole person whose identity survived betrayal, distance, and time. Leaders, parents, pastors, and business owners learn here that identity precedes interpretation. If you do not know who you are, you will interpret your story through the wound rather than through your calling. Joseph also clears the room (Genesis 45:1). Confidentiality is wisdom. Not every sacred conversation belongs in a crowded space. Parents learn to protect the moment for their children. Pastors protect a penitent's dignity. Executives protect the team from unnecessary spectacle. Identity anchored, environment stewarded, proximity invited. Integration begins.

Reframing the Trauma Without Erasing the Truth (Genesis 45:5–8)

Joseph does not pretend the betrayal didn't happen. He does not rewrite evil as misunderstanding. He does not absolve them prematurely. He names the truth with clarity: "You sold me..." (Genesis 45:5). That is accountability. He names what they did. He names what it cost. He names the wound honestly. But he does not stop there: "...God did send me before you to preserve life... God sent me before you... God made me lord of all Egypt" (Genesis 45:5–8). Joseph reframes, not to erase pain, but to redeem it. He introduces God's meaning without denying their malice. This is not spiritual bypassing. This is spiritual integration. This is where trauma becomes testimony, survival becomes assignment, and wounds become wisdom.

Genesis shows Joseph stepping away to weep more than once. Again, he does not suppress emotion. He regulates it. He feels deeply, but he does not let feeling dictate outcome. Authority without emotional regulation becomes vengeance with a title. Joseph continues to stabilize himself before he makes decisions that affect nations.

Driver Seat Quote: "Maturity is not denial of pain. It is integration of purpose."

Genesis shows Joseph stepping away to weep more than once. Again, he does not suppress emotion. He regulates it. He feels deeply, but he does not let feeling dictate outcome. Authority without emotional regulation becomes vengeance with a title. Joseph continues to stabilize himself before he makes decisions that affect nations.

There is a point here worth pausing on. Joseph is a powerful man, yet he weeps over and over again. This is not weakness. It is strength. It is the sign of a healthy man whose heart is still alive. Power did not harden him. Authority did not numb him. Leadership did not require him to abandon his humanity. His tears reveal something profound: emotional expression and emotional stability are not opposites. They belong together.

In many cultures men are taught that weeping signals fragility, that strength means emotional silence. But Joseph contradicts that narrative. His ability to step away, feel what he feels, and return with clarity shows emotional maturity. A weak man explodes or suppresses. A strong man processes. Joseph weeps privately so that he can lead publicly with sound judgment. His tears do not control him; they cleanse him. They allow him to release pain without allowing pain to control his decisions.

The sequence matters. First truth, then transcendence. First accountability, then alignment. Leaders must learn this order. Parents teach children to name harm and also to trust God's hand. Pastors name sin yet announce sovereign purpose. Business leaders face market failures, then articulate redemptive strategy. Joseph's words model a two-handed leadership. One hand holds truth firmly. The other holds sovereignty humbly. Together they carry the future without dropping the past. He refuses to let evil be edited out, and he refuses to let evil be the editor.

The Blessing of Meaning-Making

Meaning-making is one of the highest forms of leadership maturity. It is the ability to interpret your story through the lens of divine purpose without minimizing the cost of the journey. Joseph reaches the point every leader eventually must reach: the ability to look back without bitterness and look forward without fear. He sees what the pit did. He sees what the house built. He sees what the prison formed. He sees what the waiting refined. What once felt random now feels synchronized. What once felt cruel now makes sense. What once felt wasted now looks intentional. Purpose gives pain language. Meaning gives trauma context. Integration gives leaders stability.

> **Driver Seat Quote:** "When God restores meaning, pain loses its power to define you."

Here the text widens beyond one family to a nation. "To preserve life" becomes Joseph's organizing theology and operating strategy. Leaders discover their own sentence that summarizes calling. Parents say, I am here to cultivate wholeness across generations. Pastors say, I am here to form a people who can weather famine and flourish in faith. Entrepreneurs say, I am here to build systems that serve people, not merely profit. Meaning-making is not sentiment. It is strategy. It sets priorities, budgets, boundaries, and timelines. It quiets the nervous system because purpose tells pain what it built.

Leadership Is Generational, Not Situational

Joseph does not just forgive offenders. He provides for generations. He preserves not only his family but entire nations. He engineers economic systems that carry Egypt and surrounding regions through seven years of global famine. He becomes a cultural stabilizer. A governmental strategist. A generational anchor. Joseph's leadership outlives the moment, the famine, Pharaoh, the crisis that elevated him, and the pain that built him. Joseph proves that true leadership is not based on situation. It is based on stewardship across time.

Driver Seat Quote: "Leaders don't just survive seasons. They shape systems that survive them."

Genesis records the contours of those systems. During the seven years of plenty, Joseph organizes storage at a fifth of the produce (Genesis 41:34–36). During the famine, he orchestrates distribution, negotiates land and labor arrangements, secures seed for the future, and establishes a sustainable structure that endures beyond his tenure (Genesis 47:13–26). Parents learn to think beyond one semester or one crisis and set rhythms that will strengthen grandchildren. Pastors build discipleship pathways that endure staff changes and trends. Business owners design processes that outlast leadership cycles and market shocks. Generational leadership asks, what will still be standing five leaders from now because we stood faithful today.

The Hard Truth

Some of the people who wounded you will one day need what you built without them. Some of the doors that closed on you will reopen from the inside. Some of the rooms that rejected you will one day need what you carry. The question is not whether elevation will come. The question is who you will be when it does. Power without healing is dangerous. Power with healing is redemptive.

Final Forgiveness and Post-Traumatic Growth (Genesis 50:19–21)

Years later, when Jacob dies, the brothers panic again. Joseph reassures them: "Fear not" (Genesis 50:19). And then the verse that defines his entire life: "As for you, ye thought evil against me; but God meant it unto good..." (Genesis 50:20). Joseph names the evil, names God's intervention, names the outcome, names his identity. This is full-circle healing. Not avoidance. Integration.

Forgiveness here is not amnesia. It is alignment. Alignment with God's sovereignty without denying human responsibility. Joseph refuses to let evil be the final author of his story, but he also refuses to pretend it was not evil.

Joseph does not deny the wound. He interprets it. He does not dismiss the pain. He assigns purpose to it. He does not erase the past. He reclaims authorship of it. This is post-traumatic growth in Scripture's purest form.

> **Driver Seat Quote:** "Healing is not forgetting what happened.
> Healing is remembering who you became through it."

Notice three additional moves in the narrative. Joseph asks, "Am I in the place of God" (Genesis 50:19). He renounces vengeance jurisdiction and returns judgment to the Judge (God). Then he reframes again, **"to preserve many lives,"** keeping mission central when memory could have been vindictive. Finally he embodies provision, "I will nourish you and your little ones," and he speaks kindly to their fears (Genesis 50:21). Leaders, parents, pastors, and business owners learn that full-circle forgiveness includes relinquishing God's seat, re-centering on purpose, and responding with provision. This is the fruit of integrated healing. It yields tone, not just truth.

The Blessing Defined

Joseph's blessing was not the palace, the robe, the ring, the chariot, or the authority. Joseph's blessing was that he lived long enough to see his worst seasons make sense. That is blessing. That is closure. That is restoration. That is divine reversal. Not to erase the pain but to integrate it into purpose.

Blessing, in Joseph's frame, is revelation in hindsight. It is the grace to witness harvest in fields you once wept over. It is watching the same hands that harmed you carry bread you baked for them. It is seeing systems you designed rescue the people who doubted you. For the leader, blessing is clarity that steadies decisions. For the parent, blessing is a home where old patterns are broken. For the pastor, blessing is a people formed by presence, not performance. For the entrepreneur, blessing is a company stewarding trust as well as revenue. In every role, blessing is alignment.

Prayer

Lord, teach me to see my life through Your meaning, not my memory. Help me interpret pain with truth, integrate trauma with purpose, and walk in maturity that outlives every season that tried to break me. Let my leadership be generational, my forgiveness be wise, my identity be whole, and my purpose be aligned with Your sovereignty. Thank You for being the God who turns hard seasons into holy outcomes. Amen.

Driver Seat Key Takeaways

- Completion of the arc: Joseph moves from pit to house to prison to palace to purpose. This movement is not merely biographical. It is pedagogical. Expect God to use dislocation to produce discernment, restriction to produce resilience, responsibility to produce rule, and revelation to produce readiness.

- Leadership is generational: Joseph's influence shapes nations and preserves bloodlines. Measure success not only by quarterly health but by generational health. What you build should feed people you will never meet.

- Meaning-making is maturity: Pain becomes purposeful when reframed by sovereignty. When leaders can narrate their story without bitterness or bravado, they become safe people who create safe systems.

- Forgiveness is alignment: Joseph does not deny trauma. He integrates it. Forgiveness returns the gavel to God, retains boundaries with wisdom, and releases provision with kindness.

- Purpose is bigger than pain: What was meant to break him becomes the platform that elevates him. Let assignment interpret adversity. When purpose is clear, pain becomes raw material.

- Driver Seat Principle: Blessing is when God lets you see why the hard seasons were necessary. Ask God for hindsight humility and foresight stewardship. See and then serve.

***

Joseph's story now stands full and complete. The pit has spoken, the prison has shaped, the palace has revealed, and purpose has been fulfilled. But the conclusion of Joseph's journey is not the end of yours. Every chapter of his life now asks a question of yours. Every wound he integrated, every boundary he set, every moment he regulated, and every purpose he embraced calls something out of you. His story was not recorded merely to inspire you, but to instruct you. It was not preserved to entertain your faith, but to expand it.

But before fulfillment came silence. Before the palace came the pit. Before the system came the stillness. Before the interpretation came immaturity. There was a moment in a field when Joseph spoke too soon. There was a disclosure that cost him proximity. There was a dream that had to survive years without being repeated.

Leadership requires revisiting what hurt you without becoming what hurt you. It also requires learning when to speak and when to steward. Joseph had to outgrow the need to announce what God was forming. He had to survive the space between revelation and realization. He had to learn that destiny does not need constant advertisement. It needs endurance.

Chapter 12 now turns toward the quiet years. Toward the last time Joseph spoke his dream before silence began its work. Because destiny does not hand you the wheel until you are ready to drive. And sometimes the loudest part of your calling is the season when you say the least.

The only thing stronger than Joseph's story is what God wants to write next in yours.

CHAPTER TWELVE

THE DRIVER SEAT: WHEN DESTINY FINALLY HANDS YOU THE WHEEL

The last time Joseph spoke about his dream to his brothers, he did not know it would be the last time. That is the quiet cruelty of beginnings, you rarely recognize them as fragile until they fracture. He stood in a field young, certain, untested, holding revelation like it was meant to be repeated. The dream had heat in it. The kind of heat that makes you speak before you study the temperature of the room. He believed clarity guaranteed celebration. He believed proximity guaranteed protection. He believed that if something was from God, it would automatically be received by man. And so he told them. He told them about sheaves bowing. He told them about stars lowering themselves. He told them about a future larger than the soil beneath their feet. What he did not know was that this would be the final time his dream would pass his lips in their presence. After that moment, silence began its long work on him.

There is something deeply human about wanting the people who knew you before to witness who you become after. We crave continuity. We want the same faces that saw our immaturity to applaud our maturity. Joseph's disclosure was not just arrogance, it was longing. Longing to be understood. Longing to be affirmed. Longing to belong while becoming. But the field turned into fracture, and fracture turned into a pit. The very audience he hoped would celebrate his destiny became the environment that accelerated his isolation. And the silence that followed would mature him more than the dream itself.

Some of you remember the last time you spoke your vision out loud in a room that misunderstood you. You can trace the moment. The shift in the air. The subtle withdrawal of support. The tension that entered relationships that once felt safe. And ever since, you have been more careful. Not because the dream died, but because disclosure taught you discernment. Joseph learned what many leaders, creatives, entrepreneurs, pastors, parents, and pioneers eventually learn, not every revelation requires repetition. Some dreams are meant to be carried quietly until character can sustain fulfillment.

The pit did not give Joseph a platform to clarify himself. Slavery did not provide him with an opportunity to defend his innocence. Prison did not invite him to narrate his calling. Entire chapters of his life unfolded without the reinforcement of his own voice. And this is where suspense deepens. Because the question becomes: What happens to a dream when it is no longer spoken? Does it shrink? Does it rot? Does it harden into resentment? Or does it deepen into resolve? Joseph's silence did not suffocate his vision; it strengthened it. What was once announced immaturely became guarded intentionally. What was once spoken impulsively became lived faithfully.

Driver Seat Quote: "Maturity is when you no longer need to repeat the dream to prove it."

The last time Joseph spoke about his dream with his brothers, he still needed their reaction. That is what makes that moment so tender. He wanted acknowledgment. He wanted validation. He wanted to know he was not imagining what God revealed. But silence became his tutor. In the pit, he learned that destiny does not collapse when applause disappears. In slavery, he learned that calling can survive captivity. In prison, he learned that character is built where recognition is absent. His dream did not need defending; it needed forming.

And here is the tension that makes this chapter personal: many of you are living in the space between the last time you announced your dream and the day it manifests. You are in the quiet corridor where no one is asking about it anymore. The conversations have shifted. The enthusiasm has cooled. The support feels conditional. And it would be easy to either overexplain or completely withdraw. Joseph did neither. He stopped narrating and started stewarding. He did not abandon the dream; he allowed it to mature without an audience.

There is a discipline in being voiceless that the hero complex cannot survive. The hero complex feeds on reaction. It thrives on visibility. It requires acknowledgment to feel alive. But Joseph's silence starved it. When he stood before his brothers years later, the dream had already come true, and he did not have to mention it. They bowed without him reminding them. Fulfillment arrived without vindication. And the suspense of that moment is almost unbearable because we expect a speech. We expect a replay of the field. We expect him to say, "Remember what I told you?" But he does not. He weeps instead.

That weeping is the evidence that silence did its sacred work. The boy who once needed affirmation had become the man who needed alignment. The last time Joseph spoke his dream to his brothers was before the pit. Everything after that was lived, not announced. And that shift, from proclamation to embodiment, is what marks the strength of the silent seat.

Driver Seat Quote: "Silence is not the death of your dream; it is the discipline of it."

The beauty of Joseph's evolution is not that his dream came true, it is that he did not become smaller while waiting for it to. Silence can either shrink you or strengthen you. It can make you insecure or intentional. It can make you reactive or rooted. Joseph chose rootedness. He allowed God to develop substance where once there was only spectacle. And in doing so, he freed himself from the need to perform his destiny for those who once doubted it.

As this closing chapter unfolds, you must wrestle with a simple but piercing question: when was the last time you felt misunderstood for speaking your vision? And what did that misunderstanding produce in you, bitterness or discipline? Joseph's silence was not surrender. It was stewardship. It was the quiet recalibration of a man who learned that destiny does not need constant advertisement. It needs obedience.

As a pastor, I have learned that not every vision needs defending. The last time I explained certain dreams to certain rooms, it cost energy I could not afford to lose. I have preached in spaces where faith was celebrated and in spaces where it was scrutinized. I have cast vision that was applauded and vision that was questioned. And I learned something Joseph learned long before me: God fulfills what He authors without my constant narration. The dream does not need my anxiety. It needs my obedience.

There were nights I sat in empty sanctuaries long after everyone left, re-playing conversations in my mind. Wondering if I shared too much. Wondering if I said it too soon. Wondering if silence would have been wiser. And in those moments, I sensed what Joseph must have sensed in prison: quiet does not mean canceled. It means cultivated.

The last time Joseph spoke his dream in a field, he was young. The next time his brothers encountered the outcome of that dream, he was formed. Between those two moments lived years of obscurity, betrayal, waiting, and growth. And that is where most of us are shaped, not in the announcement, but in the aftermath.

The silent seat is not glamorous. It is not celebrated. But it is sacred. Because it is where God separates your need for recognition from your call to responsibility. And by the time Joseph's dream stood face to face with his past, he no longer needed to narrate it. He simply lived it. The field was loud. The fulfillment was quiet. And somewhere between those two spaces, a boy who once needed to be heard became a man who no longer needed to explain.

The Driver Seat: Leaders Navigating Transitions, Trauma, and Triumph

Now we turn to you. Because this book was never only about Joseph. It was about the leader God is forming inside you.

You, too, have walked through pits, betrayals, delays, misunderstandings, and seasons where your voice felt muted. You have known the weight of being overlooked and the ache of being misread. You have carried dreams you could not speak, promises you could not explain, and wounds you could not perform your way out of. And yet here you are, still standing, still growing, still becoming.

This is your Driver Seat moment.

Joseph did not choose every road, but he chose who he would be on the road. And now it is your turn to reclaim authorship of your direction. Leaders do not get to choose all their transitions. Leaders do not get to predict every collision. Leaders do not get to prevent every disappointment. But leaders do get to decide how they rise through them.

You are stepping into a season where God is handing you the wheel again. Not because you earned it, but because He formed you for it. Every pit taught you perspective. Every betrayal sharpened your discernment. Every delay expanded your stamina. Every collision matured your emotions. Every quiet season clarified your identity. And every silent chapter strengthened your soul.

Do not let the drama behind you distract you from the destiny before you. Do not let the trauma you lived through convince you that triumph is out of reach. Do not let old triggers negotiate your new trajectory. God has not forgotten your dream, He has been building the leader who can carry it.

So let this be the reminder you hold in your spirit as you take your place in the Driver Seat of your own life: You are not who the pit said you were. You are not who betrayal suggested you were. You are not who silence tried to convince you, you were. You are who God formed you to be.

Joseph regained his voice long before he regained his position. That is why the palace could not corrupt him. His voice was anchored before his influence expanded.

And the same God who was with Joseph in the field, in the pit, in the house, in the prison, and in the palace is with you now. Take your seat. Take your place. Take your authority. Take your identity. Take your future. You have survived enough. You have matured enough. You have healed enough. And God has trusted you with enough.

There comes a moment in every life where God places something in front of you that no past pain can sabotage, no past betrayal can cancel, and no past season can disqualify. It is the moment destiny finally hands you the wheel. Not because you earned it. Not because you performed for it. But because God has crafted a version of you who can finally carry it.

Now go sit in the driver seat of your life.

Sitting in the Driver Seat is not about control. It is about conscious partnership. It is the alignment between divine sovereignty and human obedience. God directs and you respond. The wheel is not about speed. It is about stability. It is not about acceleration. It is about accuracy. Calling does not require perfection. It requires presence.

Destiny is not waiting on your perfection. Destiny is waiting on your participation.

Rise. Speak. Lead. Drive.

SECTION FIVE

THE MODERN DRIVER

A Final Invitation: The Most Important Decision You Will Ever Make

SALVATION

As you close this book, there is one question more important than every leadership principle, every insight on identity, every moment of breakthrough, and every chapter you have just journeyed through. Do you have a relationship with Jesus? Not religion. Not routine. Not theory. A real and living relationship.

The God who walked Joseph through the pit, the prison, and the palace is reaching for you right now. He has been present in every chapter of your life, even the chapters you thought He skipped. He knows your scars. He knows your secrets. He knows your potential. And He loves you with a love that is deeper than your history and stronger than your pain.

God wants a relationship with you. God wants your heart. God wants your life. God wants you.

The Bible gives us a clear promise: "If you confess with your mouth the Lord Jesus and believe in your heart that God raised Him from the dead, you will be saved." (Romans 10:9)

That means salvation is not complicated. It is not earned. It is not achieved.

It is received.

If you are ready for a fresh start, if you are ready to be forgiven, if you are ready for the love of God to meet you right where you are, here is what you do. Believe that Jesus died for you. Believe that He rose from the grave. Ask Him to forgive your sins. Surrender your life to Him. Invite Him into your heart.

That is salvation. That is new life. That is the beginning of everything God created you for. And if you are ready, it begins with a prayer. A cry of a heart turning toward God. If you mean it, God hears it.

Pray This Prayer Out Loud

Father, I come to You today because I need You. I believe that Jesus died for my sins and that He rose again so I could have new life. I ask You to forgive me of every sin I have ever committed. Wash me. Cleanse me. Make me new. Jesus, I invite You into my heart. I surrender my life to You. I confess with my mouth that You are Lord, and I believe in my heart that God raised You from the dead. From this moment forward, I am Yours. Save me. Heal me. Lead me. I give You my life, and I receive Your salvation today. In Jesus' name, Amen.

If you prayed that prayer, heaven heard you. God has received you. Your past is forgiven. Your heart is new. Your future is open. You belong to Him.

And hear this clearly. God wants a relationship with you. God delights in you. God will walk with you from this moment forward. Just like Joseph, your story will not end in the place where it began. God is with you now. God is for you now. God is guiding you now. And God is writing the rest of your story with grace, strength, and purpose.

You are loved. You are chosen. You are forgiven. You are His.

NOTES

Chapter 4

1. Judith Herman, *Trauma and Recovery: The Aftermath of Violence—from Domestic Abuse to Political Terror* (New York: Basic Books, 1992); Bessel van der Kolk, *The Body Keeps the Score: Brain, Mind, and Body in the Healing of Trauma* (New York: Viking, 2014).

2. Judith Herman, *Trauma and Recovery*; Bessel van der Kolk, *The Body Keeps the Score*. Herman's work describes trauma recovery as involving safety, narrative processing, and reconnection, while van der Kolk discusses the restoration of agency and integration of traumatic memory as central components of healing.

3. Judith Herman, *Trauma and Recovery*, especially the discussion of adaptive containment and survival responses under prolonged loss of control; Bessel van der Kolk, *The Body Keeps the Score*, on emotional regulation and behavioral restraint in conditions of sustained threat.

4. Judith Herman, *Trauma and Recovery: The Aftermath of Violence—from Domestic Abuse to Political Terror* (New York: Basic Books, 1992); Bessel van der Kolk, *The Body Keeps the Score: Brain, Mind, and Body in the Healing of Trauma* (New York: Viking, 2014). Both authors discuss trauma recovery as involving the restoration of agency and the integration of traumatic experience into a coherent personal narrative, enabling survivors to re-enter their story as participants rather than victims.

5. Judith Herman, *Trauma and Recovery: The Aftermath of Violence—from Domestic Abuse to Political Terror* (New York: Basic Books, 1992); Bessel van der Kolk, *The Body Keeps the Score: Brain, Mind, and Body in the Healing of Trauma* (New York: Viking, 2014). Both authors discuss heightened vigilance and threat anticipation as common adaptive responses in individuals who have experienced prolonged loss of control or captivity.

Sources & References

Bureau of Justice Statistics. *Jail Inmates in 2023 – Statistical Tables.* U.S. Department of Justice, 2024.

Bureau of Justice Statistics. *Parents in Prison and Their Minor Children.* U.S. Department of Justice, 2016.

Bureau of Justice Statistics. *Mortality in Local Jails and State Prisons, 2000–2019.* U.S. Department of Justice.

Council of State Governments Justice Center. *Recidivism Trends in State Prisons: 2008–2019.*

Second Chance Act of 2008, Pub. L. No. 110–199.

Thank You!

For riding with me...

Armon Dauphin
Dauphin Tales Photography
Dauphintales.com
@dauphintales_ [IG]

CTS Graphic Designs
cts.graphics.com

Alvianne Brule'
The Eight XVIII Agency
TheEightXVIII.com
@Alviannebrule [IG]

ABOUT
Jonathan Everett

AUTHOR ⚜ SPEAKER ⚜ MINISTER ⚜ TEACHER

Bishop Jonathan Everett is a nationally recognized pastor, teacher, and global faith leader based in New Orleans, Louisiana. Grounded in strong family values and a deep faith, he answered the call to ministry at a young age, which opened doors to preach and lead across the United States and internationally. Known for his authentic teaching and people-centered leadership, Bishop Everett carries a message that connects faith to everyday life and empowers individuals to live with purpose.

He currently serves as Senior Pastor of Rock of Ages Baptist Church, where he began his pastoral assignment with just three members. Through faithful leadership, vision, and service, the church experienced unprecedented growth—expanding from three members to over 600 and now flourishing as a ministry of more than 3,500 members. Under his leadership, Rock of Ages has become a catalyst for spiritual growth, community outreach, and global ministry, impacting lives far beyond the walls of the church.

Come Rock with us:

-WORSHIP WITH US IN PERSON
-WATCH THE WORD ONLINE VIA YOUTUBE OR IG
-JOIN OUR DAILY PRAYER LINE VIA IG
-STAY CONNECTED ON SOCIAL MEDIA

Rock of Ages Baptist Church

2515 FRANKLIN AVE., NEW ORLEANS, LA 70117
@ROCKOFAGESBC @ROCKINNOLA
www.rockinnola.com

www.JeverettMinistries.com

Jonathan Everett
@paseverett

SHOP
BISHOP
ESSENTIALS

ORDER
NOW

Bishop Jonathan Everett's apparel collection is designed to reinforce faith, purpose, and identity beyond the page. Each piece carries a message meant to be lived, not just worn. To view and purchase official Bishop Jonathan Everett merchandise, including t-shirts and apparel, scan the QR code.

9 798234 015396